RISE AND FALL OF THE COSMIC RACE

The Cult of Mestizaje in Latin America

MARILYN GRACE MILLER

UNIVERSITY OF TEXAS PRESS

Austin

Requests for permission to reproduce material from this work should
be sent to Permissions, University of Texas Press, P.O. Box 7819,
Austin, TX 78713-7819.

⊗ The paper used in this book meets the minimum requirements of
ANSI/NISO Z39.48-1992 (R1997) (Permanence of Paper).

LIBRARY OF CONGRESS CATALOGING-IN-PUBLICATION DATA
Miller, Marilyn Grace
  Rise and fall of the cosmic race : the cult of mestizaje in Latin
America / by Marilyn Grace Miller. — 1st. ed.
      p.   cm.
  Includes bibliographical references and index.
  ISBN 0-292-70572-7 (cloth : alk. paper) — ISBN 0-292-70596-4
(pbk. : alk. paper)
    1. Latin America—Civilization—20th century.   2. Mestizaje—Latin
America—History.   3. Miscegenation—Latin America—History.
4. Mestizaje in literature.   5. Latin America—In art.   6. Latin
America—Race relations.   I. Title.
F1414.M545   2004
980.03′3 — dc22

                                                    2004002952

For my brothers

CONTENTS

PREFACE

This book sprang from ideas that began to intrigue me when I was at work on a doctoral dissertation in comparative literature at the University of Oregon. My dissertation, titled "Miscegenation and the Narrative Voice," explored the relationship between the notion of "mixed race" and narrative production. While addressing textual representations of miscegenation in Latin America, the English Caribbean, the United States, and South Africa within a temporal frame that stretched from the colonial moment to the late twentieth century, I noticed that radically different vocabularies and discourses were used to describe the phenomenon.

The most glaring difference, perhaps, was between the vocabulary of the United States and that of Latin America. These "other" Americas provided a showcase of historical engagements with *mestizaje*, a term that may concurrently signify both biological and cultural mixture. In the United States, the absence of a corollary term or suitable translation revealed the refusal to create a parallel ideological space in the national imaginary and its projects. This crucial distinction was nowhere more evident than in modernist approaches to peoples whose backgrounds combined indigenous or Native American and European or Euro-American elements: in Latin America they were "mestizos," a name with an enormous range of meanings and a centrality to discussions of citizenship; in the United States they were referred to pejoratively as "half-breeds," as subjects who were somehow incomplete or fragmented, and whose status was marginal to these same national discussions.

Despite this fundamental difference between the United States and its southern neighbors, the impetus for the current project was the degree of cultural difference I experienced, not in moving from the United States to Latin America, but from living in different sites within Latin America. I had been educated to conceive of Spanish America as a unified space, and I had been inculcated with the precept that *mestizaje* was the predominant characteristic which distinguished Latin from North America. As a result, I was surprised by how appropriations of *mestizaje* could differ so dramatically *within* Latin America.

A profound paradox became increasingly evident: whereas numerous intellectual and political leaders, including Simón Bolívar, José Martí, José Vasconcelos, and others, had enlisted *mestizaje* as a way of ascertaining Spanish American difference when confronted by cultural and political pressure from Spain or the United States, intellectuals in Latin America and especially in North America responded by reifying *mestizaje* as the mark of Latin American *sameness*, as the most recognizable and pervasive condition of all peoples and cultural productions found south of the Rio Grande, as the mark of *la raza*.

This leveling gesture seems to have survived the recent deepening of interest in Latin America in a wide range of disciplines, including literary and cultural studies, that, in the wake of poststructuralist and postmodern thought, might have dismissed similarly essentializing identity formulations. The United States now arguably boasts the best resources— bibliographic, economic, and human—for scholars and students of Latin America. But despite privileged access to the subject, including the presence and collaboration of an unprecedented number of Latin American scholars in the North American academy, generalized and generalizing notions of *mestizaje* are still commonplace, so commonplace, in fact, that a pan–Latin American conception of *mestizaje* is now routinely enlisted in neoliberal and globalizing political and economic discourse throughout the Americas. This book attempts to illuminate just how uncommon configurations and experiences of *mestizaje* are across Latin America and the Caribbean, and how those experiences are so historically complex and intricate that they can never be fully explicated, understood, or consumed.

ACKNOWLEDGMENTS

The presence and *convivencia* of many academic friends and intellectual kin sustained this project in different moments of gestation in the United States, Ecuador, Mexico, Brazil, and the Caribbean. Among them, Leslie Bary, Laura Bass, Leslie Bayers, Jerome Branche, Guillermo Bustos, Luisa Campuzano, Luis Cárcamo, Elizabeth Claman, Thomas Cohen, Luis Correa Díaz, Laurence Denié, Christopher Dunn, Leonardo García Pabón, Lisa Gitelman, Roland Greene, Juan Carlos Grijalva, Barbara Guetti, Angela Leonard, Yolanda Martínez-San Miguel, Cristina Ortiz, Julio Ramos, Fernando Rosenberg, Ana Serra, Peter Shoemaker, Eileen Suárez Findlay, Javier Villa Flores, and Ari Zighelboim provided a wealth of fresh ideas, cautions, and timely encouragement. I would also like to acknowledge the members of the Global Culture Reading Group in Washington, DC, as well as Idelber Avelar, Robert Irwin, and other members of the *Latinoamericanismo* reading group in New Orleans. My students at the University of Oregon, the Pontificia Universidad Católica del Ecuador, the Catholic University of America, and Tulane University have all taught and inspired me in distinct and profound ways.

I have had the privilege of working in two fine libraries: the Library of Congress, where David Kelly and Anthony Mullen proved to be outstanding librarians as well as good friends; and the Latin American Library at Tulane University, where Paul Bary has been a consistent source of knowledge and assistance.

During the period in which the book was taking shape, I benefited from two National Endowment for the Humanities summer fellowships, one in 1998 to attend the institute titled "Roots: The African Background of American Culture through the Atlantic Slave Trade," directed by Joseph Miller and Jerome Handler, and another in 2002, to participate in "The Invisible Giant: The Place of Brazil in Latin American Studies," directed by Lúcia Helena Costigan.

A research fellowship from Tulane University provided me with time to make final revisions on this manuscript during a semester in Puerto Rico, where I also taught in the Department of Comparative Literature at the Río Piedras campus of the Universidad de Puerto Rico. The camaraderie and intellectual example of Susan Homar, Rubén Ríos Ávila, and María Elena Rodríguez Castro enriched my experience there tremendously.

Theresa J. May and her staff at the University of Texas Press have been gracious and encouraging allies in the lengthy process of book production, and Kathy Bork deserves many thanks for her careful and thoughtful editing.

Several soul mates fortuitously positioned outside (or after) academia provided the immeasurable gift of unwavering friendship and unconditional affirmation; foremost among them are Kenny Bagley, Diego Castaño, Kristi Drake, and David Wilson. My mother, whose avid curiosity and ever-inquiring mind helped me develop a sense of scholarship informed by social and spiritual concerns, remains a shining example.

Excerpts from the poems of Nicolás Guillén reprinted courtesy of Fundación Nicolás Guillén.

Fragments from "Copla Mulata" by Luis Lloréns Torres; from "Trópico suelto" by Manuel del Cabral; and from "Ñáñigo al cielo," "Mulata-Antilla," and "Ten con ten," by Luis Palés Matos reprinted courtesy of Editorial de la Universidad de Puerto Rico.

Excerpts from "Ay, ay, ay de la grifa negra," by Julia de Burgos, from *Song of the Simple Truth*, reprinted courtesy of Curbstone Press.

Excerpts by Luis Palés Matos are reprinted with permission of the publisher of *Selected Poems/Poesía selecta*, Julio Marzán, ed., (Houston: Arte Publico Press—University of Houston, 2000).

"Biconception" copyright © 1993 by Guillermo Gómez-Peña, reprinted from *Warrior for Gringostroika*, with permission of Graywolf Press, Saint Paul, Minnesota.

RISE AND FALL OF THE COSMIC RACE

All kinds of crossbreeds infest the land. The result is incredible
rottenness . . . The men stand on the corners talking scandal,
and utter obscenities whenever a woman passes.
The streets of the cities swarm with beggars.

ALFRED SCHULTZ, *Race or Mongrel*

The word mestizaje has become the object of a
true cult and the symbol of nationality.

MAGNUS MÖRNER, "EL MESTIZAJE EN LA
HISTORIA DE IBERO-AMÉRICA"[1]

Accepted miscegenation leads to ambiguous and fluid interracial
boundaries. It transforms race into an achieved quality that
diffuses and dilutes the power of racist thinking.

MAURICIO SOLAÚN AND SIDNEY KRONUS,
Discrimination Without Violence

Observation shows us that, in the case of America, the sole
invariable characteristic in the mosaic of its ethnic
makeup has been its constant and rich mestizaje.

MANUEL ZAPATA OLIVELLA, *¡Levántate Mulato!*[2]

I. OUR MESTIZO AMERICA

Perhaps no part of the sum total of the historical formation and configuration of Latin American national and regional identity has been as pervasive or comprehensive as the elaboration and employment of the concept
of *mestizaje*. The genetic and cultural admixture produced by the encounters or "dis-encounters" (*desencuentros*) between Europeans, the Africans
who accompanied them to and in the New World, indigenous groups, and
various others who arrived in the Americas from regions such as Asia, was

sometimes condemned, sometimes celebrated, but nearly always productive of an animated discussion of what it meant to inhabit the ground on which such confrontations occurred. This discussion crescendos, it seems, with the publication in 1925 of the Mexican educator José Vasconcelos' *The Cosmic Race*. This book argued for a pan–Latin American embrace of racial and cultural mixture as progressive rather than regressive, as a boon rather than a bane to ongoing deliberations concerning questions of local and regional identity.

The rise of this idea of a beneficial mixed race was riddled with the numerous obstacles and contradictions imbedded in a colonial history in which questions of racial difference and distinction were paramount. The complexity of the racial discourse produced in the colonies is most graphically portrayed, perhaps, in several sets of paintings which catalogued racial types, or *castas*. Proceeding from a strange racial alchemy, earlier broad divisions of Spaniard, Indian, *negro*, and mestizo or mulatto were splintered into retrograde hybrids such as the *lobo* (wolf) and the *salta-atrás* (jump-back).[3]

With this already turbulent history as a backdrop, *mestizaje* has been employed in radically distinct ways in Latin America's collective consciousness since the uneven transition from colony to independence. The range of meanings it has conveyed and continues to represent is surprisingly extensive and often frustrates attempts at providing coherent contexts for its examination.[4] It is no wonder, then, that the most prevalent characteristic of a historiography of *lo mestizo* is its lack of uniformity and, indeed, its pervasive susceptibility to contradictions. Richard Graham notes in *The Idea of Race in Latin America* that "the mestizo and mulatto played an important part in the thinking both of racists and antiracists in Mexico, Brazil, and Cuba" (4), producing commentary on the symbolic significance of these figures that ranged from the lamentable to the laudatory. The same incongruence can be found in other regions of privileged *mestizaje*, such as the Andes, as well as in Latin American territories in which the effects of the phenomenon have been judged to be negligible, notably, Argentina.

Indeed, *mestizaje* can be used as a lens through which to read the complexities and contradictions of Latin American social and literary history at both the regional and the local levels. Such an enterprise is extremely illuminating, even when summarizing the multitudinous effects of *mestizaje* as a racial discourse is ultimately impossible. The novitiate in the cult of Latin American *mestizaje* is confronted, on the one hand, with the intensely dynamic rites and litanies of appropriation, and, on the other, with the knowledge that *mestizaje*, like all racial discourse in Latin America, is "imbedded in social relations that are themselves often masked by simulation, dissimulation, and pretense" (Graham, 71). Despite these restraints, close examination of select moments of literary and cultural expression in which *mestizaje* is conspicuously embraced or vehemently denied offers rich lodes of knowledge concerning local, national, and transnational social relations and cultural production.

While ambivalence and mixed feelings toward racial contact and its results are apparent in all eras following the European arrival in the Americas, social historians have frequently associated the nineteenth century with the condemnation of *mestizaje* (despite the examples of Simón Bolívar and José Martí), and the twentieth with its renovation as a positive, even providential, phenomenon. Thus, it is commonplace for students of Latin American history, literature, and culture to learn that the maturing of national discourses and their attendant notions of unique national character and culture depended on a complex ontology that diffused or subsumed racial, linguistic, and performative differences under the banner of multiracial or multiethnic unity that translated into an integrated and integrative "spirit" or "soul."

By the middle of the twentieth century, this idea was so common that Salvador de Madariaga could assure readers in a 1945 publication that since the Spanish conquest of the Americas, Indians, whites, and blacks had "combined in all kinds of proportions, and beyond the strictly corporeal mixtures, life also churned and mixed the three human types and their combinations in constant colorations, so that the truly representative class and type of the Indies was the man of mixed blood—mestizo or mulatto. Whatever the statistics, the soul of the Indies is, then, in its essence, *a mestizo soul*" (in Mörner, "El mestizaje en la historia de Ibero-América," 11; my emphasis).

This notion of a "mestizo soul," indicative of the elision between physical and spiritual definitions of the condition, will show up again and again in equations which restate the idea that "mestizaje and Latin Americanness are indissoluble terms" (Basave Benítez, *México mestizo*, 17). So pervasive was the concept in this period that Antonio Cornejo-Polar would later write that *mestizaje* was a "conciliatory and comforting utopia that seems to gather into one unique torrent the many rivers that converged in this physical and spiritual geography we call Latin America" (*The Multiple Voices of Latin American Literature*, 23).

Until the last decade of the twentieth century, such generalizations were generally seen as positive. Many early nation builders viewed *mes-*

tizaje and its rehabilitation as a vital key to progress and development. Even when these same nationalizing projects were criticized for reifying colonial structures and practices, notions of *mestizaje* were usually not attacked. In many early texts of postcolonial criticism, at least, *mestizaje* still provided an effective tool with which centuries of colonial domination based on racial and cultural difference could be halted or reversed. Throughout this period, *mestizaje* — especially in counterdistinction to the racial practices of the United States which allowed little room for such ideas — was generally considered antiracist, anti-imperial, and more inclusive of a greater portion of Latin America's diverse citizenry in political and cultural engagements than ever before.

But late in the twentieth century, scholars began to reveal the links between the cult of *mestizaje* and earlier forms of colonial domination. Many of these scholars concluded that, in fact, *mestizaje*'s positive retooling had not solved problems of race and class in Latin America, but instead had compounded them by employing a rhetoric of inclusion that operated concurrently with a practice of exclusion. As Alan Knight puts it, "Racism can be driven underground (not necessarily very far underground); it can shift its premises (e.g., from biological to other, ostensibly more plausible, determinants) without that ideological shift substantially affecting its daily practice; and daily practice may even acquire added virulence as a result of official attempts at positive discrimination" (in Graham, 98).

Largely through the intervention of social scientists, literary critics began to see *mestizaje*'s darker side, its negative effects. These included the subsequent erosion of "regions of refuge" such as autonomous indigenous communities, whether geographic or linguistic, and the romanticization or folklorization of the Indian and the black, thereby dismissing their active engagement with contemporary political practices. Analysts who typically focused only on texts had to admit that through the symbolic portrayal of *mestizaje* in material projects such as the Plaza de las Tres Culturas (Plaza of the Three Cultures) in Tlatelolco, Mexico, attention could be deflected from the everyday experience of nonwhite or nonurban communities that did not share the values and goals of the mestizo majority. It soon became evident, on the ground and in the text, that the privileging of whiteness continued concurrently with the deployment of *mestizaje* as a national and regional doctrine. Categories such as *"indio"* and *"negro"* were still routinely used in pejorative ways, while official ideology declared the worth and occasionally even the superiority of the nonwhite. Despite this exaltation, however, sociopolitical circumstances continued to display the reality of prejudice (Graham, 101).

A second, related, problem was theoretical: due to overuse, the term *mestizaje* now suffered from "epistemological poverty and inherent conceptual obliqueness" (De Grandis and Bernd, *Unforeseeable Americas*, x).[5] *Mestizaje* was often used interchangeably with terms such as "hybridity," "transculturation," "creolization," "*métissage*,"[6] and "heterogeneity," while other critics rejected it outright as a synonym of any of these, because of its historical associations with questions of race. In some cases, even those words associated with *mestizaje* became theoretically tainted. Walter Mignolo, for example, insists on the unwieldy alternatives of "colonial semiosis" and "pluritopic hermeneutics" as ways to avoid the "shadows of 'mestizaje'" in the term "transculturation" (*Local Histories/Global Designs*, 14).[7] Mignolo recognizes that these terms were too frequently employed in postcolonial criticism that ignored the colonial underpinnings of postindependence American cultures (*Local Histories/Global Designs*, 94): "It is confusing when 'hybridity,' 'mestizaje,' 'space-in-between,' and other equivalent expressions become the object of reflection and critique of post-colonial theories, for they suggest a discontinuity between the colonial configuration of the object or subject of study and the postcolonial position of the locus of theorizing . . . Thus, postcoloniality or the postcolonial becomes problematic when applied to either nineteenth- or twentieth-century cultural practices in Latin America."

The late Peruvian scholar Antonio Cornejo-Polar, whose work has been so fundamental to an understanding of Andean negotiations of mestizo identity, in his later work called for a new emphasis on "migrancy" as an alternative to *mestizaje*. He feared the term had exhausted almost all its explanatory capacity ("A Non-Dialectic Heterogeneity," 114).

This revelation of the problematic and even pernicious fallout of the cult of *mestizaje*, though now fairly widespread in Latin American academic studies, nonetheless seems at times to have had little practical effect. When convenient, *mestizaje* is still often seized upon in both political and artistic engagements that strive to define nations or the region. It appears that in the twenty-first century, the concept is again being retooled, this time alongside a call for the dissolution of frontiers and differences where they might provide obstacles to a full assumption of transnational neoliberal ideologies. In the hyperglossy millennial text *Mestizo America: The Country of the Future* (Villegas, 17), globalization and *mestizaje* cooperate, allowing the "new nations" of Latin America to integrate while still maintaining their cultural and regional differences. On the one hand, hundreds of full-color photographs demonstrate both the geographical and the cultural diversity of the Latin American terrain. On the other, the book documents the increasing frequency with which "traditional" and "new" cultural elements provide a palimpsest of premodern, modern, and postmodern in the myriad corners of the continent. In one shot, a Mexican in typical *charro* attire, including a huge sombrero, rides down a Zacatecas street on horseback between late-model cars (306). In another, a young girl with indigenous features, a soiled gray dress, and flat canvas shoes peeks across the back of a pickup at three light-skinned women wearing high heels and skin-tight minidresses advertising Mexican beers Carta Blanca and Tecate (336–337). These everyday juxtapositions, increasingly common throughout the region, are evidence, for the collaborators, of an "ideal that is becoming a reality," that is, true continental integration. The volume notably presents the incorporation of a postnational mestizo ideology as a *future* project, rather than one of the most prevalent intellectual and literary gestures of the now-past twentieth century. "How can we not wish that someday, when neighborliness, cooperation and mutual respect are truly honored, the American continent will become, by virtue of its shared languages and traditions, a vast alliance of dignity and civilization!" proclaims William Ospina (27). Clearly, *mestizaje* is not dead, despite its legacy of semantic ambiguity, political incorrectness, and subsequent dismissal by many cultural critics. This study looks closely at the construction of specific national and regional engagements with *mestizaje* in Latin America to better understand why it was such an essential part of these localized histories, why it reached its public apogee—or, conversely, its rejection—in particular sites at particular moments, how it differed from one area to another, and how it continues to be rhetorically produced, internally or externally, despite its fall from grace in the wake of revelations of its complicity with coloniality. Even in its most celebrated moment, *mestizaje* was riddled with ambiguities, ambivalence, contradiction, and doubt, and its fall is already present in the work of those cultural icons (both personal and national) that plot its rise to fame.

By exploring certain thickets of the semantic jungle that *mestizaje* represents in Latin America, I reveal how its invocation is always framed by local histories and contemporary sociopolitical conditions, contexts, and conditions which, in turn, re-dress it according to specific national and transnational concerns. Whereas *mestizaje* has been taken as a monolithic discourse and a commonplace of *latinoamericanismo*, a tour of its myriad appearances in textual and other expressive formats divulges a trajectory of tremendous variance, polarization, juxtaposition, and opposition. The most obvious juxtaposition is between its use as a term indicating racial or ethnic lineage or physical characteristics and its elaboration as an aesthetics or stylistics of cultural production. The first definition is associated with the colonial period, the second with the contemporary, though both are clearly at play in both moments.[8] Chilean writer Jorge Guzmán, in developing a theory of the "mesticity" of Latin American texts, explains, "Of course, I understand the category 'mestizo' in the first place, as a characteristic of the Latin American semiotic system, and only in secondary terms as a topic related to genetics, that is, as something which has to do with the form and color of our bodies" (*Contra el secreto profesional*, 21). But historians and sociologists have not always maintained this emphasis, and Guzmán admits that "the two components, semiotic and somatic, are inseparable, and in a certain way, indistinguishable" (21).

The slipperiness of *mestizaje* as a somatic or semiotic category of signification should be seen in the context of several centuries in which "race" was considered a viable and, indeed, inescapable determinant of Latin American and Caribbean character and, ultimately, of cultural ontology. In this taxonomy, the mestizo was frequently converted into an essential racial type who possessed specific traits that were alternately positive or negative, thus casting him and his counterparts (the mestiza, the mulatto, the mulatta, etc.) as either villains or heroes in the drama of identity. This idea of a fixed mixed race crystallized, perhaps, in the late nineteenth century, when "empirical" theories of positivism, social Darwinism, and geographic determinism restricted the play of meanings attributed to racial or ethnic indicators. While such notions were frequently imported from countries that Latin Americans considered their models and mentors,[9] their application to local situations had to account for unprecedented numbers of peoples who exhibited mixed lineage (and therefore challenged facile categorization) and for the cultural intersections implied by these populations.

II. EARLY NEGOTIATIONS

While the term "*mestizaje*" is used—even by some of the writers examined here—to refer to distant parts of the world, no region, it is repeatedly claimed, boasts the degree of *mestizaje* brought about by the colonial encounter of Iberia and the territories convened by Spanish and Portuguese expansionism as Latin America. It is there where "there exists a case unique to *the entire planet*: a vast zone for which mestizaje is not an accident but rather the essence, the central line" (Fernández Retamar, *Caliban and Other Essays*, 4; original emphasis). The cult of *mestizaje* renders particular homage, therefore, to revolutionary leaders such as Simón Bolívar and José Martí, who presided over the century that marked the uneasy and fitful transitions of Spanish colonies to new American republics. Two texts by Bolívar, a letter written from Jamaica in 1815 and an address read to the Venezuelan Congress at Angostura four years later, are often considered the anchor documents of Latin American *mestizaje*.[10] In the first, Bolívar responds to the governor of Jamaica concerning current conditions in the colonies and provides details of specific revolutionary efforts throughout Spanish America. He dreams of an "America fashioned into the greatest nation in the world," but admits that such a dream is grandiose and distant from the complexities faced by the "Creole," or American-born, leaders sketching out national and regional autonomy.[11] Other fallen empires, notably Rome, could build new governments on historical precedents; America was different (*Selected Writings of Bolívar*, 110): "But we scarcely retain a vestige of what once was; we are, moreover, neither Indian nor European, but a species midway between the legitimate proprietors of this country and the Spanish usurpers. In short, though Americans by birth we derive our rights from Europe, and we have to assert these rights against the rights of the natives, and at the same time we must defend ourselves against the invaders. This places us in a most extraordinary and involved situation." Though he invokes the categories of European and Indian, Bolívar's "midway" species is defined more in political than in ethnic terms. Thus it finds itself caught in an "extraordinary situation" between legitimate proprietorship and usurpation.

The same ideas are strikingly recycled in the address delivered at the inauguration of the second national congress of Venezuela in February of 1819, this time in the context of the future of Bolívar's national home. Again, Rome is held up as a model of reconstruction, whereas, "we, on the contrary, do not even retain the vestiges of our original being. We are not Europeans; we are not Indians; we are but a mixed species of aborigines and Spaniards. Americans by birth and Europeans by law, we find ourselves engaged in a dual conflict: we are disputing with the natives for titles of ownership, and at the same time we are struggling to maintain ourselves in the country that gave us birth against the opposition of the invaders" (*Selected Writings of Bolívar*, 176). The difficulty of rendering the notion of biological *mestizaje* into English is more apparent in this passage (thus the clumsy use of "aborigines"), but the equation between *mestizaje* and a unique political destiny is exactly the same. Latin America can no longer be ruled by Spain, because its people are not Spanish, and the proof of this difference is the presence — not of an indigenous, or "aboriginal," remnant—but of a "mixed species" engaged in a "dual conflict." Bolívar's formula notably leaves out the "pure" Indians in the same way that it rejects the Spanish in the configuration of the republic, although he ultimately dismisses the notion of purity as well (*Selected Writings of Bolívar*, 181):

> We must keep in mind that our people are neither European nor North American; rather, they are a mixture of African and the Americans who originated in Europe. Even Spain herself has ceased to be European because of her African blood, her institutions, and her character. It is impossible to determine with any degree of accuracy where we belong in the human family. The greater portion of the native Indians has been annihilated; Spaniards have mixed with Americans and Africans, and Africans with Indians and Spaniards. While we have all been born of the same mother, our fathers, different in origin and in blood, are foreigners, and all differ visibly as to the color of their skin: a dissimilarity which places upon us an obligation of the greatest importance.

In this second segment of his address, Bolívar acknowledges the fundamental importance of peoples of African descent to the constitution of American ontology, questions the notion of European racial purity, and recognizes the role of the indigenous woman (though not, perhaps, indigenous women, since all are reduced here to the "same" mother) in the genealogy of the peoples of the Americas.[12] He insists the *dissimilarity*, or difference, between these social mixtures and cases elsewhere obliges Latin Americans to respond to their destiny in an autochthonous way.

Bolívar's famous words, so often recalled, are tempered by others in which this characteristic difference is lost in generalizations that stereotype the Indians and blacks of nineteenth-century Latin America and subsume their quotidian experiences of inequality and injustice within a pervasive "spirit of gentleness" (*The Hope of the Universe*, 119). In a draft written in Jamaica about 1815 titled "Racial Harmony in the Mixed Society of the New World, and Other Thoughts in Jamaica," Bolívar contends with the notion that the main obstacle to independence "lies in the difference between the races that make up the people of this immense country" (*The Hope of the Universe*, 118). He addresses the specific fear raised for Euro-Americans by the Haitian Revolution in 1791 (the first successful large-scale revolutionary movement of nonwhites in the New World), namely, that where *criollos* or whites did not constitute the majority, a similar rebellion of blacks or Indians might occur. Bolívar concurs that whites are in the minority, "but it is also certain that the latter possess intellectual qualities which confer on them relative equality and an influence which may seem excessive to those who have not been able to judge for themselves of the moral situation and material circumstances in South America" (*The Hope of the Universe*, 118). This argument is, of course, much closer to the ideas of just conquest and providential expansion by Europeans and their descendants than are the references to the "midway species" in the texts examined above.

In the wake of the French Revolution and its emphasis on the implementation of majority rule, Bolívar seeks here to justify a situation in which the minority exert the greater power by reverting, implicitly, to the claim of rational (and racial) superiority: what whites lack in numbers, they make up in smarts. And he provides further proofs of why racial strife is unlikely. First, he points out that since the conquest, the Indians have thought the Europeans to be "a race of mortals superior to ordinary men," an idea which lingers, "owing to the strong influence of superstition, fear of brute force, displays of disproportionate wealth, the wielding of authority, intellectual superiority and any number of circumstantial advantages" (*The Hope of the Universe*, 118). While Bolívar acknowledges abuses of power by the white minority, such as the exercise of brutality, economic practices that are inherently unequal, and an ominous-sounding "wielding of authority," he nevertheless unflinchingly proclaims the intellectual superiority of Euro-Americans. The Spaniard and his New World descendant, gentle by nature (despite the aforementioned brutality and repression he inflicts) treats his servants well, and "is rarely driven by greed or necessity" (*The Hope of the Universe*, 119). Similarly, the Indian "is so peace-loving by nature that he desires only rest and to be left alone"; he has no ambition to prevail over outsiders. He is friendly toward all, enjoying his full rights before the law. Given this high measure of gentleness, peacefulness, and friendliness between whites and Indians, and those of mixed race, who presumably share all these qualities, "the threat of hostility between races decreases" (*The Hope of the Universe*, 120).

But the most difficult element to square with a vision of the great Liberator as a staunch opponent of race-based discrimination and a champion of racial mixture and harmony is his portrayal of the enslaved Latin American (*The Hope of the Universe*, 120): "The slave in Spanish America vegetates in complacent inertia on his master's estate, enjoying all the benefits that accrue from being part of such an establishment, as well as a considerable degree of freedom. Since religion has taught him that to serve is a sacred duty, and since all his life he has lived in this state of domestic dependence, he feels that he is leading a natural life, as a member of his master's family, whom he loves and respects." Though Bolívar never describes this slave as either African or black in this text, his previous characterization of Creoles, Indians, and mestizos makes clear the unstated obvious: black and slave have become synonymous or interchangeable in early-nineteenth-century Spanish America.

Despite the considerable "freedom" the slave population reportedly enjoyed, in 1816 Bolívar issued a decree declaring "absolute freedom for the slaves" (*The Hope of the Universe*, 123) who had "suffered under the Spanish yoke for the past three centuries." Much of his motivation was clearly tactical: the decree also states that within twenty-four hours of its publication, every able-bodied man between the ages of fourteen and sixty was to report to his district parish to enlist for military duty. "Any new citizen who refuses to take up arms to perform the sacred duty of defending his freedom shall remain in servitude, and not only he but also his children, even if under the age of 14, his wife, and his parents, even if elderly" (*The Hope of the Universe*, 123–124). Despite the clear linkage of emancipation and military service, Bolívar's strategy drew protests, and he had to reiterate his policy in 1820 and again in 1821, demonstrating that slave owners were not at all convinced that service to one's country should be paid for with freedom papers.[13]

Where difference was perceived to be an asset, that is, *mestizaje* as proof of an American political destiny separate from Spain, Bolívar was careful to accentuate it. Where difference was a potential liability to his struggle for autonomy, as in the distinction between blacks and whites and between slave and master, he sought to minimize it, so that, ultimately, all Americans, whether white, black, or Indian, could unite in the defense of the homeland. Bolívar is ultimately unique in his recognition of an Afro-Euro-indigenous American *mestizaje*, since most early references typically portrayed the mestizo as the cross between a Spanish man and an indigenous woman and discounted African contributions. In this acknowledgment of Africans as Americans, Bolívar prefigures, to some extent, Caribbean approaches to *mestizaje* which lament the decimation of indigenous peoples and focus on the Afro-European encounter. Beginning with the 1815 Letter from Jamaica, then, the Caribbean begins to constitute itself as an epicenter both productive and reflective of *mestizaje*, producing a long line of central figures and a condensed list of key terms and critical comments which together provide a textual map of its impact in the rest of Latin America.[14]

If Bolívar is the reigning figure in the cult of *mestizaje* which we have begun to chart and question, José Martí (1853–1895) may be considered its most ardent champion prior to the full elaboration of a mestizo apologetics in Vasconcelos.[15] Martí clearly considered Bolívar an ideological mentor and a model for his own attempts to question racial hierarchies and discrimination. In an effusively laudatory essay on Bolívar, he wrote, "The hero wrapped himself in this Indian, [mestizo] and white soul merged into a single flame, and found it constant and inextinguishable" (*José Martí Reader*, 167).[16] In another passage, he specifically ties Bolívar's independence projects to an explicitly emancipatory rhetoric, asking, "Did he not unshackle races, disenthrall a continent, bring nations into being?" (165).

Drawing on the example of collaboration between blacks and whites in earlier attempts at gaining Cuba's independence from Spain, especially during the Ten Years' War (1868–1878), the gifted Creole statesman-poet proclaimed that "there can be no racial animosity, because there are no races" (*José Martí Reader*, 119). He also addressed the lingering fears of a race war, still felt eighty years after Bolívar assured his readers that such a struggle would not occur (*José Martí Reader*, 161): "In Cuba, there is no fear of a racial war. Men are more than whites, mulattos or Negroes. On the field of battle, dying for Cuba, the souls of whites and Negroes have risen together into the air. In the daily life of defense, loyalty, brotherhood and shrewdness, Negroes have always been there, alongside whites." Like Bolívar, Martí championed the ideas of racial unity and cooperation in the struggle for independence, but he also expanded his predecessor's notion of *mestizaje* as a fundamental characteristic of Latin America's unique heritage and destiny. In the 1891 essay titled "Our America," which still enjoys enormous popularity among scholars of Latin American and trans-American studies,[17] he proudly proclaims the rise of the mestizo as the guarantee of Latin American autonomy in the face of the United States' expansionist designs on Cuba, Puerto Rico, large chunks of Central America, and other regions.

Martí's ideas on race, like the subsequent notions of José Vasconcelos, should be understood, at least in part, as a reaction to official and unofficial racial discourse in the United States. Martí was convinced that the United States meant to take advantage of political disintegration in his island and impose its own government, and as Philip Foner points out in an introduction to an anthology of Martí's work in translation, "Martí's conviction that the great neighbor to the north was an omnipresent threat to Cuba's progressive and independent development stemmed as much from his fear of Yankee racism as it did from his fear of U.S. imperialist ambitions" (Martí, *Our America*, 29).

Both these fears were well-founded. A quarter decade after Martí called for an end to racial distinctions in Cuba, Edward Byron Reuter published a dissertation in the Department of Sociology at the University of Chicago titled "The Mulatto in the United States" (later published by Badger Press). Despite the title, Reuter included a long discussion of mixed-race peoples in South America, arguing that, "broadly speaking, the review seems to bear out the conclusion that in its acute and troublesome form, the 'race problem' is the problem of the mulatto . . . In every case the half-caste races have arisen as the result of illicit relations between the men of the superior and the women of the inferior race" (*The Mulatto in the United States*, 87–88). Later on he adds (317–318):

> There is no intention here to criticize the mulattoes or other men of mixed blood; quite the contrary. To recognize their desire to be white, their ambition to associate themselves through marriage or otherwise with the white race, is but to recognize their ability to appreciate the superior culture of the white group. An opposite tendency on their part would go far towards establishing the thesis of the congenital inability of the lower group to assimilate white civilization. It would show a deliberate preference on their part for the inferior in the presence of the superior.

The unperturbed certainty with which Reuter and other "men of science" fostered such notions of racial superiority would have been familiar to Martí, who lived in the United States for some fourteen years before returning to Cuba to take part (with fatal results) in the armed struggle for independence in 1895. He was also no doubt aware that many of the same ideas were prevalent in his own country and, indeed, throughout Latin America, voiced even by those attached to the long struggle to end slavery. The famous Cuban abolitionist and historian José Antonio Saco (1797–1879) had argued, for example, that once the slave trade ended and further miscegenation ensued, blacks would disappear (Graham, 39).

Despite his enormous stature in Cuban and Latin American studies today, in his own era Martí was a maverick whose ideas were dismissed by many of his Cuban contemporaries. Cuban ethnographer Fernando Ortiz (1881–1969) recalled hearing his grandfather categorize all Cubans who were separatists, or *independentistas*, as people of color. When the younger Ortiz (who later carefully researched Martí's writings on race) maintained that the revolutionary Creole leader was born in Cuba of "pure" Spanish blood, his grandfather retorted that "Martí wasn't colored, but he might as well have been; he was a mulatto on the inside" ("Martí y las razas,"

337). The comment reveals that even at the turn of the twentieth century, racial characteristics and political posture were still often considered to be mutually reflective.

Despite Martí's detractors, in the modernist Latin American ontology that emerged in the wake of the last independence struggles in the Spanish colonies in the 1890s, the discourse of *mestizaje* takes on cultlike dimensions, appearing as it does in numerous political and aesthetic projects under the banners of union, assimilation, harmony, synthesis, and cooperation. While these appropriations focused on contemporary cultural trends, they also entailed a reassessment of colonial practices or independence movements, rereading them as indicators or harbingers of the mestizo character only fully understood in modernity. In this progressive reading of mestizo phenomena, José Vasconcelos becomes the intellectual and spiritual heir of Bolívar (Zea, *Regreso de las carabelas*, 82): "Vasconcelos takes the Bolivaran utopia to its highest level."

It is the optimism and idealism of men like Bolívar, Martí, and Vasconcelos that is usually remembered, not their misgivings or fundamental changes in opinion. There is little awareness, for example, of Bolívar's later disenchantment with the notion of the "new human type" that the fusion of Indian, black, and European had produced. In October of 1830, he wrote to Gen. Rafael Urdaneta expressing pessimism about the barbarous masses (Ortega y Medina, *Reflexiones históricas*, 279), a crisis of faith that may have provided fodder for the virulent racism of Domingo Faustino Sarmiento, whose mid-nineteenth-century foundational text *Facundo* called for the reduction of "savage" Indian and black elements and the coterminous stimulation of white European immigration to Latin America.[18]

As tends to happen with martyrs and saints, any undercurrent of doubt is usually excised from the biographies of key figures associated with the defense of Latin America's unique mesticity. Consider, for example, the words of a contemporary celebrant, Mexican essayist Leopoldo Zea (*Regreso de las carabelas*, 55): "Where does this utopia that Vasconcelos, Bolívar, Martí and many other Latin Americans imagined as a universal goal come from? From history, from the historical experience of the region that emerged in the history of European consciousness October 12, 1492, that is, five hundred years ago." Zea's comment demonstrates how the historical "real" and the ideal or imaginary come together in the revolutionary configurations of *mestizaje* in Bolívar, Martí, and Vasconcelos, so that a history that is marked by war and atrocity paradoxically produces utopia.

Indeed, part of this common project of moving beyond the rancor of conquest was the adoption of the term "Latin American," which called attention to the cultural and linguistic heritage that distinguished countries south of the Rio Grande from the United States. But the "Latin" element also represented the importance of classical models to these thinkers, who, to varying degrees, looked for ways to adapt the Greco-Roman example to the new American situation—sometimes finding important distinctions, too, as had Bolívar. The heterogeneity of these cultures of antiquity was particularly attractive to these nineteenth- and twentieth-century contractors of Latin American identity, providing them with a tool for reinterpreting the mixture of peoples and cultures not as contamination or dilution, but as a felicitous conjoining of forces and characteristics, conjuncture that could be enlisted in the development of a regional identity that both recognized internal differences and unified Latin America in its distinction from Europe and the United States.

These early engagements with *mestizaje* by Bolívar and Martí left an enormous imprint on Latin American intellectual culture, and there can be little doubt that *The Cosmic Race* is in many ways a companion text to other writings by Vasconcelos in which these independence leaders figure prominently, such as *Bolivarismo y Monroísmo*. When Roberto Fernández Retamar revisited *mestizaje* in light of the 1959 Cuban Revolution in "Caliban: Notes toward a Discussion of Culture in Our America" (*Caliban and Other Essays*, 3–45), he cited both Bolívar's address to the Congress of Angostura and Martí's famous designation of "our Mestizo America." For Fernández Retamar, Martí's *mestizaje* serves as a harbinger of the full realization of Latin American identity within the Cuban Revolution, in which "*mestizaje* is not an accident but rather the essence" and "the distinctive sign of our culture—a culture of descendants, both ethnically and culturally speaking, of aborigines, Africans, and Europeans" (4).[19] Here, Fernández Retamar seems to again equate "race"—or at least ethnicity—with culture, although in a footnote, he clarifies that what interests him "is not the irrelevant biological fact of the 'races' but the historical fact of the 'cultures'" (113). He enlists Martí's emphasis on *mestizaje* to prove his common cause with the oppressed, explaining that "Martí is radically antiracist because he is a spokesman for the exploited classes, within which the three races are fusing" (27). Though Fernández Retamar judges both Vasconcelos and his cornerstone essay to be "confused," he nevertheless considers the text to be "full of intuitions" that would be later illuminated by revolutionary events.

III. TRANSCULTURATION AND ITS BY-PRODUCTS

Beginning in the nineteenth century, written commentary on racial or cultural mixture and its ramifications for emerging Latin American nations began to have a deep impact on such diverse issues as immigration, the classification and management of criminal behaviors, religious practices and their promotion or suppression, and the enactment of a variety of juridical and economic policies. Bolstered by the "hard science" of positivism and determinism, intellectuals and policy makers generally found it unproblematic to equate physical characteristics with specific socioeconomic indicators or cultural behaviors. While this tendency produced obvious problems in terms of the discourse of *mestizaje* or hybridity,[20] it also stimulated an examination of these ideas within a broadly interdisciplinary frame of inquiry. The study of science and culture often converged, as is the case in the work of Fernando Ortiz, whose *Cuban Counterpoint: Tobacco and Sugar*, first published in Spanish in 1940, attempted to chart cultural modes alongside economic developments and structures in Cuba.

Ortiz used the term "*transculturación*" to refer to the process of complex cultural transmutations produced in Cuba through contact between Amerindians, Spaniards, Africans, Asians, and others, a phenomenon especially in evidence, he believed, in the juxtapositional cultures that grew up around tobacco and sugar production. This process was itself a multiplication of elements already "transculturated" before their insertion into the Cuban scenario: the colonial population that arrived from a wide variety of geographies and cultural experiences in Spain; the diverse "human flood" of Africans of distinct cultures and races; and the successive waves of immigrants from Asia and other parts of the globe. Ortiz argued that the conceptualization and employment of transculturation accomplished two things: first, it acknowledged the mutual processes of influence and adaptation between these different members of classes, races, stations, and settings in the emerging Cuban society; and, second, it disabled the Anglo-American models of acculturation, which recognized only a unidirectional cultural influence of dominants over subalterns (*Cuban Counterpoint*, 98).

There is a clear, if implicit, connection between Ortiz' transculturation and the discourse of *mestizaje* in the work of Bolívar, Martí, and others.[21] The most apparent change is the weight shift from *mestizaje* as a result of a biological genealogy to transculturation as the result of the specific local economy. While observable racial phenomena may still be present in Ortiz' survey, they are secondary to cultural emanations. And as with previous theories of *mestizaje*, Ortiz' work on transculturation presents certain elements that complicate a history of contact as productive of harmony and positive synthesis. Significantly, he sees contemporary transcultural processes as the legacy of the Spanish colonial project, a project he identifies with the famous sixteenth-century Dominican friar Bartolomé de las Casas' condemnation as the "destruction of the Indies." In his famous chapter entitled "On the Social Phenomenon of 'Transculturation' and Its Importance in Cuba" (*Cuban Counterpoint*, 97–103), Ortiz' description of transculturation employs a form of terror in five different instances, alongside notions of destruction, failure, cruelty, brute force, injustice, and pain. Thus, despite insisting on the creative collaboration of oppressor and oppressed groups in the formation of Cuban and other American cultures, Ortiz acknowledges that such a process was frequently violent and, in fact, productive of violence.

The challenge to rethink transculturation in a broad trans-American frame was taken up by Ángel Rama in his influential *Transculturación narrativa en América Latina* (Narrative Transculturation in Latin America), published four decades after Ortiz popularized the term. Rama focuses on the creative possibilities implied by transculturation as a form of *narrative* transitiveness between cultures, even when those cultures stand in unequal relation to each other, and he explores these possibilities in relation to Latin American novels from the 1960s to the 1980s.[22] Whereas Ortiz focused on performative discourses such as music and dance as the best examples of transculturation, for Rama, literature is in fact its privileged staging ground, and a model for its expression in other cultural forms.

Transculturation has since had a quite successful career in Latin American studies. It appears prominently in the work of Mary Louise Pratt, who borrows an ethnographic understanding of the term to describe "how subordinated or marginal groups select and invent from materials transmitted to them by a dominant or metropolitan culture" (*Imperial Eyes*, 6), an application somewhat distant from the term's employment by Ortiz. One element of Pratt's work that had substantial impact in further developing the theory of hybridity and *mestizaje* was the development of the notion of the "contact zone," "the space in which peoples geographically and historically separated come into contact with each other and establish ongoing relations, usually involving conditions of coercion, radical inequality, and intractable conflict" (*Imperial Eyes*, 6). While this contact is never explicitly sexual, miscegenation is implicitly evoked as one of its immediate results, and *mestizaje* as a product of its "ongoing relations." For Pratt, as for Ortiz, such relations were often uneven, conflictive, and frequently violent or coercive.

Another supporter of the term is critic Nelly Richard, who has sought ways to "de-symbolize difference" and open it to a differential multiplicity of practices. Richard suggests a strategy of "appropriation-reconversion" in which hybridism and other figures "bear on *local* problematics of our histories and societies: the role of racial-cultural *mestizaje* and other forms of Transculturation in the formation of Latin America" ("The Latin American Problematic of Theoretical-Cultural Transference," 230; original emphasis).[23]

Recognizing various historical deployments of transculturation in the writing of Ortiz as well as in works by colonial chroniclers, the artists of the Cuzco school, twentieth-century Peruvian writer José María Arguedas, and contemporary Latino narrators, Silvia Spitta's *Between Two Waters* defines transculturation as "the complex processes of adjustment and re-creation — cultural, literary, linguistic, and personal — that allow for new, vital, and viable configurations to arise out of the clash of cultures and the violence of colonial and neo-colonial appropriations." Whereas notions such as acculturation, adaptation, assimilation, Manifest Destiny, and the melting pot represent for Spitta one axis of (bleakly) interpreting the conquest of the Americas, transculturation, miscegenation, hybridization, syncretism, *métissage*, and heterogeneity are proposed as tools for an alternative, more promising, understanding (Spitta, 2). Moving between the colonial and the contemporary, Spitta argues that the Latin American subject is always "in process" and situated along a "continuum of mestizaje" (23). At the same time, she recognizes the complexity and difficulties of this process and urges us to read transculturation as a colonially produced space of "extreme ambiguity" and contradictory meanings (24).[24]

From different corners of the field, other noteworthy critics have weighed in for transculturation (Román de la Campa,[25] Françoise Perus, Abril Trigo) or against it (Neil Larsen, Martín Lienhard, Antonio Benítez-Rojo). In his 1990 study of the colonial chronicle in Mexico and Peru, Lienhard rejects both the notion of cultural *mestizaje* and its recuperation in the idea of transculturation, because of the tendency to "erase the pluricultural reality, and above all, the permanent discrimination of those sectors marginalized culturally or socially" (*La voz y su huella*, 132), thereby leaving unresolved the problem of political evaluations of cultural interactions (134).[26] Antonio Benítez-Rojo, in *The Repeating Island*, the most ambitious study to date of hybridity and similar concepts in the context of Caribbean postmodernity, dismisses both *mestizaje* and transculturation as suggestive of synthesis, rather than as an ongoing, insoluble (cultural) equation of differences (26). He recommends instead "syncretism," a term, in his estimation, too often restricted to descriptions of religious practices. What all these reflections reveal, perhaps, is the semiotic variance and susceptibility of *mestizaje* and its sequels, including transculturation and hybridity.

IV. BAKHTIN IN THE AMERICAS

Another important critical event which contributed significantly to the interest in terms such as "hybridity," "liminality," and "*mestizaje*" in Latin America was the translation of M. M. Bakhtin's essay "Discourse in the Novel" into English by Caryl Emerson and Michael Holquist in 1981. Before this, Bakhtin was an "obscure Russian critic" known in a few quarters for an overstated book on Dostoevsky and an idiosyncratic study of Rabelais (Morson, *Bakhtin*, vii). With the publication of "Discourse in the Novel" and three other essays included in *The Dialogic Imagination*, Bakhtin quickly became one of the most frequently cited critics in the West. Responding in large part to the microscopic study of aesthetic structures practiced by the Russian formalists, Bakhtin calls for a poetics that celebrates "unfinalizedness" as an irrefutable characteristic of any speech or text act and argues that the formalists' presumption of the fixedness of literary structures prohibits a full understanding not only of ideological meanings inherent in words, but, indeed, of the "idea system" of speech, a system which is fluid and dynamic. Bakhtin seeks to expose both the dogma and the fragility of forms in his investigation of Rabelaisian carnival, a trope which he says ironizes, satirizes, and, ultimately, jeopardizes formal fixity.

In "Discourse in the Novel," Bakhtin uses hybridity in its philological sense to describe the phenomenon of multivoicedness within a single speech act as a linguistic and social act: "What is hybridization? It is a mixture of two social languages within the limits of a single utterance, an encounter, within the arena of an utterance, between two different linguistic consciousnesses, separated from one another by an epoch, by social differentiation or by some other factor" (Bakhtin, 358). Bakhtin recognizes two basic kinds of hybridity. Organic, "unintentional, unconscious" hybrids are those in which the mixture of languages is fused into a new system, while "intentional" hybrids are "internally dialogic" forms in which languages and idea systems are set against each other. He sees the first kind of hybrid structure as characteristic of any living, evolving language, while he associates the second specifically with the development of language in the novel (361; original emphasis): "The novelistic hybrid is *an artistically organized system for bringing different languages in contact with one another, a system having as its goal the illumination of one language by means of another, the carving-out of a living image of another language.*"

According to Bakhtin, the multivoicing that is representative of novelistic language comes into play as the contours of everyday society allow for the interaction of dissimilar languages. His description of the circumstances in which this phenomenon can and does occur is broad enough to allow for many kinds of social and structural confrontation that he never addresses. The intentional hybrid structure of the novel may result from the presence of two linguistic systems separated by geography, class, time, or by some "other factor" (358). While Bakhtin's examples of the novelizing force of heteroglossia are most often based on class differences, very often his "other factor" is the focus of contemporary scholars applying Bakhtin to the fields of postcolonial criticism, "race" theory, and regional studies of culture, including Latin American studies.

Bakhtin's insistence on the dynamic quality of language is undergirded by the anti-Romantic belief that no speech act is autonomous, that "everything means, is understood, as part of a greater whole—there is a constant interaction between meanings, all of which have the potential of conditioning others" (Bakhtin, 426). By defining meaning as conditioned by multivoicedness or heteroglossia, Bakhtin is also arguing that interpretation is about context as well as text. The commitment to context and the insistence on multivoicedness are two aspects of Bakhtinian theory that many Latin Americanists recognize as characteristic of both primary and secondary sources within their own canon, including many theoretical texts that predate the appearance of Bakhtin's essays in English or Spanish. Thus, while many critics in North America working in postcolonial theory, New Historicism, and cultural studies began to talk about Bakhtinian hybridity as a tool for application to minority, "subaltern," or revisionist texts, scholars in Latin America took note of the affinity of his concepts not only with several historiographies and novels important in the continent, but also with "general" works of literary criticism and theory such as Ortiz's *Cuban Counterpoint* and Rama's *Transculturation in Latin America*.[27] Françoise Perus is one prominent Latin American scholar who has noticed the affinity between Bakhtinian theory and two important currents in late-twentieth-century critical theory in Spanish America: Cornejo-Polar's commentary on cultural heterogeneity as characteristic of *indigenista* narrative, and Rama's appropriation and expansion of Ortiz' transculturation as applied to regionalism in narrative. Both ideas, like Bakhtinian dialogism, are attempts to find a bridge between cultural discontinuities and narrative fiction ("El dialogismo y la poética histórica Bajtinianos," 31).

Certainly, there are striking, if not eerie, similarities between Cornejo-Polar's comments on Latin American discourses and Bakhtin's conceptualization of the chronotope. Bakhtin used the term *"xronotop"* to refer to a unit of analysis in which neither time nor space is privileged, and in which both categories are interdependent. The editors write in the glossary that "the chronotope is an optic for reading texts as x-rays of the forces at work in the culture system from which they spring" (Bakhtin, 426). Cornejo-Polar combines the idea of dialogism with the concept of time-space (*The Multiple Voices of Latin American Literature*, 21; my emphasis): "There are discourses from diverse historical planes, sometimes incompatible discourses, that coexist in a *common space and time*. More importantly yet, within one and the same text different voices can be heard. Sometimes multiple voices, voices that come from those 'different histories' but that are coetaneous, and that at the same time can articulate a common consciousness in one enunciation that chronologically might be perceived as separated by the barrier of the centuries." In fact, Cornejo-Polar goes as far as to describe Latin America as a "dialogic culture, a culture that in this sense is profoundly democratic, as in fact is seen in the great texts of Spanish-American literature" (25). The easy shifting in the last sentence between the languages of linguistics, politics, and literary criticism is typical of much interpretive work in Latin American literary studies and clearly exceeds the Bakhtinian example of reading principally for stylistics. As Perus has demonstrated, however, "the insistence of the Russian critic and historian on encounters, moments of culture shock, on transitional periods, on historic forms of separation and contact between historically separate traditions, living languages and canonical forms, 'high' and 'low' genres, orality and writing, etc., reveals preoccupations that go well beyond the formal boundaries of changes in linguistic or stylistic registers" ("El dialogismo y la poética histórica Bajtinianos," 34).

Both Cornejo-Polar and Rama relate the formal phenomenon of the dialogic to the idea of cultural confrontation or resolution based on social, economic, political, and linguistic differences. Thus, the varied phenomena of *mestizaje*, both material and immaterial, are linked through sociolects of both verbal and nonverbal codes. Bakhtin's ideas have also been traced in the work of Néstor García Canclini, particularly in his widely read *Hybrid Cultures,* first published in 1992. Although García Canclini does not, perhaps, recognize an explicit debt to Bakhtin, "dialogism is implicitly alluded to in his idea of cultural hybridization, because hybridity implies the coexistence of different conflictive belief systems, languages, styles, and linguistic consciences" (De Grandis and Bernd, 221). Undoubtedly, *mestizaje* and/or hybridity offered many Latin Americans outstanding examples of what Bakhtin's "other factor" could be.

V. THE CHANGING FACE OF *Mestizaje*

In Colombian author Fernando Vallejo's much-discussed 1994 novel *La virgen de los sicarios* (Our Lady of the Assassins, 2001), the narrator pronounces an indictment of mestizaje that would seem to signal its complete disintegration as a unique and advantageous characteristic of Latin Americanness (97–98):

> Bad blood, bad race, bad character, bad reputation, there's no worse mix than that of the Spanish with the Indian and the black: they produce throwbacks, that's to say monkeys, simians, apes, capuchins with tails so they can go back up into the trees with them. But no, here they walk the streets on two feet, crowding the centre. Uncouth Spaniards, wily Indians, sinister blacks: mix them together in the crucible of copulation and see what explosion that produces with the blessing of the Pope and all. What comes out is a crooked, self-seeking, slothful, covetous, mendacious, loathsome, treacherous and thieving, murderous and pyromaniac riffraff. This is the doing of Spain the Promiscuous, that's what they left us with when they made off with our gold.

In the same way that he sets about to dismantle other values and virtues revered in Latin American societies—Catholicism, heterosexual romance, prohibitions against gratuitous violence, for example—the author here disdains *mestizaje* and the redemptive doctrine that historically has accompanied it. Even within the context of the cynicism which permeates Vallejo's novel, such a dismissal is jarring. It would seem that the notion of *mestizaje* has hit rock bottom, not because of quibbles with its implicit claims of European or white superiority, but because, according to the novelist, racial mixture has produced a regressive, rather than a progressive, people. But what prompts such a reaction, what makes *mestizaje* such an important target of Vallejo's withering gaze?

Pointing to the hyperviolence that surrounds him, Vallejo's protagonist dismisses earlier enlistments of redemptive *mestizaje* as lies. His text spits (in the form of gunfire) in the face of a pioneering national logic in which mestizo formulations are prevalent and overwhelmingly positive, as can be seen in fellow Colombian Otto Morales Benítez' 1984 *Memorias del mestizaje* (Memories of *Mestizaje*). That work hails the syncretic process as a "poem of optimism to the future" and interprets all movements toward independence in Latin America—cultural and political—as results of the mestizo presence (78): "In the historic moment in which the mestizo shows himself and his personality, America begins to feel its fighting spirit. Its passionate historic destiny." But despite this all-encompassing embrace of mixture, the everyday experience of *mestizaje* remains, in Colombia and elsewhere, a site of continual rupture, disjunction, contradiction, and opposition.

As Vallejo's text so graphically suggests, the Latin American literary canon is rich with cases in which the mestizo is the embodiment of betrayal, deception, craftiness, opportunism, and moral degradation. Whereas abstract theorizations insisted on the fundamental ambiguity of the figure, the mestizo or mestiza was rarely so ambivalent in specific contexts. The foremother of this pack of treasonous mestizos is, of course, Doña Marina, or La Malinche, Hernando Cortés' Mexican "lover" and interpreter, the matriarch of mixed blood, the indigenous woman betrayed by the conquista(dor) who, in turn, betrayed her own people by giving up Aztec imperial secrets to the Spanish, thus earning her the moniker "La Chingada" (the Screwed One) and all Mexicans after her the insult "hijos de la Chingada."[28]

Her emblematic value is reiterated in a wide variety of explorations of *mestizaje*, ranging from the conservative (Octavio Paz, Tzvetan Todorov, etc.) to the more radical (Anzaldúa, Alarcón, etc.). Todorov says of her (*The Conquest of America*, 101): "I myself see her . . . as the first example, and thereby the symbol, of the cross-breeding of cultures; she hereby heralds the modern state of Mexico and beyond that, the present state of us all, since if we are not invariably bilingual, we are inevitably bi- or tricultural. La Malinche glorifies mixture to the detriment of purity—Aztec or Spanish—and the role of the intermediary." But while La Malinche may "glorify" mixture in this figuration, she is also maligned, accused of disloyalty and treason. As the mother of a nation that began to define itself as mestizo from the moment of conquest, La Malinche carries with her the stigma of sexual violence and illegitimacy, a status repeatedly evoked in literature that deals with *mestizaje*, even in the contemporary period.

By instigating or authoring *mestizaje*, La Malinche is either the face of disaster, "La Chingada," or a pillar of resistance and survival, the womb of cultural annihilation, or the fertile ground of cultural diplomacy. This duality seems inescapable, so that at times *mestizaje*'s "rise" and "fall" appear to occur simultaneously. "On the one hand, we have mestizaje as a liberating force that breaks open colonial and neocolonial categories of ethnicity and race. This is a resistant mestizaje, one that questions authenticity and rejects the need to belong as defined by those in power," explains Florencia Mallon. But as is true in many of the examples studied here, "mestizaje also emerges as an official discourse of nation formation, a new claim to authenticity that denies colonial forms of racial/ethnic hierarchy and oppression by creating an intermediate subject and interpolating him/her as 'the citizen.' As a discourse of social control, official mestizaje is constructed implicitly against a peripheral, marginalized, dehumanized Indian 'Other' who is often 'disappeared' in the process" ("Constructing Mestizaje in Latin America," 171–172). Sometimes, this Indian is not disappeared, but integrated into a taxonomy of *mestizaje* in which the physical figure is represented as monstrous, asymmetrical, or hideous, as Vallejo's novel demonstrates.

The reading of the European arrival in the Americas as providential discovery or as brutal invasion has not necessarily translated into similarly polarized positions on *mestizaje*, although this might be expected. In fact, *mestizaje* offers itself as a site of accommodation for *both* positions. The late Oswaldo Guayasamín, an Ecuadorian painter credited with being one of Latin America's finest plastic interpreters of the indigenous reality, demonstrated this in a 1996 interview in his home and studio, when he claimed that *mestizaje* signified both the death of indigenous cultural expression and the most profound expressive reality of Latin Americans. Guayasamín's invocation of *mestizaje* as both cultural resistance and cultural devastation is not unusual in a review of primary and secondary literatures (though it is unusual to find it in a single conversation). As in Guayasamín's commentary, and often in his paintings, the figure of *mestizaje* often appears as two-sided and thus two-faced: certain aesthetic traits are associated with the European progenitor, others with the indigenous participant. Ernestina Avedaño de Vargas and Elva Liliana Patiño, the authors of *Mestizaje en la literatura iberoamericana a partir de la raíz aborigen* (*Mestizaje* in Ibero-American Literature, Starting with the Native Race) write, in this vein, "We think that in the integration of the rational (European contribution) with the mythical-symbolic (indigenous contribution), our literature originates, and within which unity prevails over juxtaposition, because we are not a literature of transplant but rather of *synthesis*" (1; original emphasis). This formulation of "unity" suggests that little has changed since Bolívar compared his rationally superior whites or Creoles to the numerically superior indigenous inhabitants.

In some sense, both the condemnatory vision of *mestizaje* offered by Vallejo and the redemptive versions of the authors cited above have failed. That is, *mestizaje* and its variants have been claimed in a vast array of political and cultural projects in the Americas in attempts to solve the riddle of identity for the diverse inhabitants of the area, and in efforts to project this identity to geographical and cultural neighbors. Most of these projects and efforts have not produced measurable local or regional cohesion, however, nor have they provided substantial protection against U.S. political control or cultural infiltration. At times, the practices associated with *mestizaje* are seen as proof of assimilation and the attendant loss of indigenous cultures, a move toward "whiteness." Larsen and others have argued that transculturation, like *mestizaje*, amounts to a "surrogate hegemony, a strategy of containment of subaltern groups by a state power camouflaged beneath a populist aestheticism" (Trigo, "Shifting Paradigms," 86). In other moments, the mobilization of *mestizaje* is viewed as reluctance to recognize or adopt mainstream values located in the centers of metropolitan power, and the mestizo is seen as an Indian resistant to this same "whitening" influence. Peruvian author and ethnohistorian José María Arguedas writes that "the majority of people who are racially mixed remain Indian in their customs and in their social condition; their life is indigenous in all its manifestations, and all are called 'Indians' . . . The artistic production of these people is indigenous; I refer to the conceptualization of its production, its soul, and to what we might call its 'aesthetic content'" (*Canto Kechwa*, 13–14). While Arguedas recognizes that contact with nonindigenous peoples and cultures signifies, on the one hand, new elements of expression and, on the other, new emotional experiences, he maintains that "amongst mestizos, the Indian element has greater weight . . . the mestizo is much closer to the Indian" (13–14).

Despite these (con)founding contradictions, *mestizaje* has been one of the most attractive features of Latin Americanness for those reading and interpreting the region from the outside, especially from the North. It is undeniable that successful exportation of Latin America to its American and European neighbors has depended, in large part, on variations of that discourse. The so-called Boom that brought Latin American authors such as Gabriel García Márquez and Carlos Fuentes into the university classrooms and bookstores of an international public, but especially of the English-speaking United States, emerged in the contexts of magical realism, *lo real maravilloso*, and other stylistic and thematic practices that were, at least to some extent, versions of or responses to *mestizaje*.[29] Uruguayan writer Mario Benedetti titled a 1967 collection of short stories *Letras del continente mestizo* (Letters from the Mestizo Continent), explaining, "I have the impression that the rich inventory of contemporary Latin American letters owes its vitality and fecund imaginary in part to conscious processes and in part to random chance, but always to that conjugation of races and immigrations, of influences and worldviews, of seething and fervor, of conformity and rebellion, that constitute our *mestizaje*" (7). That is, the twentieth-century Latin American textual imaginary is necessarily the result of the "conjugation of races . . . , influences and worldviews." One could even conclude that North American resistance to forms of Latin American expression in which *mestizaje* is *not* presented as an anchoring logic results from the belief that such representations must be "false" or "unauthentic." This suspicion may be at play in the debates about the value of truth and the degree of accountability in the work of Mayan activist Rigoberta Menchú, whose testimonial text speaks for a specific, marginalized group, rather than a composite dominant (mestizo) national or regional identity. Arguably, the United States has now come to read a mestizo or hybrid version of Latin America as the only "authentic" portrayal of the Latin American reality.

The following chapters display a few of the many faces of *mestizaje*, framed by local contexts as well as within transnational relationships. As we view their features and account for their gestures from different disciplinary vantage points, we begin to perceive how the rites and tenets convened in the cult of *mestizaje* make manifest a novel and intensely complex historical discourse.

Por mi raza hablará el espíritu.

JOSÉ VASCONCELOS

I. THE MISSION OF THE COSMIC RACE

Although celebrated figures such as Simón Bolívar and José Martí had already posited equations between mixed race and Latin American identity, the 1925 publication of Mexican educator and politician José Vasconcelos' *La raza cósmica: Misión de la raza iberoamericana* (The Cosmic Race: Mission of the Ibero-American Race) marked the inception of a fully developed ideology of *mestizaje* that tied political and aesthetic self-definition and assertion to a racial discourse at both the national and the regional levels. The book elaborated on the slogan Vasconcelos (1882–1959) had coined in 1921 for the Universidad Nacional Autónoma de México in Mexico City, a phrase that was to be emblazoned on a map of Latin America to form the institution's coat of arms. Vasconcelos explained that the phrase "Por mi raza hablará el espíritu" (The spirit will speak through my race) corresponded to an era in which the organization of peoples and nations was being transformed, so that old constituencies based on war and politics could now be substituted with states built on commonalities of blood and language. In the wake of the Mexican Revolution and the demise of the dictatorship of Porfirio Díaz in 1910, Mexico's emerging intellectuals should recognize "the necessity of founding their own fatherland with the great Hispanic-American fatherland that will represent a new expression of human destiny" (Taracena, *José Vasconcelos*, 19).[1] In *The Cosmic Race*, Vasconcelos thus insisted on what Bolívar had campaigned for but later rejected as impossible: an understanding of Latin American identity that was continental as well as national, and that superseded conditions of race. "Race is therefore everything we are in spirit," he said, explaining that this spirit was the result of a common history which "fixed the Spanish and

Catholic character of our peoples" (Taracena, 32). He later clarified that the spirit of the famous phrase was in fact the Holy Spirit, further delineating his understanding of the national and regional subject as Christian, and the political project as inherently tied to the Catholic Church.

In his role as one of Mexico's most prominent figures of the early twentieth century, the "Teacher of America" thus attempted a renovation of the understanding of "race" in the Latin American context, reconceptualizing *mestizaje* as providential, progressive, and beneficial for Mexico and Spanish America.[2] Although a quarter century earlier, José Enrique Rodó had, in *Ariel*, advanced the notion of a regional Latin American corpus and identity in the face of North American commercial and cultural pressures, he had steered clear of any somatic descriptors.

Vasconcelos' project was so provocative that Peruvian essayist José Carlos Mariátegui wrote that "no one has imagined the future of America with so much ambition or with such vehement hope as José Vasconcelos" (*Temas de nuestra América*, 78). Vasconcelos' invention of an all-encompassing Latin American "race" did not receive unanimous approval, however. His critics, using as their starting point the controversial slogan which graced the university, denounced his use of "race" as messy or erroneous. Alfonso Toro complained that nobody knew exactly what the rector had in mind, since it was impossible to talk about a Hispanic American race in ethnographic terms (Taracena, 19).

Nor was Vasconcelos the first to invent the notion of fortuitous Mexican *mestizaje* in the service of nation or region building. In the first half of the nineteenth century, two priests devised a plan to proclaim a mestizo monarchy, in which a congress formed of the twelve closest relatives of Montezuma would elect an emperor, who would marry a white woman if he were Indian and a "pure Indian" if he were white (Basave Benítez, 22). In 1884, Vicente Riva Palacio proclaimed that true emancipation from Spain was the result of racial fusion (Basave Benítez, 30), and Justo Sierra also contributed to a rethinking of *mestizaje*, calling it the dynamic element of the Mexican population (Basave Benítez, 33–36).

But the leading figure who preceded Vasconcelos in the development of *mestizofilia*, that is, *mestizaje* as thoroughly desirable (Basave Benítez, 13), was Andrés Molina Enríquez, who came to completely equate Mexico and *lo mestizo*, an equation seconded by Manuel Gamio in 1916 (Graham, 85). Certainly, by the time of the Porfirio Díaz regime (1876–1911), most Mexicans were—at least physically—mestizos, according to demographic reports. But the process of documenting this mestizo majority revealed a new problem: the tendency to underestimate Indian populations in Mexico. Graham (73) notes that estimates of the Indian population in Chiapas during this period ranged from 38 percent to 80 percent, for example, suggesting that even as Vasconcelos was polishing his ideas, *mestizaje* was already subject to a variety of definitions, and was already being manipulated for political ends.

The title and the subtitle of *La raza cósmica: Misión de la raza ibero-americana* (the latter often dropped in translations) allude to several important elements in Vasconcelos' thinking. The reference to race as "cosmic" shifted the semantic weight from the material to the spiritual, from corporeal to aesthetic *mestizaje*, "not race in the biological sense, but as an attitude" (Zea, "Vasconcelos y la utopía de la raza cósmica," 23). Drawing on the ideas of those revolutionary statesmen who had envisioned the political and cultural unification of the Americas (Bolívar is mentioned repeatedly), Vasconcelos called on fellow Mexicans and (Latin) Americans to reject Anglo-Saxon models from North America and find in themselves and in their own cultural history a true "spiritual synthesis" (Domínguez Michael, "Estudio preliminar," xxi). As the complete title suggests, Vasconcelos' vision was focused not so much on the present as on a coalescence still to be realized. While purportedly bearing witness to historical processes that could be documented or measured, and thus presented as empirical data, he undercut this same discourse by insisting on metaphysical, or "spiritual," experience.

An often unwieldy interdependence of the mystical and the material thus permeates Vasconcelos' work, prompting many critics to label it inconsistent and contradictory. He countered these criticisms with the argument that "whoever studies scientific progress within the field of natural systems of knowledge realizes that there is no biological phenomenon which is not also psychic, nor a psychic phenomenon which is not also biological. We can also affirm that each science is philosophy and each philosophy, science. There is in both a fundamental identification of the problem of ontology, although seen from two different viewpoints . . . Philosophers and scientists have realized that ideas are the synthesis of life and establish new points of contact with the absolute" (Nicotra Di Leopoldo, *Pensamientos inéditos de José Vasconcelos*, 72).

The elaboration of this pseudoscientific ontological formula was the necessary precursor of Vasconcelos' seemingly contradictory contention that the new *aesthetic* order he proposed would come about through the *biological* process of blood mixture: "Whatever opinions one may express in this respect, and whatever repugnance caused by prejudice one may harbor, the truth is that the mixture of races has taken place and continues to be consummated. It is in this fusion of ethnic stocks that we should look for the fundamental characteristic of Ibero-American idiosyncrasy" (*The Cosmic Race*, 19). Vasconcelos' work on *mestizaje* thus epitomized a position which allowed biological and aesthetic definitions of race to coexist and envisioned a dual "mission of ethnic and spiritual fusion of peoples" (*La raza cósmica* [1966], 28).

Although the notion of a "cosmic race" had social, ethical, and political dimensions, for Vasconcelos, it was ultimately a spiritual cause. "Our race will develop a culture of new tenderness, of a spiritual essence, absolutely free," he proclaimed (*Discursos: 1920–1950*, 13). This tendency to seek refuge from the frustrations and shortcomings of social and public life in the spiritual world is graphically revealed in a statement he made during his unsuccessful bid for the Mexican presidency in 1929.[3] In the midst of a tense political situation, and sensing a defeat which most acknowledged was fraudulent, he exclaimed, "I don't know what I'm doing here. My kingdom is not of this world!" (Taracena, 84).

Virulently anti-Protestant, Vasconcelos had absorbed many ideas from Chateaubriand's eighteenth-century tome *The Genius of Christianity*, which linked art, theology, and religious practice and lamented the disintegration of religious experience as a result of Enlightenment ideals. Vasconcelos' insistence on Christian love as a core value of the cosmic race provided him with another way to distance his notion of race from biological constraints and to offer it as a metaphor for "pure" and metaphysical communion. Indeed, writing itself would increasingly become for him a confessional act, full of accounts of his sins of commission and omission, his loss of faith, and his falls from grace. One of his biographers even refers to the era of his life in which he completed *The Cosmic Race* as the culmination of a spiritual pilgrimage (Domínguez Michael, xxxvii): "Like a saint who prepares himself spiritually in a hermitage for evangelism, Vasconcelos makes the romantic pilgrimage to Holy Ground and like Chateaubriand, finds in these lands the origin of his strength for overcoming adversity. That year, he publishes the milestone of his utopia: *The Cosmic Race*." The Mexican educator believed that the Latin American population was a "chosen people" with a "divine mission" to integrate and consolidate whites, blacks, and Indians. North Americans, who did not have "in their blood the contradictory instincts of a mixture of dissimilar races," had committed the sin of destroying other races, while the Spaniards and American-born Creoles had assimilated them, thus providing "new rites and hopes for a mission without precedent in history" (*The Cosmic Race*, 17–18). Only in Latin America could one find "a thousand bridges . . . available for the sincere and cordial fusion of all races" (*The Cosmic Race*, 20).

Vasconcelos himself was "not quite what Latin Americans call a *mestizo*" (Jaén, in Vasconcelos, *The Cosmic Race*, xx), although he was born in Oaxaca, a region with a particularly rich indigenous presence, and he claimed some Indian blood. Like many other intellectuals of his day, his inclusion of the Indian in the projects of regional and national citizenship focused on pre-Columbian contributions. In 1909, Alfonso Reyes, Pedro Henríquez Ureña, and Vasconcelos founded the Ateneo de la Juventud, which created a venue for scholarly activity and supported educational reforms. Early in his career, Vasconcelos was also heavily influenced by Indian philosophy, spiritualism, and the Theosophists, who listed as one of their aims, "To form a nucleus of universal brotherhood of humanity without distinction of race, creed, or color" (*Webster's International Dictionary*, 1950). *The Cosmic Race*, published when Vasconcelos was in his early forties, represents the fruition of a line of thought which began in 1920 with *Prometeo vencedor* (Victorious Prometheus), in which he proclaimed that "a new humanity with the best of all its cultures" would form, "harmonized and ennobled within the Spanish mold" (41).

II. TRAVELING THE AMERICAS

While Vasconcelos' first frame of reference for his ideas on race and race mixture was his experience in Mexico, he believed, like Bolívar and Martí, that *mestizaje* was a regional, not just a national, issue. Thus the second mention of "*raza*" in his original title is not spiritual, but geographic, calling up all those American territories colonized by Spain. Like his predecessors (whose point of departure was frequently the Caribbean), the Mexican author acknowledged the heterogeneity of this vast territory (*The Cosmic Race*, 15): "Our geography, for example, was and continues to be an obstacle to unity, but if we are to overcome this obstacle, it will first be necessary to put our spirit in order, purifying ideas and signaling correct orientations." But while he believed that spiritual oneness could triumph over geographic difference, he also believed in a "promised land" *within* Latin America that would be most propitious for the growth of the cosmic race, provided scientific advances in making that region more comfortable did not outpace the "ethnic process."

Vasconcelos' delineation of this zone—"all of Brazil, plus Colombia, Venezuela, Ecuador, part of Peru, part of Bolivia, and the upper region of Argentina"—prompts several questions (*The Cosmic Race*, 24). Why are many nontropical areas included in his model and so many tropical regions excluded? Why does his "promised land" have such an arbitrary relationship to Latin American territories where processes of *mestizaje* were already highly developed at the time he was writing? Brazil and Ecuador (two examples of exemplary *mestizaje* studied in Chapters 4 and 5 here), are included, but Mexico, Central America, and the Caribbean are not. Why is Argentina on the list, if Vasconcelos himself lauded it as a region without a significant Indian presence (*La raza cósmica* [1966], 148)? The surprising, seemingly fanciful, demarcations of this tropical (racial) paradise are symptomatic of the disconnect in the text between lived conditions in the Americas and Vasconcelos' philosophical prophesies.

Geography was not the only defining characteristic of Latin American ontology for Vasconcelos. Like several other Latin American intellectuals mentioned in this volume, he found music a helpful metaphor for describing cultural identity. In *The Cosmic Race*, he compared Ibero-America to North America, which seemed to him the "uninterrupted and vigorous *allegro* of a triumphal march." "How different are the sounds of the Ibero-American development! They resemble the profound *scherzo* of a deep and infinite symphony" (*The Cosmic Race*, 21). In his 1936 work *Estética* (Aesthetics), he speaks again of rhythm, melody, harmony, accord, symphony, and counterpoint, concluding that Mexican philosophy is a philosophy of the auditory. As Joaquín Sánchez MacGrégor points out, music functions for Vasconcelos like an epistemological model in which the metaphor of the symphony calls attention to the felicitous intermingling of the qualities of a variety of types of instruments (Sánchez Macgrégor, 248).

While the first quarter of *The Cosmic Race* is dedicated to this spirited defense of Latin America's unique relationship with racial amalgamation, the rest of the original text, usually ignored by critics, comprises a travel memoir of a 1922 diplomatic mission to Brazil and Argentina in which Vasconcelos participated. While certain reflections on cultural phenomena in Brazil—including its high incidence of racial mixture—would seem to be in keeping with the initial argument of the essay for the creation of a "synthetical race, the integral race, made up of the genius and the blood of all peoples and for that reason, more capable of true brotherhood and of a truly universal vision" (*The Cosmic Race*, 20), the final chapter, on Argentina, weakens Vasconcelos' argument for *mestizaje* considerably. The country is praised as the "Paris of our America," the most European of all Latin America's territories, the most civilized, and the least mestizo. Buenos Aires is "ultra-Spanish," demonstrating a force of colonial assimilation comparable only to the English, in which in the space of a few years,

Italians, Jews, Poles, the French, and the English themselves are absorbed. Whereas the environment in Mexico is Indian, and that in Cuba is mulatto, only Buenos Aires is cosmopolitan, representing the Spanish spirit in its "universal expression," home to a race that is healthy and new (*La raza cósmica* [1966], 148).

Vasconcelos' travels in Brazil, Argentina, and the United States, and his contacts and conversations with fellow diplomats and dignitaries along the way, clearly shaped the ideas of *The Cosmic Race*, and the book should be understood as more than the abstract reflection on *mestizaje* that characterizes the first section. At the beginning of his notes on his trip to Brazil, Vasconcelos speaks of a particularly disagreeable conversation he has en route to the port city of Bahia with an anthropologist from the "Instituto XX" in Washington, presumably the Smithsonian. To his colleague's insistence that New York should be the model for all the cities of the world, Vasconcelos replies that each true civilization should make an effort to avoid imitating New York, fatherland of Mammon and one of the world's "defects." A few nights earlier, this "Darwinist" had claimed that the human species was most advanced in the white race, and that within the white race, the most perfect examples existed in the United States, declarations that drew from Vasconcelos rancorous laughter (*La raza cósmica* [1966], 62). The Mexican assured his colleague that travels in South America would change his views.

The first stop on their journey was the Brazilian port city of Salvador, Bahia, where Vasconcelos witnessed the suppression of the black element firsthand. Later, he visited Rio de Janeiro, São Paulo, Santos, Minas Gerais, Belo Horizonte, and Juiz de Fore before embarking anew for Buenos Aires. An essay titled "El bronce del indio mexicano se apoya en el granito bruñido del Brasil" (The Bronze of the Mexican Indian Is Supported by the Burnished Granite of Brazil), published prior to *The Cosmic Race*, demonstrates the importance of Brazil and Brazilian intellectual currents in Vasconcelos' elaborations. In these early texts, Vasconcelos worked with two principal ideas: he decried the importation and imposition of U.S. ideas and institutions in Latin America, including official North American policies regarding race; and he called on his compatriots to reject an official discourse which considered miscegenation the chief evil of interethnic contact and coexistence.

One of the "scientific" voices in the chorus of U.S. doctrines championing racial purity was Alfred P. Schultz, whose 1908 *Race or Mongrel* featured this subtitle: *A Brief History of the Rise and Fall of the Ancient Races of Earth: A Theory That the Fall of Nations Is Due to Intermarriage with Alien*

Stocks: A Demonstration That a Nation's Strength Is Due to Racial Purity: A Prophecy That America Will Sink to Early Decay unless Immigration Is Rigorously Restricted. On the subject of racial mixture in South America, Schultz wrote, "The fusion of whites and Indians produces mestizos, the fusion of negroes and Indians produces Zambos. Both mongrels are vastly inferior to the pure Indian. It has been said that it is physiologically inexplicable why only the bad qualities of the whites and of the negro are transmitted to the mongrel offspring and never the good qualities of the Indian. All laws of nature are inexplicable; we recognize them, but we cannot explain them" (150).

Less than two decades later, Vasconcelos would react with a defense of miscegenation and *mestizaje* that he claimed was intellectually, morally, and biologically grounded. This position held that the four main racial stocks—"the Black, the Indian, the Mongol, and the White" (*The Cosmic Race*, 9)—would fuse and harmonize in a fifth, universal race, imbued with the best traits and characteristics of all its constituencies. "Dispersion will come to an end on American soil; unity will be consummated there by the triumph of fecund love and the improvement of all the human races" (*The Cosmic Race*, 18).

Schultz had claimed that Mexico was inhabited by two groups: one-fifth of the population was of Spanish origin, "men of whom the white race has no reason to be proud"; and the other four-fifths (Indians, blacks, mestizos, and mulattos, presumably) were "slow-witted, stupid, without individuality. They are animals, and their only human qualities are their superhuman mendacity and their ability to consume pulque" (151). Although we have no indication that Vasconcelos had read Schultz, his own racial categorizations clearly turned the earlier writer's exercise in fractions inside out, triumphantly announcing the advent of a fifth, mixed, race that was superior to all others. In an essay titled "Raza pura y raza mezclada" (Pure Race and Mixed Race), Vasconcelos said, "Our task is to demonstrate that the mestizo and indigenous populations are capable of assimilating and equaling, at the very least equaling, white culture. Understand here that this does not mean we should organize for a struggle against the white man. Just the opposite. The white man is our half-relative by blood and our teacher in culture" (*Qué es la revolución*, 218).

III. THERAPEUTIC EFFECTS

Against the backdrop of the ideology of white supremacy and superiority in Europe and the United States, Vasconcelos' comments were radical and innovative, despite the obvious privileging of Western culture and the implicit deprecation of indigenous and black factors which would be "improved" and "instructed" by admixture with whites. His idea of a cosmic race provided a therapeutic response to an old malaise in Latin America and continued an intellectual trajectory that was more than a century old: the unification of Central and South America as a postcolonial territory of peoples who, as Bolívar had pointed out, were a composite. De Beer writes that "it was a theme that was filled with hope and optimism and, thus, served as an inspiration for many people" (*José Vasconcelos and His World*, 290). Vasconcelos, however, rejected the notion that his ideas appealed only to the emotions, insisting that "science" would prove their veracity (*The Cosmic Race*, 35):

> The doctrine of sociological and biological formation we propose in these pages is not a simple ideological effort to raise the spirits of a depressed race by offering it a thesis that contradicts the doctrine with which its rivals wanted to condemn it. What happens is that, as we discover the falsity of the scientific premise upon which the domination of contemporary power exists, we will also foresee, in experimental science itself, orientations that point the way, no longer for the triumph of a single race, but for the redemption of all men.

If science could be redefined, then *mestizaje* could be offered as a cure for the "depression" that had plagued the Latin American populace, could, in fact, be used to reject the diagnosis of pathology used by those who would condemn it.

Although Vasconcelos' elaboration of *mestizaje* ultimately elicited more ideological than scientific support, his reading of the beneficial effects of racial and cultural mixture has retained its popularity, despite obvious problems with a denial of social diseases perpetuated or created by such an ideology. One of his most fervent admirers has been Mexican essayist Leopoldo Zea, who wrote in 1993 that Vasconcelos' utopian notion of a cosmic race, in its development of the potential for integrating the diverse, could still serve as an example to peoples in other parts of the world without denying diversity, but, instead, affirming it in a "horizontal relationship of solidarity and no longer one of dependence" ("Vasconcelos y la utopía de la raza cósmica," 36).

Despite Zea's homage, it is difficult to find evidence of this "horizontal relationship," during Vasconcelos' lifetime or since. Alan Knight raises three problems with this and similar appropriations of *mestizaje*. First, it is an epistemology imposed on Indians from the outside—instead of from remaining indigenous communities—that proceeds to speak for the Indian. Second, it assumes that acculturation can and should proceed in a guided, enlightened fashion, retaining the positive and discarding the negative. Third, Vasconcelos' ideas reproduced many of the racist assumptions of Western European thought, and thus allowed for the continuation of racist paradigms and practices in postrevolutionary Mexico (in *The Idea of Race in Latin America*, 86–87).

Basave Benítez, situating Vasconcelos in a broader spectrum of *mestizofilia* in Mexico, recognizes that even in his most fervent moments of supporting the mestizo model, Vasconcelos' brand of mixture is not very equitable; ultimately, in Vasconcelos' thought, Latin America owes what it is to the contribution of white Europeans (133). Or, as Rubén Ríos Ávila succinctly observes, "the cosmic race is another name for Hispanism, its mestizo name" (*La raza cómica*, 155).

IV. CHICANO AND CHICANA APPROPRIATIONS

Surprisingly, none of these problems—the privileging of the European element in Latin American mixed race, the manipulation of demographic data to emphasize mestizo populations and to deemphasize black and Indian populations, the imposition of Creole cultural systems in existing indigenous and other nonmestizo communities, and the general failure to implement public policy and practice based on a valorization of *mestizaje* that provided for true horizontal relationships of solidarity—seem to have constituted serious obstacles for a number of Chicano and Mexican American critics in the United States who have treated *The Cosmic Race* as a hallmark text of cultural and racial vindication. Although "his essay has traditionally been taken as a racist theory for the encouragement of a people with deeply rooted feelings of inferiority" (Jaén, "Introduction," x), the early Chicano movement embraced Vasconcelos' "cosmic race" as a variant of "la raza," a term resurrected to address the sociopolitical realities of Mexican Americans and other immigrants from Spanish-speaking countries living in bilingual and bicultural zones of the United States (Jaén, "Introduction," xv–xvi). "Vasconcelos seemed emphatically to regard such mixing of the races, or mestizaje, especially as it is given in Latin America, as the fundamental requirement for the emergence of the new age," writes Didier Jaén in his introduction to an English-language edition of *The Cosmic Race* sponsored by the Department of Chicano Studies at the University of California at Los Angeles. Certainly, Vasconcelos himself knew something of the borderlands and the contact zone, having attended school in Eagle Pass, Texas, while his father worked across the river in Piedras Negras.

Chicano and Chicana critics, including Gloria Anzaldúa, have identified with Vasconcelos' ideas in a number of ways, sometimes positing Latin (American) experience in the United States as the fulfillment of the cosmic race, and the Chicano community as the standard-bearer of quintessential *mestizaje*. Anzaldúa's work has been extremely influential in this regard, advocating an approach to Vasconcelos that integrates a focus on gender issues. She modifies Vasconcelos' slogan for the National University, beginning her essay "La Conciencia de la Mestiza: Towards a New Consciousness" with the epigraph, "Por la mujer de mi raza hablará el espíritu" (The spirit will speak through the woman of my race). Her first paragraph prominently features the inventor of the cosmic race (765): "José Vasconcelos, Mexican philosopher, envisaged *una raza mestiza, una mezcla de razas afines, una raza de color—la primera raza síntesis del globo*. He called it a cosmic race, *la raza cósmica*, a fifth race embracing the four major races of the world . . . From this racial, ideological, cultural and biological cross-pollenization, an 'alien' consciousness is presently in the making— a new *mestiza* consciousness, *una conciencia de mujer*. It is a consciousness of the Borderlands."

Few readers have realized how radically Anzaldúa had to revise (or misread) Vasconcelos to suit her theoretical argument.[4] Vasconcelos makes little explicit reference to gender in *The Cosmic Race* other than to praise the "beautiful race" of the marvelous Argentinian women he watched on the streets of Buenos Aires, who, according to him, possessed a svelte firmness and a luxuriance unequaled elsewhere. Whereas in other cities (and one surmises here that Vasconcelos had in mind the rest of "mestizo" America), the majority of women were ugly, here in this "European city," it was rare to see a woman who was not beautiful, so much so that Vasconcelos wondered, "Perhaps monogamous love is a thing of the village," not necessary in the urban centers (*La raza cósmica* [1966], 148).[5]

Anzaldúa's revisionist reading of Vasconcelos is even more radical, given writings after *The Cosmic Race* in which Mexicans and Mexican Americans living north of the Rio Grande are frequently the target of criticism and sometimes scorn. In one essay, for example, Vasconcelos denounces *pochismo*, a hybrid Mexican-U.S. cultural phenomenon and important antecedent to Chicano aesthetics ("The Latin-American Basis of Mexican Civilization," 11–14).

Still, Vasconcelos continues to provide inspiration for Anzaldúa and others, particularly in terms of the room he allows for cultural confrontation. "The new *mestiza* copes by developing a tolerance for contradictions, a tolerance for ambiguity," Anzaldúa writes ("La Conciencia de la Mestiza," 766). "The work of *mestiza* consciousness is to break down the subject-object duality that keeps her a prisoner and to show in the flesh and through the images in her work how duality is transcended. The answer to the problem between the white race and the colored, between males and females, lies in healing the split that originates in the very foundation of our lives, our culture, our languages, our thoughts" ("La Conciencia de la Mestiza," 767). As she later points out, though, in the personal and collective effort to winnow out the "oppressive traditions of all cultures and religions" from the repertoire of identity (769), it is often difficult to differentiate between the inherited, the acquired, and the imposed, and there is a sense in which Vasconcelos' ideology of the cosmic race belongs to this last category, an icon of Chicano identity that is revered without being understood or sufficiently questioned.

The call for a "new" *mestizaje* that draws a causal connection between Vasconcelos and his reappearance in late-twentieth-century negotiations of "radical" bicultural experience in the United States also glosses over the fundamentally "mestizo" history of the area now known as the American Southwest, as well as the tendency to perpetuate that same history as "white" in official historical discourse. Dworkin writes, for example, that despite the claim that the City of Los Angeles was founded in 1781 by "pure Spaniards," "it is now known that settlers were from the *criollo, mestizo, indígena*, and *mulatto castas* (racial classes)" ("The Peoples of La Raza," 169). Arguably, "La Raza" is a strategy which, while serving as a counterideology to "Anglo" superiority and Manifest Destiny (Dworkin, 182), suppresses historical and contemporary differences among Spanish Americans, making all the heirs equal, biologically and culturally, in the wake of Columbus.

Another problem that has been rarely discussed in terms of Chicano/a appropriations of Vasconcelos is the tendency to ignore that part of the U.S. population which would stand most directly parallel to the Latin American populations the Mexican educator and philosopher was describing, that is, "Native Americans." Advocates for Native American groups, among them, contemporary authors, acknowledge that the overwhelming majority of North Americans who claim Indian descent are "mixed bloods" or "mixed race," people for whom this characteristic "*mestizaje*" functions in very distinct ways from elsewhere in the Americas. In an essay titled "America's Mestizos," Brewton Berry writes that in the eastern United States alone "there are some two hundred communities of people whose racial ancestry is uncertain and whose lives are profoundly affected by that uncertainty" (191).[6] These groups claim a variety of relationships to "white," "Indian," and "black" identity and bear names that strangely resemble the old categories of the *castas*, such as Brass Ankles, Redbones, Redlegs, Pondshiners, Buckheads, Guineas, and Bushwackers. Although "mestizo" is sometimes used for these widely varying if officially marginal groups, "in the literature they are often called 'raceless people,' 'racial orphans,' 'mystery people,' 'half-castes,' 'half-breeds,' or merely 'breeds,'" notes Berry (193).

For the most part, efforts to enunciate "mixed-race" identity or cultural autonomy by Native Americans or U.S. "mestizos" have not been examined in the context of Vasconcelos' writings, despite the adoption of his ideas by many Chicanos and Chicanas.[7] The profound marginality of such groups within North American identity configurations would seem to present an excellent opportunity for examining *mestizaje* both as a differentiating sign of Latin Americanness and as a figure of racial redemption. In Berry's comment that "most mestizo groups, in all probability, represent an amalgam of Indians, adventurers, traders, runaway slaves, *outlaws, deserters, and deviants of all types, both white and black*" (196; my emphasis), we see the degree to which *mestizaje* is still frequently considered pathological or deviant in the context of the United States.

According to Jaén, the most common critical error committed by readers of *The Cosmic Race* is to view it "from a strictly sociological point of view" ("Introduction," xviii–xix), when its ideas are built on a philosophical system marked by esoteric characteristics. Vasconcelos called this system "aesthetic monism," arguing for a single, final essence of the universe. The cosmos for Vasconcelos had three levels: atomic, which governed mechanical movements and was in the intellectual purvey of science and logic; living matter, governed by ethics; and the human psyche or soul, characterized by creative or aesthetic acts. This system was clearly hierarchical, and Vasconcelos believed that the third level was the site of one's most profound perception of the true essence of the universe. His work elaborated on this predominance of the aesthetic-metaphysical over the merely numerical or mathematical. Jaén finds these philosophical underpinnings fundamental to an understanding of the Mexican writer ("Introduction," xxix): "It is clear, for instance, the close relationship of Vasconcelos' description of the aesthetic mode with the state of bliss described in all mystic traditions. So that what Vasconcelos predicts for the future of mankind . . . is akin to a universal state of mystical union. The mixture of the races is but one aspect in which this tendency to an integration of rhythms guided by the aesthetic experience is manifested." Jaén returns here to the key argument (and paradox) of Vasconcelos' cosmic race: mystical transformation in a universal subject through biological race mixture. Even the idea's author would soon recognize certain idealistic weaknesses in his formulation.

V. ABOUT-FACE ON THE COSMIC RACE

Almost immediately after the publication of *The Cosmic Race*, Vasconcelos began to backtrack and lose faith in the notion of Latin America as providentially mestizo.[8] In his later writing, he often limited his discussion of race to a comparison between Mexico or Latin America and the United States, where he and other Mexicans were frequently victims of racial discrimination. But when speaking of *mestizaje*, he became increasingly despondent and insistent on the necessity of preserving and enhancing the white contribution to Spanish American culture. In the prologue to *Indología*, the book that followed *La raza cósmica*, he figures himself as a lover so infatuated with his beloved (idea) that he fails to see its imperfections. He suggests that the Spanish conquistadors' propensity to mate with indigenous women contributed to the Indians' salvation, whereas North Americans' repugnance for miscegenation resulted in genocide. The tragedy of Mexican history lies in the watering down of the blood of the Spanish conquistadors, whereas nearby Costa Rica, with its "pure race of Gallic origin" and its absence of Indians and negligible populations of blacks, has escaped the malaise of *mestizaje* (De Beer, 313). Not only did such comparisons reflect Vasconcelos' increasingly racist ideas, they also revealed his lack of knowledge and erroneous assumptions regarding other parts of the Americas, none of which (especially Costa Rica) were inhabited by a pure Gallic race.

By the 1940s, Vasconcelos had made a complete or nearly complete about-face in his views on *mestizaje*. "One of my silly notions," Vasconcelos told an audience in 1944, "perhaps one of my most notorious mistakes, was the idea that I drew from my adolescence in the tropics, the idea that proclaimed my faith in our mixed race and potent future" (*Discursos: 1920–1950*, 210). This reversal is perceptible, though not explicit, in the prologue to the 1948 edition of *La raza cósmica*, where the author explains that the essay was written in response to social Darwinism and the writings of Gobineau.[9] He writes that the central thesis of the book he had published more than two decades earlier was that "the various races of the earth tend to intermix at a gradually increasing pace, and eventually will give rise to a new human type, composed of selections from each of the races already in existence." The aftermath of World War II had seen the establishment of organizations such as UNESCO, "which proclaim the need to abolish all racial discrimination and to educate all men in equality." "In short," Vasconcelos wrote, "present world conditions favor the development of interracial sexual unions, a fact which lends unexpected support to the thesis which, for lack of a better name, I entitled 'The future Cosmic Race'" (all quotations from *The Cosmic Race*, 3). Vasconcelos seems to acknowledge here the disconnect between his utopian, future-oriented vision and the historical reality of a country *already* racially and, thus, politically complex.

Vasconcelos highlights a key rupture from his earlier ideas on *mestizaje* when he notes in the 1948 edition of *La raza cósmica* that "it remains to be seen whether the unlimited and inevitable mixture is a favorable factor to the increment of culture or if, to the contrary, it will produce a decadence which now would no longer be of merely national but of worldwide proportions" (3–4). He makes a halfhearted attempt at hoping for the best, advising his readers that Egypt produced a "flourishing First Great Empire" when it was "predominantly white and relatively homogeneous," that this empire was "weakened" by "black penetration" from the south, but that, ultimately, a Second Empire arose, "a new, mestizo race, with mixed characteristics of both the white and the black," an empire that was more advanced and flourishing than the First. "The period in which the pyramids were built, and the Egyptian civilization reached its summit, is a mestizo period," he concludes (*The Cosmic Race*, 4).

Mestizaje in other parts of the New World is also reconsidered, and it is surprising to see how much Vasconcelos has tempered his diatribe against the United States, simultaneously adopting some of its generalizations and stereotypes regarding its own nonwhite populations. He now sees Mexico's neighbor to the north as "nothing but a melting pot of European races" (*The Cosmic Race*, 4) where, although blacks have not contributed to the "creation of power," they have achieved "spiritual penetration" (*The Cosmic Race*, 5) through music, dance, and other aspects of artistic sensibility. In Latin America, Vasconcelos' prime example of "productive" *mestizaje* is the Argentine Republic, "where the *mixture of similar races, all of them of European origin*, is again repeated" (*The Cosmic Race*, 5; my emphasis). Vasconcelos finally concludes (5):

> Thus, it can be readily stated that the mixture of similar races is productive, while the mixture of very distant types, as in the case of Spaniards

and American Indians, has questionable results. The underdevelopment of the Hispanic American peoples, where the native element predominates, is difficult to explain, unless we go far back in time to the first example cited here of the Egyptian civilization. It so happens that the mixture of quite dissimilar elements takes a long time to mold . . . At any rate, the most optimistic conclusion that can be drawn from the facts here observed is that even the most contradictory racial mixtures can have beneficial results, as long as the spiritual factor contributes to raise them . . . A religion such as Christianity made the American Indians advance, in a few centuries, from cannibalism to a relative degree of civilization.

This passage encapsulates an astounding microhistory of the ascent and descent of theories of *mestizaje* in Latin America and, as we shall see, situates Vasconcelos in a historical discourse that expands on the civilizing rhetoric that was built into and, to some extent, generated the conquest of the Americas. Like his Spanish forbears, Vasconcelos maintains the preeminence of religious practice in the promotion of "civilization."

Besides this explicit backpedaling by Vasconcelos in texts published after *The Cosmic Race*, problems of terminology and style also became more apparent. As a philosophical essayist, Vasconcelos often reacted to contemporary trends by employing an antiscientific, antirational mode of writing to challenge point by point the criteria of the scientific discourse that characterized his period. As David William Foster points out (*Para una lectura semiótica del ensayo latinoamericano*, 70), this antiscientific approach was also marked by high levels of ambiguity in the use of specific terms, not the least of which was the word "race" itself, a term whose usage repeatedly raised questions for Vasconcelos' readers, as noted above. Sometimes anthropological in Vasconcelos' wide-ranging appropriation, as in "white race" or "black race," "race" more frequently came to refer to a group of people with a shared history and common set of cultural values, a meaning quite distant from ethnic or racial characteristics.

This is important not only because it reflects a principal intellectual tension of the period, but also because it mirrors the central debate in the cult of *mestizaje*: is it a physical, quantitative category, or is it a social, cultural, or even spiritual phenomenon? Although Vasconcelos never answers this riddle, he does denounce scientifically proven theories of racial superiority by focusing on the spiritual benefit and enrichment of people of mixed descent. It is this questioning of a dominant ideology in both formal and thematic terms that has made Vasconcelos' ideas so seductive for Third World readers, according to Foster. Vasconcelos' rhetoric of inversion did not so much challenge racial stereotypes as reformulate them. What was once the largest defect of Latin America, its "racial mongrelization," becomes in his writing its best quality. The Mexican author took the markers of perceived national and regional inferiority, such as irrationality, emotiveness, unbridled enthusiasm, and sensitivity, and redrew them as the characteristics of a privileged people.

Although few could argue with Vasconcelos' prominent position in the chief philosophical arguments of his era, or with the hope and pride many found in his texts, there were many who reacted to his writings with worry or even disdain, recognizing the dangerous consequences of his ideology for the cultural autonomy and political agency of those individuals and groups who identified first or solely as indigenous, black, mulatto, and so on. "The 'cosmic race' might be the product of *mestizaje*, but one in which the Hispanic elements would predominate," comments Carlos Tur Donatti, echoing the frequent critical charge that Vasconcelos always took a pejorative view of the indigenous element, despite including it rhetorically in the national project ("La utopía del regreso," 171). Other critics rejected his ideas on the basis of rhetorical and intellectual failures. Uruguayan Rómulo Nano Lottero condemned him for favoring some regions of Latin America, discrediting others, and thus developing a theory of a fifth race that was contradictory and utopian (*Palabras para América*, 55).

The cult of *mestizaje* that Vasconcelos shepherded in *The Cosmic Race* proved susceptible to harsh criticism both for its providential reading of colonial history and for the blind eye it turned to contemporary problems facing both mestizo and nonmestizo populations. Vasconcelos' mission, which recognized and built on a colonial substructure both material and discursive — "The Spanish colonization created *mestizaje*" (*La raza cósmica* [1966], 27) — is perhaps merely typical of other modernist nation-building efforts that tend to assimilate and thus cancel difference and dissent. Still, the degree to which Vasconcelos dismissed historical or *present* conditions of *mestizaje* is striking. When he does enlist these precedents for the future fulfillment of a complete human fusion, his version of historical contact is resolutely glorious, created in the "abundance of love that permitted the Spaniards to create a new race with the Indian and the black, profusely spreading white ancestry through the soldier who begat a native family, and Occidental culture through the doctrine and example of the missionaries who placed the Indians in condition to enter into the new state, the stage of world One" (*The Cosmic Race*, 17).

Such comments reveal, finally, the affinity of Vasconcelos' thinking about race, even early in his writing career, with projects of eugenics and *blanqueamiento,* or whitening, in other parts of the hemisphere. He admits that "perhaps the traits of the white race will predominate among the characteristics of the fifth race," but urges that this "supremacy" result from free election, and not violence or economic pressure (*The Cosmic Race*, 26–27). Peter Earle notes that "a sour epilogue is written in 1939 and 1940, when Vasconcelos passes from the Fifth Race to the Fifth Column, contributing to a series of vehemently pro-Axis and pro-Hitler editorials to an ephemeral journal in Mexico City, *El Timón*" ("Utopía, Universópolis, Macondo," 148–149).

Who could have predicted that the effusive praise of miscegenation and mixed race in *The Cosmic Race* would be replaced by ideas more closely aligned to the white supremacist ideology of Naziism? Perhaps a certain sense of foreboding can be teased out of the comments of some early critics. Nonetheless, Vasconcelos' about-face clearly received much less press and had much less impact than his earlier triumphant celebration. Ultimately, his vision of *mestizaje* inspired writers, artists, and others throughout Latin America to consider the importance of mixed-race phenomena and ideas in their own countries and specific histories. Vasconcelos left in his wake a Latin American racial discourse that remains "a continuing paradox of harmony and struggle" (Earle, 157), but one in which the inherent contradictions were frequently set aside in order to answer pressing questions of local and regional identity and citizenship. The inherent paradoxes in these processes is the subject I take up in subsequent chapters.

Y así estás, mi verde antilla,
en un sí es que no es de raza,
en ten con ten de abolengo
que te hace tan antillana . . .
Al ritmo de los tambores
tu lindo ten con ten bailas,
una mitad española
y otra mitad africana.

LUIS PALÉS MATOS[1]

Aquí todos somos café con leche; unos más café, otros más leche.

VENEZUELAN PROVERB[2]

I. *Mestizaje, Mulatez,* AND *Negrismo*

In the prologue to *Indología*, published soon after *The Cosmic Race*, José Vasconcelos spoke favorably of the specific *mestizaje* of the mulatto, calling it the "most illustrious document of American citizenship" (6).[3]

But the place of the mulatto or the mulatta in the rhetoric of Latin American citizenship has not always been as prestigious as Vasconcelos' comment would suggest. The mulatto usually occupied an ambiguous, overwhelmingly negative, position in narratives of the colony or emerging nation; the mulatto or the mulatta was a threat to unity or coherence, a contaminant, a stain, a temptation, or a force beyond the control of vested powers. This legacy of the mulatto as a metaphor for corruption or fracture is common to social and literary discourse throughout Latin America, but nowhere more crucial than in the Caribbean. As Rubén Ríos Ávila notes, "Situated along the navel that divides both hemispheres of the American world, the Caribbean is the heterotope that defracts the illusions of totality with which North America and Latin America saturate and suture their identity discourses [*discursos identitarios*] . . . An unsolvable puzzle of language and race, one could say that the Caribbean is the party pooper which spoils the festivities of both continents during their Día de la Raza celebrations, the trope which trips them up" (*La raza cómica*, 158).

Beginning, perhaps, with the work of the Puerto Rican poet Luis Palés Matos, several Caribbean poets and essayists more or less contemporary with Vasconcelos engage in a rich "counterpoint" with this idea,[4] challenging historical reprobation and marginalization of the mulatto or the mulatta and resituating him (or, more often, her) in the middle of debates around citizenship and cultural currency. In Palés' writing and that of later practitioners such as the Cuban Nicolás Guillén and the Dominican Manuel del Cabral, the mulatto or the mulatta's fundamental ambiguity persists, but is recast as an asset. This literary representation of the mulatto or the mulatta in the first half of the twentieth century in the former Spanish colonies of the Caribbean reveals the successes and failures of Latin American *mestizaje* in general, as well as the specific difficulties of incorporating the African and African American into such national and regional ideologies. In a dramatic shift that takes shape in various Caribbean literatures, the mulatto or the mulatta as a sign of alarming dilution or contamination is transformed into the incarnation of advantageous admixture.

Certainly, such attempts reflected desire rather than daily practice (Williams, *Charcoal and Cinnamon*, 94), and often had a limited relationship to enactments within everyday "race relations." The iconic encoding of the mulatta as the symbol of national identity and synonym of *mestizaje* often highlighted the stark contrast between the cultural visibility and social *invisibility* of certain sectors of the society (Kutzinski, *Sugar's Secrets*, 7). Nonetheless, this aesthetic counterpoint to nineteenth-century condemnations of the black or mulatto presence constitutes one of the most dynamic engagements with *mestizaje* in Latin America, an engagement that would, in turn, produce or influence numerous key texts written throughout the continent.

Vasconcelos had initiated an important discussion by constructing providential Latin American *mestizaje* in spiritual terms, incorporating the contributions of white, indigenous, black, and Asian peoples to create a future, amorphous "fifth race" in the Americas.[5] But his model was a difficult fit in the Caribbean for two reasons: the near-total disappearance of indigenous populations in the Spanish Caribbean early in the Spanish colonization of the islands; and the subsequent pronounced presence there of Africans and their descendants, often in numbers that exceeded those of "white" populations.[6]

Faced with a colonial history that distinguished the Caribbean region from the rest of Latin America and resident populations that did not match old notions of *mestizaje* as a mix of Indian and Spaniard, intellectuals in the islands attempted to redress (or undress) their own racial "problem" in carnal or material terms, very frequently focusing on the body of the mulatta as the quintessential site of felicitous mixture. This foregrounding of the mulatta coincided with aesthetic experiments which dramatized racial contact, confrontation, and interpenetration between blacks and whites, resulting in a movement that was labeled "*mulatez*" or "*mulataje,*" a particularly Caribbean response to the cult of *mestizaje*. Vasconcelos' essay undoubtedly contributed to this new movement, since a review of *La raza cósmica* appeared in the Havana daily paper *El Diario de la Marina*, suggesting that the book was read in the Spanish Antilles and was assessed from the perspective of the Caribbean. The same newspaper would later serve as the first public venue for many works associated with both *negrismo* and *mulatez* (Kutzinski, *Sugar's Secrets*, 147).

It should be noted from the outset that the poets associated with this new aesthetics of *mulatez* differed widely in terms of their acceptance of racial terminology to describe their work. Within social and economic contexts still quite rigidly divided by race and, by extension, by class, a poetics of *mulatez* was invariably read by most as a black poetics—even when the authors were white. But authorship was only one of the terrains in which these writers questioned notions of black and white as fixed markers of identity and, instead, called for a textual space marked by synthesis and integration. In the introduction to his second book of poems, *Sóngoro cosongo: Poemas mulatos*,[7] published in 1931, the Cuban poet Nicolás Guillén clarifies his own poetics of *mulatez* (in *Summa poética*, 39–40):

> I'm not unaware, of course, that these poems are repugnant to many people, because they deal with matters of blacks and of the community. I don't care. Or better stated: I'm pleased. What I mean to say is that such sharp characters are not part of my lyric agenda . . .
>
> Let me say finally that these are mulatto verses. They are formed, perhaps, of the same elements which are present in the ethnic composition of Cuba, where we are all of a rather uncertain background. Does this hurt? I don't think so. In any case, it's important to say this before we forget it. The African injection is so deep in this land, and so many capillary currents cross and intersect in our well-irrigated social

hydrography, that untangling this hieroglyphic would be the task of a miniaturist.

Thus, I believe that we won't have a well-developed Creole poetry if we forget the black. The black—in my judgment—provides essential ingredients in our cocktail.[8]

With these words, Guillén sets out to invoke a social or at least textual terrain in which black and white elements are equally valued as essential ingredients in the formation of the Cuban people and their cultural expression. In this respect, Guillén does not differ radically from the ideas José Martí expressed in "Nuestra América," but we should notice his insistence on poetry, and not political activity, as the privileged domain for the valorization of *mestizaje*. Guillén is not calling just for a poetic response, but for poetry that depends on the synthesis of speech forms and themes usually segregated from each other: popular black speech with traditional Spanish verse forms, the daily preoccupations of the working class with the more ethereal concerns of the educated class, and the like. With the reference at the end of the citation to "our cocktail," Guillén emphasizes the social, everyday dimension of Caribbean experience. In a prodigious blend of metaphors, his prologue incorporates references to the spiritual, the literary, the scientific, the hieroglyphic, and, finally, the mixological, the science of the cocktail.

The title of Guillén's collection can itself be read as a nod to *mulatez*. As the anecdote goes, the North American poet Langston Hughes wrote Guillén a letter in which he praised his early poems, but found difficulty in discerning the meaning of the untranslatable "sóngoro cosongo." According to Guillén, the phrase used to appear on restaurant menus in Havana, and when he asked a waiter what it meant, his server replied, " 'Good morning' in African" (Sardinha, *The Poetry of Nicolás Guillén*, 13). Whether or not this is true, the term provides a microhistory of the interchange of Spanish and African elements in the Cuban lexicon, part linguistic modification, part invention, part myth, part celebration of an orality that privileged rhythmic rather than grammatical meaning.

Guillén's poetry from this period was enormously successful, even if it elicited a wide range of response from readers. One reviewer wrote, "Among us only Nicolás Guillén has created and discovered anything. He is, then, something more than a great poet. He is the poet of Cuba whose muse is mulatto," to which another retorted that "he is a national poet. His lyric poetry cannot be confined to the 'mulatto muse' " (Sardinha, 18). Guillén, on the other hand, seems to dispense with such debates in the poems themselves. In "Palabras en el trópico" (Words in the Tropics), he writes, "Dice Jamaica/que ella está contenta de ser negra,/¡y Cuba ya sabe que es mulata!" (Jamaica says/that she's content to be black/and Cuba already knows that she's mulatta!) For him, the Cuban condition was unavoidably mulatto/a, and his poetry merely another proof or symptom of that condition.

Luis Palés Matos was less comfortable with a description of his verses as reflective of a "mulatto poetics" and refused to use racial labels to describe his poetry. In a response to his friend José I. de Diego Pardó, he attested, "I have not spoken of a black poetry nor a white one nor a mulatto one; I have only spoken of a Caribbean poetry" (Vázquez Arce, "*Tuntún de pasa y grifería*," 94). Much less explicit than Guillén in terms of the relationship between his lyric production and the island's racial makeup, Palés repeatedly reaffirmed the fundamental *Antillean* condition of his work when critics dismissed his "mulatto poetry" as the inauthentic expression of a white author, or his "arte negro" as a poetic project with no place in Puerto Rican letters (*La poesía de Luis Palés Matos*, 3).[9]

These various appropriations and rejections bear out that, as with other key terms in the discourse of *mestizaje*, and, indeed, *all* identity markers in Latin America, the term "*mulatez*" and its employment in both literary and popular agendas is inherently problematic. Still, a study of literary works which invoke the phenomenon brings to light the central position of the Antilles in any discussion of Latin American *mestizaje*. An exploration of *mulatez* thus provides an opportunity to question the specific place of the Caribbean within the complex rhetorical matrix of Latin American *mestizaje*, and the connection between this rhetoric and subsequent cultural and social behaviors which confirm or challenge it. Lourdes Martínez-Echazábal recognizes the importance of comparing and contrasting *mulatez* to other forms of rhetorically sanctioned hybridity in *Para una semiótica de la mulatez* (Toward a Semiotics of *Mulatez*, 5–6):

> In Hispanic America, racist ideology has manipulated and mystified the notion of racial difference, inscribing its values not only in popular language, but also in academic and political language, through the use of racial tropes; tropes which configure our actions and contribute to the sustenance of a specific vision of the world. Thus the primordial task of this work is to uncover the mechanisms which have made of *mulatez* a sign/signifier of difference, an essential part of the political and intellectual rhetoric and the aesthetic production of those Spanish-speaking countries which Fernando Ortiz would call Afro-America.

An exploration of *mulatez* also allows us to consider the possibility of an inter-Caribbean expression that goes beyond the categories and limitations typical of modern identity, such as language, national boundaries, type of government, current relationship with colonial powers, and religion. Antonio Benítez-Rojo has addressed this question with interesting results in *The Repeating Island*, which places Caribbean cultural phenomena within a context which is concurrently premodern, modern, and postmodern. Such an inquiry may also provide an avenue to what Vèvè Clark has called "diaspora literacy," interpretive work that takes up literatures (and other discourses) of Africa, Afro-America, and the Caribbean in relationship to each other in a necessarily multicultural and multilingual frame ("Developing Diaspora Literacy and Marasa Consciousness," 42).

Early-twentieth-century critics who read the works of these writers associated with this new aesthetics of *mulatez* often responded by relegating the mestizo of African descent to a peripheral position within an already marginalized "subcategory" of *negrismo*, a vanguard movement in Spanish American literature valorizing the black experience in the Americas. This critical segregation of *mulatez* within *negrismo* is revealing of various tendencies within Caribbean racial discourse. First, though blacks and mulattos were rarely collapsed into a single racial group in Caribbean social praxis (C. Williams, xi), the tendency to do so in literary representations exposed *mestizaje* as a rhetoric distanced from everyday experiences. Second, while most recent studies insist that the ideology of *mestizaje* always assumes an implicit project of whitening and the superiority of mixed race to black or indigenous identity, this argument is harder to sustain in an examination of the Caribbean, where instances of *mulatez* are still inevitably tied to the vindication of black identity. Clearly, *mulatez* should not be considered an exact parallel to Vasconcelos-style *mestizaje* or to the development of other black literatures in the Americas.

II. GENDER TROUBLES

The fraught relationship between the discourse of *mestizaje* and somatic features shows the extent to which *mulatez* or any other mestizo logic is based in a reading of the body, a reading which cannot avoid being intersected by the binary of gender.[10] As Kutzinski's important research has revealed, *mulatez* is generally enunciated from the position of the male writer, and, historically, the mulatta has been represented as the focus of colonial desire and aggression in the Caribbean. She is subordinated to both males and females in the dominant class because of her color, and because in Western thought, the man is traditionally associated with the mind, soul, and spirit, while the woman is associated with the body.

With rare exceptions, Caribbean literatures from the late nineteenth and early twentieth centuries restrict the mulatta's beauty to physical characteristics, while her moral and intellectual traits remain suspect or unclean. Many "empirical" studies of the African female body were used in early-nineteenth-century Europe to justify intellectually sanctioned racism at the same time that a body of Romantic literature grew around the mythic portrayal of the native woman of color in the European colonies, praising her beauty and ardent sensuality. The Caribbean mulatta is heir—and, to some degree, product—of these two traditions, appearing first as the dazzling but doomed beauty hoping to improve her situation through intimacy with white men and white culture, and later as the figure of favorable mixture which provides the outline and form of literary *mulatez*.

In no other Latin American literary history is the elaboration of locally specific *mestizaje* so tied to the emblem of the female figure.[11] As a result, the notion of *mulatez* has often been reduced to a summary of the representation of the mulatta in verse and prose, and the construction of a mulatto or mulatta aesthetics over her mute body. Kutzinski writes that "at the center of this frustrated, deeply romantic search or self-invention, the mulata is the inscription of a desire for cultural synthesis upon a field of sociopolitical contingencies that is accordingly distorted" (*Sugar's Secrets*, 165). Predominantly male and white writers' appropriation of the mulatta in the development of Caribbean aesthetics follows certain notable precedents in social history. For example, for most of the nineteenth century, Cuban law decreed that a white man could marry a mulatta, but a white woman could not marry a man of color (Rivas, *Literatura y esclavitud*, 78). Thus, at the point that the mulatta became the focus of a literary movement valorizing Caribbean *mestizaje* or hybridity, she was already functioning, in many respects, as an agent of racial destabilization.

In Cuba, the beloved and archetypal figure of this earlier representation of the mulatta (robust and delightful exterior but blighted interior) is Cecilia Valdés, the protagonist of Cirilo Villaverde's nineteenth-century short story (1839) and novel (*Cecilia Valdés o, la loma del ángel*, 1882). In a melodramatic tale that prefigures William Faulkner's *Absalom, Absalom!*, a wealthy white family man has an affair with a light-skinned mulatta. They have a daughter whom he separates from the mother and denies publicly but maintains economically during her childhood. Years later, the lovely adolescent Cecilia is courted, seduced, "kept," and ultimately rejected by her half-brother Leonardo without either one's being aware of their blood ties. En route to his wedding with a more suitable white spouse, Leonardo is killed by Cecilia's spurned mulatto suitor. As Madeline Cámara has pointed out, the Cecilia whom Villaverde fashions after more than four decades of revision is, in fact, more heavily t(a)inted by racial determinism than the original protagonist: her voluptuousness belies weakness of character, and her face would be the model of beauty were it not for her malicious, even malignant, expression.

The incorporation of the mulatta into the discourse of *mulatez* in the early twentieth century perpetuates this stereotype of fulsome sensuality and ardent sexuality, but reinvests it with productive creativity, rather than predestined tragedy. Still, the mulatta's physical contours change very little in this rehabilitation, and she rarely has a speaking part in the verses Caribbean writers penned during the period. Claudette Williams argues that the obsession with the Afro-Caribbean woman as an erotic creature, in fact, had the effect of obscuring her social situation (130–131). "Returning the voice to the text of *mulatez* symbolically inscribed on the body of the woman could be a liberating way to re-read the Cuban nation, in which hybridity might stop being the utopia of racial conciliation," Cámara suggests ("¿Dónde está la hija de Cecilia?").

III. CUBAN *Ajiaco*

Cuba has historically constituted a privileged space of *mestizaje* in Latin American and Caribbean imaginaries, due to historical processes within the island that contributed to a high level of miscegenation and to Havana's importance as a principal port of maritime traffic, a "crossroads of the world" between Spain and other European powers and the New World colonies. José Martí's reference to Spanish America as "our mestizo America," distinguishing it from the northern neighbor and its history of antimiscegenation and racial segregation by law, may be considered an early building block in a prodigious elaboration of *mestizaje* by Cuban intellectuals writing in a variety of genres. These include poetic engagements with *mulatez* by a number of authors during the first half of the century, Fernando Ortiz' development of the notion of transculturation in *Cuban Counterpoint*, and Alejo Carpentier's invocation of the "marvelous real" in the prologue to *The Kingdom of This World*. In all of these cases, aesthetic engagements with questions of race and mixed race represented complex negotiations that, on the one hand, vindicated the nonwhite presence in both low and high culture, and, on the other, mediated that presence through its incorporation into established Creole and post-Creole institutions and registers. In this sense, these authors populated and occupied the space between historically segregated peoples and forms of expression, becoming themselves mediators and procurers of hybrid phenomena.

But such negotiations were not without their obstacles and pitfalls. The death of Martí and of the mulatto general Antonio Maceo, who had fought alongside him in the revolutionary effort, left Afro-Cubans without an important spokesman in the early twentieth century. The peculiar interest the public took in Maceo after his death highlighted the gulf between Martí's ideal of a raceless society and everyday social practice. In 1900, Maceo's bones became the subject of an official study, which found—after careful research, no doubt!—that Maceo's skeleton attested to his black origin, but that his skull was that of a white man (Graham, 47).[12]

Similar studies and similar results were not unusual in the period, and, in fact, Fernando Ortiz initially became interested in the African element in Cuba in terms of its relationship to criminal behavior. His 1906 text *Hampa afro-cubana: Los negros esclavos* (Afro-Cuban Underworld: The Black Slaves), which explored the criminality of blacks in the island, revealed a much different position on race from the posture with which Ortiz is routinely identified in *Cuban Counterpoint*.[13] As becomes evident in the ethnologist's later work, his ideas were also significantly influenced and modified by his close examination of the poetry of *mulatez*.

Besides the term "transculturation," Ortiz used "*ajiaco*," a Cuban stew composed of various meats, vegetables, potatoes, and hot peppers, to describe the cultural composition of the island.[14] As he saw it, this complex "pepper-pot" had been brewing since the earliest moments of the conquest. Beginning in 1502, Africans from diverse nations and speaking a wide variety of languages were brought to Cuba as slaves, and by the middle of the nineteenth century, they constituted more than half of the population.[15] Other political and economic developments in the late eighteenth century brought French subjects from Haiti and Louisiana, and in the nineteenth, Chinese peoples from Canton and Macao, as well as indigenous peoples from the Yucatan Peninsula and parts of Central and South America. European immigration also contributed to Cuba's multifarious population. Late colonial Cuba did indeed resemble an *ajiaco*, and the same stew, with somewhat different ingredients, could be savored throughout the Caribbean.

Although *mestizaje* was never accepted as a national characteristic by all, Kutzinski argues that by the early twentieth century, terms such as "*cubanidad*" and "*cubanía*," both versions of Cubanness, "were for all intents and purposes, synonymous to *mestizaje*" (*Sugar's Secrets*, 7).[16] In the 1970s, Salvador Bueno explained that "*mestizaje* is the characteristic that best defines Latin American society and culture, and within this subcontinent that José Martí correctly called 'our mestizo America,' Cuba is one of the countries that presents the highest level of mixture in all areas, since it integrates not only ethnic *mestizaje*, but also a cultural *mestizaje* in which the most diverse elements interconnect and embrace" (89–90).

Within a complex set of aesthetic and rhetorical maneuvers that retooled *mestizaje* to suit local needs, Cuban writers attempted to redraw or repaint the characteristics of national identity. As was true elsewhere in the Caribbean, the most successful challenges to old definitions of cultural citizenship would arguably be staged in a space of lyric expression.

IV. MULATTO VERSES

The notion of *mulatez* as an aesthetic movement reached its zenith in Spanish America between 1920 and 1940, a period simultaneous with the production of several key *negrismo* texts, including the early novel *Écue-yamba-ó!* by Alejo Carpentier (1933), the *Cuaderno de poesía negra* (Notebook of Black Poetry) by Emilio Ballagas in Cuba, *Doce poemas negros* (Twelve Black Poems) by the Dominican Manuel del Cabral in 1937, and the elaboration of *négritude* in French by poets Jacques Romain and León Damas from Haiti and French Guiana, respectively. In Mexico, José Juan Tablada published "Canción de la mulata" (Song of the Mulatta) in 1928, and in Venezuela, Andrés Eloy Blanco wrote a poem titled "Píntame angelitos negros" ("Paint Me Little Black Angels"), which would later be set to music and broadcast throughout the continent. On the Caribbean coast of Colombia, a young poet named Manuel Zapata Olivella began to compose verses, an effort he would recall many years later in his 1990 autobiography, *¡Levántate mulato!* (Rise Up, Mulatto!), which recycled Vasconcelos' famous phrase, "The spirit will speak through my race" in the subtitle. "I had been born of the crossing of many bloods and I felt the creative potential of the young man who reclaimed a place on my turf without any reverence or halting before a master or foreign lord," Zapata Olivella wrote (18). Recounting a personal history in which all the grandfathers of the family were the offspring of Indian or black women, he wonders, "Hybrid or new man? Am I really a traitor to my race? A slippery *zambo?* A mulatto sellout? Or simply an American mestizo who seeks to defend the identity of his oppressed bloods?" (21)

In poetic texts from this period, typically massed under the heading of "black literature," mulatto identity is a recurring theme, either as it pertains to specific characters, or as a condition typical of the nation or region. This slide between mulatto protagonists and regional *mulatez* appears repeatedly in the work of Nicolás Guillén. In Guillén's famous poem "Balada de los dos abuelos" (Ballad of Two Grandfathers), the speaker invokes the two ancestors who escort him, one black and the other white, mirroring exactly each other's stature and actions, as he declares his role in bringing them together:

Yo los junto.
—¡Federico!

¡Facundo! Los dos se abrazan.

Los dos suspiran. Los dos
las fuertes cabezas alzan;
los dos del mismo tamaño,
bajo las estrellas altas;
los dos del mismo tamaño,
ansia negra y ansia blanca,
los dos del mismo tamaño,
gritan, sueñan, lloran, cantan.
Sueñan, lloran, cantan.
Lloran, cantan.
¡Cantan! (Morales, *Poesía afroantillana y negrista*, 354)

I bring them together.
—Federico!

Facundo! They embrace.
They sigh. They both
lift their strong heads;
both the same size,
under the lofty stars;
both the same size,
black longing, white longing,

both the same size,
they call, they dream, they weep, they sing.
They dream, they weep, they sing.
They weep, they sing.
They sing!

If in the essays of Martí, there can be no race hatred because there are no races, in Guillén's poetics, black and white not only coexist, they also appear together on equal terms. The titles which distinguish the two grandfathers' social class at the beginning are dropped in the last stanza as they embrace each other and mirror each other's actions. But the biological agents of this coming together of black and white, the women who engender mulatto offspring, are absent or erased, as this function is transferred to the domain of the poet. As Kutzinski reads the poem, "*mestizaje* becomes legitimated as an exclusively male project or achievement in which interracial, heterosexual rape can be refigured as a fraternal embrace across color (and in this case, class) lines and, significantly, across a female body absented by rape . . . Guillén's conception of a racial (or raceless) utopia in 'Balada' is predicated on the erasure . . . of a black woman, the one in whose violated body the two races actually met" (*Sugar's Secrets*, 168).

While the mulatta may be absent from "Ballad of Two Grandfathers," she certainly plays a concrete, though not always endearing, role in other examples of Guillén's poetry. In "The Mulatta," from 1930, the poetic speaker disdains the mulatta's scorn for his overtly African features, warning that she, too, has a big mouth and nappy hair, and besides, his black woman is enough for him. As Claudette Williams has grasped, here Guillén leaves aside literary rhetoric for "lived reality," showing that the mulatta can serve as a spokeswoman for a color-coded racist discourse which reads "pure" white as the highest value and "pure" black as the lowest, even as she herself is used to personify national unity (99–100).

A more complex problem than the neglect of the woman of color in Guillén's portrait of his grandfathers is the implicit erasure or silencing of the mulatta in her transformation into a metaphor, rather than an active agent of history. An example of this strategy is Guillén's conception of a "mulatta land" in "La canción del bongó" (Song of the Bongo), also part of *Sóngoro cosongo*. Translated by Langston Hughes and Ben Carruthers and included in a collection titled *Cuba libre* (1948),[17] the poem offers a ground for the ideal association of African and Spanish elements, distant from the feudal domains of the sugar plantation. What is interesting about the notion of a "mulatta" land is its clearly utopian logic: neither Spaniards nor Africans had any indigenous connection to the Caribbean geography; thus the land could be "mulatta" only within a cultural matrix that reinvented it as such, subsequent to conquest and colonization. In fact, the poem sets up culture as more powerful than nature:

> Pero mi repique bronco,
> pero mi profunda voz,
> convoca al negro y al blanco
> que bailan al mismo son,
> cueripardos o almiprietos
> más de sangre que de sol,
> pues quien por fuera no es noche,
> por dentro ya oscureció.
> Aquí el que más fino sea
> responde, ¡si llamo yo! (Morales, 355–356)

> But my hoarse rejoinder,
> deep, bass voice,
> calls both black and white
> to dance to the same *son*.
> Brown of skin or brown of soul
> more from blood than sun,
> those who are not night outside
> get darker deep within.
> Here even blueblood
> answers if I call. (Guillén, *Cuba libre*, 81)

As the title promises, the verses are inherently musical, interspersing, as they do, literary and percussive elements and creating a rhythm that grows in intensity and force. The voice of the poet is infectious, drawing in black and white—even the purest-blooded listener among them—to dance to the same Cuban rhythm. Among the dark-skinned or dark-souled folks who heed the call, we see various configurations of cultural, racial, and spiritual mixture, complemented in the second stanza with the invocation of the Catholic Saint Barbara alongside the Yoruba deity Changó:

> En esta tierra mulata
> de africano y español,
> (Santa Bárbara, de un lado
> del otro lado, Changó) (Morales, 356)

In this mulatto land
of Spaniard and African,
(*Santa Bárbara* on one side,
on the other *Changó*) (Guillén, *Cuba libre*, 81)

As Ortiz has noted, the *bongó* is a "mulatto" instrument and thus a musical corollary to the multicultural stew "created by Cuban genius," not brought from Africa, but imbued with Africanness and appearing in the island only "when the black soul began to feel free in Cuba and *mulatez* stopped being a sinful evocation." Ortiz associates the drum with the emergence of the independent nation and "mulatto music, engendered of its African mother and Peninsular father" ("Más acerca de la poesía mulata," 193). Ortiz noticed the specificity of these local rhythms and languages when he attempted to present some of Guillén's early poems to a group of Latin American and Spanish literary critics convened in Washington ("Los últimos versos mulatos," 171): "No one could read them or savor their *sandunga* [charm or wit], nor could they understand their musicality. It wasn't just their lack of acquaintance with vocabulary, a problem easily solved, but the lack of rhythmic articulation, and, above all, a total lack of the adequate vocal expression. Only a Cuban could read them acceptably, give them sense, transmit them with emotion, and capture their encomium." Ortiz predicted that linguistic and rhythmic barriers would limit the success of this "mulatto poetry" abroad, but not only did Guillén's verses elicit an enthusiastic response from readers outside the Caribbean, they also prompted a reevaluation of the African diasporic foundations of "mestizo" culture throughout Latin America.

While the *bongó* and the poetic voice function together in Guillén's call to the assembled to respond to the "deep voice" of each, we notice that the poet/musician and the reader/listener change places in a carnivalesque shift at the end of "La canción del bongó." While the poem recognizes both a tendency to deny one's black heritage ("there's always a grandpa missing") and the reality of racial discrimination that still colors the Cuban experience, it also acknowledges progress and predicts a dethroning of white superiority ("you'll ask my pardon yet/. . . for top dog here is me!").

As these verses so clearly attest, Guillén's poetic expression was not limited to concerns with blackness; he was also deeply concerned with the companionship of blacks and whites, and their expressive forms, within the poetic imaginary. But in his development of a poetics of *mulatez*, Guillén has been viewed with suspicion by certain critics who see in his work just one more version of a *mestizaje* in which blacks benefit or improve from contact with whites, or, worse yet, in which African or neo-African expression is erased or annulled within the frame of *mestizaje*. "Even the affirmation of the African heritage by a writer such as the Afro-Cuban Nicolás Guillén does not preclude this ideology of racial integration," asserts Claudette Williams (13). As with other appropriations of *mestizaje*, some readers worry that an ideal of racial harmony is envisioned which minimizes remaining tensions and inequities based on race. The exiled Cuban writer Guillermo Cabrera Infante questioned Guillén's racial politics precisely *because* the poet reportedly insisted on his mulatto identity ("Nicolás Guillén," 32):

> Guillén's problems in Cuba were not all political: some in a strange way were racial. In 1961, at a party given by the party after he was unanimously elected president of the Writers Union (I was, comically, his seventh vice-president, thus making Guillén a Cuban version of Snow White and me his seventh dwarf), I introduced him to an American publisher (of sorts):
> "Ah!," she exclaimed in near ecstasy. "The great negro poet!" Guillén said quickly:
> "Negro no, mulato." [18]

Despite this anecdote, Guillén's enlistment of *mulatez* repeatedly focused on the inclusion rather than the preclusion of black identity in the national makeup. In the frequently anthologized "Son número 6" from his 1947 *El son entero* (The Whole *Son*), he speaks of "negros y blancos, todo mezclado," blacks and whites all mixed. In another famous poem, "El apellido" (The Last Name), Guillén's poetic speaker expresses "ancestral anguish" at the erasure of African genealogy through the imposition of a Spanish surname, insisting that his skin, voice, bones, and roots are a composite of Spanish and African elements.

Whether or not Guillén's persistent focus on Cuba's particular relationship to *mestizaje* makes him guilty of dis-identification with blackness—a question which should now seem more complex than Cabrera Infante's comments suggest—there are two important aspects of the Caribbean racial discourse which come to light in his personal appropriation of *mulatez*. First, in Cuba, as elsewhere in the Caribbean, "race" is configured according to a complex pigmentocracy which determines social standing not only on the basis of white and black, but also according to a broad spectrum of colors between these two poles. This caste system is so deeply entrenched that even ardent revolutionary and postcolonial arguments have not been able to eradicate it. Second, Guillén recognized that the similar colonial and economic histories shared by Caribbean territories did not result in identical racial discourses, so that, for example, Jamaica recognized itself as *negro* and Cuba saw itself as mulatta ("Palabras en el trópico" [Words in the Tropics]). The affiliation of many authors in the insular and continental Caribbean with a poetics of *mulatez* has sometimes obscured the importance of locally specific histories to each national engagement with a racial politics and poetics. Just as we should view *mulatez* as a particular and distinct approach to the dilemmas of *mestizaje*, we should also recognize that each Caribbean engagement with *mulatez* is imbedded in local enunciations of "race." Despite historical ties, Cuba, Puerto Rico, the Dominican Republic, and other Caribbean nations took up the aesthetics of *mulatez* in radically different ways.

V. IN THE ISLAND OF ENCHANTMENT

The best practitioner of the genre of "black-white verses" in Puerto Rico,[19] according to Fernando Ortiz, was Luis Palés Matos, who in a poem titled "Ten con ten" spoke of his island as "una mitad española/y otra mitad africana" (one half Spanish/and the other half African). But Palés was not the first Puerto Rican to dedicate verses to a mulatta entity or, arguably, to *mulatez*. Luis Lloréns Torres had earlier penned "Copla mulata," which proclaimed in part,

> Esta semisalvaje mediasangre,
> ibera y antillana,
> merece que la corra a todo escape
> en la pista de llamas
> sobre la mar Atlante
> tendida entre ambas razas.
> Esta hembra montañesa,
> que sabe a ron Jamaica,
> untada de ají bravo,
> que resopla mostaza,
> es en la isla caliente
> la caliente potranca;
> hecha para subir sobre ella en pelo
> la cuesta de la noche a la mañana;
> digna de ensangrentar en sus ijares
> mis espuelas de plata. (Morales, 13–14)

This semisavage halfblood,
Iberian and Antillean,
deserves that I chase her full speed
along the trail of flames
over the Atlantic sea
stretched between both races.
This mountainous female
who tastes of Jamaican rum,
anointed with fiery chile,
who breathes mustard,
in this hot island
the hot filly is
made to mount bareback,
the rise from night to morning;
worthy of bloodying in her flanks
my spurs of silver.

Lloréns Torres' "hymn" to the mulatta, included in Jorge Luis Morales' *Poesía afroantillana y negrista* (Afro-Antillean and Negrista Poetry), is typical of the Caribbean treatment of the theme prior to the interventions of writers like Guillén and Palés Matos and embodies many of the ideas associated with *mestizaje* in the late nineteenth and early twentieth centuries: primitivism, savageness, an unbridled and fiery nature, temptation.[20]

The poem registers the enactment of male violence on the mulatta body in a number of ways. The choice of the verb *correr* allows for a reading of the speaker as alternately cutting her off or chasing her along a trail of flames across the Atlantic. The poetic speaker also rides her bareback and, finally, bloodies her flanks with his spurs. Moreover, the mulatta is deserving and "worthy" of such violence, presumably because the rider's spurs are silver, a synecdoche for whiteness. The conflation of the mulatta with a hot filly is, of course, strikingly close to the animalization of the racialized subject through the use of the term "mulatto" or "mulatta," etymologically based on the notion of crossbreeding the horse and donkey to produce the mule.

In 1937, Luis Palés Matos published *Tuntún de pasa y grifería* (Tomtom of Kinky Hair and Black Things),[21] a collection which brought together more than a decade of poems which had appeared earlier in journals and newspapers, proving that Palés Matos' "black verses" preceded not only the work of Cubans Guillén, Ballagas, and Carpentier, but also that of many celebrated North American poets, such as Langston Hughes and Claude McKay.[22] His title, which announces the arrival of the black ("pasa") and the mulatto ("grifo" was a word for mulatto in Puerto Rican Spanish during the late colonial period), represented an open challenge to a national literary discourse which refused to identify with the black, to the point that his allusive title was unintelligible to many readers (Díaz Quiñones, *El arte de bregar*, 35). According to Mercedes López Baralt, the emphatic reference to race in the title corresponds to a declaration by the Martinican poet Aimé Césaire, who was the first to use the term "*négritude*," in 1934 (in Palés Matos, *Túntun de pasa y grifería*, 27): "Since Caribbean peoples were ashamed of being black, they looked for all kinds of periphrasis to refer to a black. They spoke of a 'tan-skinned person' and other stupid terms of that nature . . . so we adopted the word *negre* as a word-challenge." Puerto Rican essayist José Luis González read the Palés oeuvre as the progressive fine-tuning of a conceptualization of national genetics without precedent in Puerto Rican literature, and the signal text of the discovery of the *afroantillidad* at the root of Puerto Rican identity.

Palés Matos' contemporaries were less than supportive of this strategy of foregrounding and celebrating black expression in Puerto Rican poetry. "So-called black art has no relationship to Puerto Rico," bristled one critic, thus demonstrating that the situation in Puerto Rico was significantly different from the literary environment in Cuba in the 1930s. "The fact that the first *negrista* poems of Palés prompted a commotion which soon would take on the appearance of a literary scandal, is symptomatic of the racist attitude of the island elite at that moment," notes López Baralt in her introduction to a 1993 revised edition of *Tuntún* (40).[23]

Despite these criticisms, and the persistence of the pseudo-scientific discourses of positivism and determinism in his era, both of which relegated blacks to inferior positions in the social structure, Palés created a body of mordant and provocative lyrical work in which black culture and *lo mulato* play a central role. His frequent use of irony is evidence that, for Palés, black and white do not cancel each other out, but, rather, live together in a permanent tension of encounter and dis-encounter. As Ríos Ávila has pointed out, first in an excellent article and, more recently, in *La raza cómica* (The Comic Race), this irony is symptomatic of the suspicion with which Vasconcelos' cosmic, quintessential *mestizaje* has been regarded in the Caribbean context (11): "If the cosmic is that which is taken to be closed in on itself, controlled by a complete and invariable power, then the comic refers to whatever excess or residue which might call into question cosmic perfection. The comic is produced by the suspicion of the fraudulence of the cosmic. Everything cosmic, when viewed close up, is comic."[24]

A notable example of this comic excess in a text that in fact invokes the cosmos is "Ñáñigo al cielo" (*Ñáñigo* to Heaven). A *ñáñigo*, or practitioner of the Afro-Caribbean cult of Abakuá, meets God in heaven, where he is greeted with a cornucopia of tropical abundance. As is frequently the case in Guillén's poetry, as well, deities from both African and Western traditions share the performative and semantic space:

El ñáñigo sube al cielo.
El cielo se ha decorado
de melón y calabaza
para la entrada del ñáñigo.
Los ángeles, vestidos
con verdes hojas de plátano,
lucen coronas de anana
y espadones de malango.
La gloria del Padre Eterno
rompe en triunfal taponazo,
y espuma de serafines
se riega por los espacios.
El ñáñigo va rompiendo
tiernas oleadas de blanco,
en su ascensión milagrosa
al dulce mundo seráfico.

The *ñáñigo* climbs to heaven.
Heaven is festooned
with melons and pumpkins,
for the *ñáñigo*'s entrance.
Robed in green plantain fronds,
the angels sport
pineapple crowns
and tuber broadswords.
The Eternal Father's glory
erupts in triumphal uncorking
and a seraphim froth
spills throughout the cosmos.
The *ñáñigo* is breaking

mild waves of white
in his miraculous ascension
to the sweet seraphic world. (Palés Matos, *Selected Poems*, 34–35)

The eruption of an Afro-Caribbean deity into the heavenly domain presents an overt challenge to established authorities, over which traditional Christianity reigns supreme, whether the Eternal Father is Catholic, as in the Spanish tradition, or Protestant, as in the North American version. As Díaz Quiñones has noted, Palés' influence on *lo negro* represents not only an attempt to fully celebrate Caribbean culture, but also a desire to emphasize the differentiating element that distinguishes the Spanish Antilles from both Spain and North America (*El almuerzo en la hierba*, 85). Although a disciple of Lloréns Torres, Palés saw that his predecessor's exaltation of the *jíbaro* had devalued this element: "Lloréns, nonetheless, limits himself to painting the country *jíbaro* of pure Spanish descent adapted to the tropics, and makes abstract the other racial nucleus which has nobly mixed with us, and due to its fecund, strong, and lively nature, has imbued our psychology with unmistakable characteristics, giving it its precisely Antillean character. I'm referring to the black. An Antillean poetry that excludes this powerful element seems to me impossible" (Díaz Quiñones, *El almuerzo en la hierba*, 94). Faced with the intransigence and immobility of intellectual and racial discourses in Puerto Rico, Palés exploits movement in its most concentrated and collective forms of music, rhythm, dance, and spiritual practice.

Tuntún de pasa y grifería is divided into three sections: trunk, branch, and flower. It begins with the African trunk; continues with the branch, represented by the mulatto; and, finally, culminates in the flower, fruition of Antillean identity. The absence of roots in Palés' arboreal structure recalls Édouard Glissant's discussion of the rhizome in *Poetics of Relation* as "an enmeshed root system, a network spreading either in the ground or in the air, with no predatory rootstock taking over permanently." Thus, some sense of rootedness can be maintained, but one which "challenges that of a totalitarian root." Glissant calls for a development of "rhizomatic thought . . . in which each and every identity is extended through a relationship with the Other" (11). For Palés, this "totalitarian root" is Puerto Rico's *hispanidad*, celebrated to the exclusion of its equally fundamental *africanidad* or *negritud*.

While some critics have argued that the poems in *Tuntún* represent the author's momentary excursion into "black poetry," and that his later poems depart from black thematics (a reading frequently applied to Guillén's oeuvre as well), López Baralt upholds the unity of his work in the face of a false dichotomy of "black poetry versus white poetry" (*Túntun de pasa y grifería*, 529). We should understand the author of these poems not as the spokesperson of the black sector of Puerto Rican society, but, rather, as the one who announces blackness as a key element in the West Indian identity, distinct from dominant European and North American cultures, suggests Mayra Santos Febres (cited in Palés Matos, *Túntun de pasa y grifería*, 15). Ríos Ávila assumes a somewhat different position toward the mulatto figure, wondering to what point whiteness continues to be the master term in the Antillean *mestizaje* of poets such as Palés (*La raza cómica*, 152).

The first edition of *Tuntún* appeared only three years after the publication of Antonio Pedreira's foundational essay *Insularismo* (Insularism) (1934). Reflective of a larger project of "Latinization" in the face of North American cultural and economic imperialism—a fundamental project in the earlier texts of Vasconcelos as well—*Insularismo* declares the inferiority of blacks and suggests that the fusion of races in Puerto Rico is the cause of its cultural and political con-fusion (*con-fusión*). Pedreira blames the failure of Puerto Rican progress on two things: the North American intervention in 1898, and the racial incapacity of the island to constitute a coherent "whole" of the two hemispheres of the national collective personality (Ríos Ávila, "La raza cómica," 563). "The mulatto, who combines within himself [the two races] and usually isn't one thing or the other, is a kind of unstable and murky foundation which maintains two anthropological tendencies in agitation without being able to mark his place socially," Pedreira writes (*Obras completas*, 35). Read within the context of Pedreira's declaration of racial fracture and incoherence, Palés charts a counterspace of racial encounter, refashioning racial ambiguity as plenitude and creative infusion. While "there is probably no richer and more productive binary opposition or a more dramatic tension than that which is established between *Insularismo* and *Tun Tun de pasa y grifería* in all of Puerto Rican literature" (*La raza cómica*, 121), Ríos Ávila notes that the two authors nonetheless shared certain ideas: supporting political independence from the United States, and attacking the "North Americanization" of the island (*La raza cómica*, 120).

In their circulation in official venues and in the popular traffic of songs, dances, refrains, and public recitals of the day, Palés Matos' poems challenged prevailing etiquettes of "high" culture on both racial and formal grounds. Performance was important to Palés both for its implicit privileging of orality and the popular voice, and for its gestural richness. As Ríos Ávila points out, "To recite poetry is to enter into a verbal dance" for

Palés (*La raza cómica*, 165).[25] A culminating moment in this performance is the presentation of "Mulata-antilla" (Mulatta-Antille), which appears in expanded form in the 1950 edition of *Tuntún de pasa y grifería* and in at least one songbook from the period, which frequently published the lyrics of boleros and *guarachas* in vogue. Here, the poet's narrator addresses himself directly to the mulatta, already established as correlative to the Antilles and personified through the repeated use of direct address on the part of the poetic speaker (*Selected Poems*, 82–85):

> En ti, ahora, mulata,
> me acojo al tibio mar de las Antillas . . .
>
> En ti, ahora, mulata,
> cruzo el mar de las islas . . .
>
> En ti, ahora, mulata . . .
> ¡Oh despertar glorioso en las Antillas! . . .
>
> Eres ahora, mulata,
> todo el mar y la tierra de mis islas.
> Sinfonía frutal, cuyas escalas,
> rompen furiosamente en tu catinga.
> He aquí en su traje verde la guanábana
> con sus finas y blandas pantaletas
> de muselina; he aquí el caimito
> con su leche infantil; he aquí la piña
> con su corona de soprano . . . Todos
> los frutos ¡oh mulata! Tú me brindas
> en la clara bahía de tu cuerpo
> por los soles del trópico bruñida . . .
>
> In you, mulatta, I now embrace
> the lukewarm sea of the Antilles . . .
>
> In you, mulatta, I now cross
> the sea of many islands . . .
>
> Now in you, mulatta,. . .
> Oh glorious awakening on the Antilles! . . .
>
> Now you are, mulatta,
> all my island's landmass and surrounding sea.
> Fruit symphony whose scales
> overture furioso in your sweat.

Here in a green dress the soursop
with its fine, soft muslin bloomers;
here, the *caimito* with its
wet nurse milk: here the pineapple
crowned like a soprano . . . Every fruit,
oh mulatta, you offer me,
in that luminous bay your body
burnished by tropic suns.

As Díaz Quiñones perceptively notes, the poem represents a strange mix of the erotic and the patriotic (*El almuerzo en la hierba*, 117). We can see in the first verse of the first three stanzas, "En ti, ahora, mulata," the insistence on the relationship between the mulatta's body, the Caribbean landscape, and a Caribbean aesthetic. The Antilles do not contain her, but, rather, the earth and its phenomena—hurricanes, the night, the buzz in the air—are found within "her curves," her body outlining the boundaries of the Caribbean lyric space. In the second part of the poem, that relationship is even more emphatic: now she is all the sea and the earth, producer of a catalogue of sensations marked by synesthesia, for example, the symphony of fruit, her dress of soursop, the pineapple with its soprano's crown. "Mulata-Antilla" represents the contestation of Lloréns' abject portrayal of the mulatta and exaltation of the "white" *jíbaro*, as well as the culmination of Palés' vision of the relationship between Caribbean culture and a mulatto aesthetic. The poem is perhaps the fullest expression of the poetics of *mulatez* in Latin America. The voice which Palés employs is personal and intimate, markedly different from that of the poetic speaker in Lloréns. The figure of the woman is conflated with the warm sea; here she is a bay which receives the speaker.

It is important to read beyond or through the adoration of the mulatta's body to a conversion of that body into a metaphor for the lyric project (Ríos Ávila, "La raza cómica," 566). Whereas Pedreira develops a poetics of the pathology of the Puerto Rican soul, Palés elaborates a poetics of hybridity of the body, finding in it a semiotics of poetic being. The mulatta in Palés is "the allegory of that same irreducible *mestizaje*" (Ríos Ávila, "La raza cómica," 572), drawing the parallel between corporeal and regional cultural contours so closely that, finally, the most important element in the poem might be the hyphen that separates "Mulata" and "Antilla" in the title. Whereas in Pedreira, the two opposed values of his binary logic create inertia, sickness, and malaise, "as a poet, Palés converts these oppositions in nuclei of resistance, in radiant and productive vortices" (Ríos

Ávila, "La raza cómica," 574). The hyphen questions the binary logic in a textual environment which is unstable, indocile, and unfinished, but which is richly endowed with aromas, tastes, textures, and sounds, all of which invite the poet and reader to a banquet of lyric delicacies, displacing race as the central concept that defines the nation (C. Williams, 87). By upsetting the fixity of racial categories, definitions of the national subject are also rendered susceptible to incessant renovation.

Arcadio Díaz Quiñones reads Palés Matos as an early master of *la brega*, the specifically Puerto Rican form of perpetual negotiation or struggle, a way of managing resistance and difference that produces momentary results, but not final resolutions. He locates a potent example of this strategy in Palés' employment of the phrase "*ten con ten*," "defined as an unstable balance that is never resolved," and a synonym of *la brega*.[26] The *ten con ten* provides for an understanding of subjectivity and, particularly, racial identity that remains enigmatic or unresolved, "an origin that can be affirmed and negated" at the same time (*El arte de bregar*, 35). Díaz Quiñones highlights the lines from "Ten con ten" used in the first epigraph of this chapter, "un sí es que no es de raza" (a yes it is that no it isn't of race), as a founding moment in the elaboration of a Puerto Rican poetics of "la brega," a moment in which this struggle is epitomized in anxieties around issues of race.[27]

The poetry of Palés differs from the work of Guillén in its density and emphasis on pure sensation (what Ortiz called the "super-real"), but shares with it a transnational vision of the Caribbean experience, and of the mulatta as a symbol of suspended Antillean mixture. While in many earlier works by Caribbean poets, "the ideological coherence in these images of the *mulata* manifests itself in a Eurocentric subtext that disparages her African connections" (C. Williams, 79), both Guillén and Palés re-dress the mulatta as an agent of composite beauty and of comic resolution. However, whereas the carnal elements of the mulatta may be reason enough for celebration for Guillén, Palés Matos exploits her figure in additional ways, converting it into the medium over which or through which he travels poetically.

Some, including Ortiz, were reluctant to classify Pales' verses as mulatto or black poetry (Blanco, *Sobre Palés Matos*, 32), and, as noted, Palés himself rejected any rigid ethnic categorization of his work. But he did insist on the Afro-Antillean root of national identity, an acknowledgment essayist José Luis González judged to be unprecedented in previous Puerto Rican literature ("Literatura e identidad nacional en Puerto Rico," 78). *Tuntún*, then, is a text that opens up, rather than "solves," the problematics of "race" in Puerto Rico. "The hybridity of mulatto culture, far from resolving itself in a fusion without any residue of a third race, is staged as a struggle, as an internal tension" (Ríos Ávila, *La raza cómica*, 146). These tensions have not disappeared with Palés' canonization in Puerto Rican and Latin American literature. As is true with Guillén, he remains a point of reference in contemporary cultural production, reappearing in official formats such as elementary school textbooks and in the popular vernacular. San Juan–based musician Rayda Cotto, in fact, sings a repertory based on *bomba*, *plena*, and other popular rhythms that includes musicalizations of "Ten con ten," "Mulata-Antilla," "Preludio en Boricua," "Danza negra," and other Palés poems.[28]

Julia de Burgos, a successor to Palés who spent much of her life in the United States, also contributed to the tradition of *mulatez* with a well-known poem titled, "Ay, ay, ay de la grifa negra," (Ay, Ay, Ay of the Kinky-haired Negress). In her only "negrista" poem, Burgos pays clear homage to Palés, but the last two stanzas suggest a failed attempt to exalt blackness, predicting, instead, its absorption or erasure (*Song of the Simple Truth*, 32–33):

Ay ay ay, que la raza se me fuga
y hacia la raza blanca zumba y vuela
a hundirse en su agua clara;
o tal vez si la blanca se ensombrará en la negra.

Ay ay ay, que mi negra raza huye
y con la blanca corre a ser trigueña;
¡a ser la del futuro,
fraternidad de América!

Ay, Ay, Ay, the race escapes me
and buzzes and flies toward the white race,
to sink in its clear water;
or perhaps the white will be shadowed in the black.

Ay, ay, ay, my black race flees
and with the white runs to become bronzed;
to be one for the future,
fraternity of America!

Burgos' poem is reminiscent of an approach to Puerto Rican blackness in Palés that recognizes its fundamental importance to national identity while expressing the complex mix of fear and aversion, desire and appreciation such a recognition prompted. The end of the poem seems at once ominous and programmatic, and we can't help but be suspicious of the fraternity it finally proposes as a result of the "bronzing" process. Burgos reveals, once again, the failed project of forging a cosmic race from the ethnocultural components of the Caribbean. Her poem suggests, though with much more limited success than Palés', perhaps, the alternative aesthetic of a comic race, which Ríos Ávila describes thus (*La raza cómica*, 157): "A comic world would be precisely that world which resists being governed by the demands of coherence, a world open in the present indicative tense, positioned toward the open and incomplete form of being in the now, not toward a utopian future being."[29] Ultimately, the poetry of Palés Matos reveals the fertile susceptibility of "race" in Puerto Rico to lyric constructions, reconstructions, and deconstructions that concurrently contest and question practices and "truths" that are routinely taken for granted in nonlyric genres.

VI. *Mulatez* IN HISPANIOLA

The significant disparities between engagements with and receptions of *mulatez* in Puerto Rico and Cuba are repeated elsewhere in the Caribbean, proving yet again that each process of *mestizaje* is "locally variable, historically contingent, and exceedingly complex," and thus requires "a focus on particularity—the changing politics and identity matrices of a given time and place" (Smith, "Myths, Intellectuals, and Race/Class/Gender Distinctions," 148). Critic Franklin Franco Pichardo notes that in the Dominican Republic, where independence was achieved through confrontation with Haiti, a nation composed primarily of people of African descent, the intellectual oligarchy appropriated the independence struggle "to inculcate among our people a pseudo-nationalism tainted with profound racist prejudices" (*Sobre racismo y antihaitianismo*, 113). As a result, Dominicans suffer from what Silvio Torres-Saillant has called "deracialized social consciousness" ("The Tribulations of Blackness," 126, 134): "Blacks and mulattos make up nearly 90 percent of the contemporary Dominican population. Yet, no other country in the hemisphere exhibits greater indeterminacy regarding the population's sense of racial identity." A series of historical events are implicated in this condition, including the decay of plantation life in the early nineteenth century and the abolition of slavery in 1822, so that "gradually, the sphere of blackness became associated exclusively with slavery and subversion, fostering a conceptual space that permitted free blacks and mulattos in Santo Domingo to step outside the racial circumscription of their blackness in configuring their identities or aligning themselves politically" (Torres-Saillant, 135).[30]

Vasconcelos' proclamation of "spiritual" *mestizaje* was welcome in a society that had already arrived at a nonbiological understanding of race through the purposed erasure of its own African or Afro-American features, and in which racial hybridity was considered a "corrosive germ" that impeded civilization (Torres-Saillant, 138). An "imaginary foundational *mestizaje* with the Indian" allowed twentieth-century nation builders to deny the African component and create a new catalogue of skin color that substituted terms such as "indio puro" (pure Indian) and "indio claro" (light-skinned Indian) for indicators of Afro-Hispanic descent such as *moreno*, *mulato*, *pardo*, or *grifo*. "Ethnically, the Indians represented a category typified by nonwhiteness as well as nonblackness, which could easily accommodate the racial in-betweennes of the Dominican mulatto. Thus, the [Trujillo] regime gave currency to the term *indio* (Indian) to describe the complexion of people of mixed ancestry," explains Torres-Saillant (139).

The dissolving of mestizo or mulatto identity into the category of *indio* occurred to a certain extent in Cuba and Puerto Rico, as well, where the figures of the *guajiro* and *jíbaro* were also exploited to develop an "indigenous" history.[31] But this racial remapping is more pronounced in their island neighbor, so that "the particular racial situation of the Dominican Republic thus resembles a mirage: there is apparent racial harmony, but with a strong underlying current of 'unofficial' prejudice and racism" (Sagás, *Race and Politics in the Dominican Republic*, 2).[32]

Within this historical framework, it should come as no surprise that mulatto poetics would be enunciated in a very different way from what we have seen so far in the work of Guillén, Palés Matos, and others. A particularly striking example of this difference can be found in Tomás Hernández Franco's long narrative poem entitled "Yélida," classified as "the most elevated exaltation ever given to the mulatto," but which is nonetheless "almost unknown by the majority of Dominicans" (Franco Pichardo, 108) and even less frequently read outside the island. In "Yélida" (Morales, 207–214), a Norwegian sailor named Erick succumbs to the natural and supernatural charms of the island beauty Madame Suquí, who becomes his wife. But she continues to pray to the African orishas for her *hombre blanco*, whom she loves precisely because he is blond, a synecdoche for whiteness. The poem is written from the perspective of the white male, and despite its celebrated foregrounding of the mulatto or of *mulatez*, Hernández Franco's work exposes a horror of black power, especially when that power is exercised by a woman. The poem paints Erick as the victim of Suquiete, whose desire for (his) whiteness, a desire she continues to exercise through the use of prayer and perhaps even poison, is ultimately stronger than his own desire to be rid of her (blackness). Whereas the mulatta in Palés Matos arguably serves to enunciate the development of a trans-Caribbean lyric space, the black-white relationship in "Yélida" suggests an encounter of doomed desire, sickness, shipwreck, even death.

Manuel del Cabral is probably the best-known Dominican *negrista* poet, and his "Trópico suelto" (Free-flowing Tropics) is a title frequently associated with a mulatto poetics, although "Mulata," also included in the collection *Trópico negro*, would be another obvious choice. With its references to the "mula tropical" whose belly sweats rum and who tastes like her island of coconuts, "Trópico suelto" would seem to be a rather (stereo)typical celebration of the mulatta as the synthesis of sensual and desirable elements (Morales, 220–221):

> Mulata que te hicieron de la noche y del día
> en el café con leche
> bebo tu carne de fantasía.
> Tabaco para hacerlo picadura
> con el cuchillo de la dentadura:
> tu talle
> que le roba los ojos a la calle.

> Mulatta made of night and of day,
> in my coffee with milk
> I drink your flesh of fantasy.
> Tobacco to bite off
> with the knife of the teeth:
> your figure
> which robs the eyes of the street.

But as these lines from the first section demonstrate, the mulatta is consumed as the "flesh of fantasy" by the poetic speaker, swallowed in his "café con leche" and cut (off) as the end of his cigar. Despite these images, the poetic speaker claims *he* is the victim, and not she, since it is his gaze (and that of others) that her figure robs in the street. The male gaze in Cabral's poem does not possess but is, rather, possessed. In subsequent lines, Cabral, like Lloréns Torres, equates the mulatta with heat, flame, and *ají*—hot peppers. And like Lloréns Torres' filly, she is a "bestia divina" (divine beast) drunk on rhythm. In at least one version of the poem, the final stanzas of the fourth section are strangely ominous, associating the mulatta with death and the macabre. Like Lloréns Torres' "Copla mulata," "Trópico suelto" ends with a reference to blood, and to the wounding of the mulatta body (Cabral, *Obra poética completa*, 218):

Corta la sangre cuajada
de una rosa, que en su pecho,
revienta como una herida
que le perfuma su cuerpo.

She cuts the curdled blood
of a rose, which in her chest,
bursts like a wound,
which perfumes her body.

In both works, the mulatta's presence heralds both (his) pleasure and (her) pain, and while Cabral's mulatta arguably has a voice in the poem (although it is not clear if she or her body is speaking), the message is a plea which goes unanswered. The association of the mulatta with magic, death, and the macabre is reflective of Cabral's attempts to forge social and historical reality to a new aesthetic vision of imaginative myth. "Del Cabral fuses, then, myth and history, events and fables, occurrences and inventions," notes Candelier ("Historia y mito en *Compadre Mon*," 230). Whereas this tactic is present in nearly all the works studied here, it seems to be especially marked in the work of these Dominican authors associated with *mulatez*, suggesting that the poetic representation of the mulatta mirrors the level of mythification with which race has been addressed in the nation's official discourse.

This presents us with an important paradox: does the fusion of myth and reality in the poetic project negate the lived experience and expression of its human subjects, or does it provide a way for those same subjects to break free from the restraints of social strictures and structures? The Dominican Republic provides us with a scenario in which *mulatez* is effusively celebrated by certain authors while at the same time it is dismissed or rejected within an official discourse that repaints Afro-Dominican *mestizaje* as the blend of Indian and Spaniard.

The varied tactics of negating, recasting, or exaggerating racial (and, implicitly, cultural) mixture once again reveal how poetics of *mulatez* are framed within vastly different histories and practices in the Caribbean.[33] While the impact of these poetics of *mulatez* on Latin American poetry and literature in general is obvious, their relationship to other genres of social and cultural history is less well known. It is likely that Fernando

Ortiz' development of the notion of transculturation, so fundamental to later engagements with literary theory in the continent, was in part the result of reading the so-called mulatto verses penned by Guillén, Palés, and others.

VI. FERNANDO ORTIZ, POETRY CRITIC

Ortiz was a profoundly interdisciplinary scholar who moved with ease between the registers of social, scientific, and literary discourse. Despite university training in law and criminology, his research interests included history, ethnography, music, dance, religion, economics, linguistics, folklore, and literature, and most of his critical writing addresses several of these fields simultaneously. His 1935 essay "Los últimos versos mulatos" (The Latest Mulatto Verses), begins with a summary of the black influence in nineteenth-century popular music and dance, typically denied by historians of the *habanera, tango, danzón, cucuyé,* and other forms (156). Ortiz catalogues several of the most prominent themes of the era, such as the metaphoric reference to the body of the mulatta and the black woman. He also speaks of the rhythmic quality of mulatto poetry, borrowed from popular music and depending heavily on onomatopoeia, neologisms, and *jitanjáforas,* words which, according to Ortiz, come from the language of magic, whose semantic quality is assumed only in their performative invocation.

The following year, Ortiz published another essay on the subject, focusing on the work of Palés Matos as a kind of super-real poetry instead of an "authentic" expression of the popular voice of the sort found in Guillén's poetry. But he made it clear that his position was not based on the ethnicity of the poet (Guillén was, in fact, one of the few poets of color in a large group of *negrista* contemporaries), but on the linguistic and thematic forms of the poem ("Los últimos versos mulatos," 179): "This leads us to consider that in mulatto verses one finds all the linguistic elements which have formed the stratification of *mestizaje:* white and black voices and forms, black words and mulatto spins. We can observe mulatto verses with white language, with mestizo language, and with black language . . . This mulatto language of today is a step forward in the historic process of fusion or linguistic *mestizaje* between Spanish as it has been spoken in Cuba, and the numerous African languages brought by the slaves." As Ortiz' comments demonstrate, the experience of racial difference was being increasingly subsumed within notions of cultural *mestizaje,* so that mulatto poetry is ultimately defined as a kind of bilingual emanation, more so than a biracial or interracial expression.

In January of 1937, soon after he was named the first president of the Society of Afro-Cuban Studies, Ortiz gave a talk in the Club Atenas titled "La religión en la poesía mulata" (Religion in Mulatto Poetry). He began his lecture by stating that more than three decades earlier, he had initiated the study in Spanish America of "social phenomena produced here through the interaction of African races" (*Estudios etnosociológicos*, 141) and that he welcomed the expansion of this personal vocation into a collective endeavor. Urging his listeners to "continue the task of the liberators of old, putting science, art, and culture of the era at their service," he warned that abolitionist efforts had not ended, and that it was up to his younger contemporaries to keep alive the struggle "as long as social subordination under the pretext of color, ancestry, or caste continues, which adds greatly to economic subjugation, which in turn is aggravated by false categories of race and because of delusive preconceptions" (142).

Ortiz' lecture establishes several important precedents in terms of literary and cultural studies as related to racial discourses. First, it claims a history for the systematic study of African and Afro-Hispanic culture in Cuba and elsewhere in the Caribbean that begins with his own work at the beginning of the twentieth century. Second, it ties literary or cultural studies to political efforts both past and present that call for the vindication of that African presence within the Cuban milieu. Third, it demonstrates that Ortiz' deliberations on questions of mulatto expression and *mestizaje*, ideas that would coalesce a few years later in *Cuban Counterpoint*, were (at times, at least) taken up alongside questions of social subordination, economic subjugation, and racial categorization. Remarkably, fifty years after slavery was officially abolished in the island, Ortiz was urging his listeners to faithfully continue the work nineteenth-century abolitionists had begun, and to do so (in part) through a study of poetry.

Finally, Ortiz launches into the subject of "that beautiful flourishing of Cuban genius which is called *black poetry or mulatta poetry*, and the demopsychological elements which we can discover in it, in order to better interpret, with documentary objectivity and clear analysis, the contribution of the races to the Cuban soul" (*Estudios etnosociológicos*, 142; original emphasis). Here, Ortiz equates black and mulatto poetry and suggests that examples of either can be treated as objective proofs of the nature or "soul" of the nation. He begins with a comparison of Cuba's mulatto poetry to "Afro-Anglo" poetry and spirituals from the United States, noting that while black poetry from North America is frequently religious, "in the mulatto lyric of Hispanic America there are no sacred chants, traditionally liturgical and fixed, which are distinct from the profane" (143). Ortiz, who cites W. D. Weatherford's *The Negro from Africa to America* (1924), James Weldon Johnson's *The Book of American Negro Spirituals* (1925), Newbell Niles Puckett's *Folk Beliefs of the Southern Negro* (1926), and the famous collection by John Avery and Alan Lomax, *Negro Folk Songs as Sung by Lead Belly* (1936) as his sources, ponders the differences between the poetic and musical expression of peoples of African descent in areas of English and Spanish colonization.[34] He suggests that whereas black protestant churches provided the space for Afro-European cultural synthesis in the United States, this function is more noticeable in the textual arena of poetry in Cuba (158–159): "Mulatto poetry reflects the religious emotions of the black-white masses in their diverse positions, in the mystery of the jungle, in the temple of *santería*, in the Christian church, and in the meeting place of the philosophers . . . Afro-Cuban poetry, when it is based on religion, is almost always a ritual of conjuration, of the integration of a full liturgy, which is expressed at once in the antiphon, chorus, rhythm, melody, dance, mimesis, and ritual."[35]

While Ortiz was well known for his efforts to promote the study of neo-African cultures in Cuba and elsewhere in the Americas, he is very rarely read as a literary critic or expert on the period or movement known as *mulatez*. And few critics have examined the connections between his reading of mulatto poetry and his engagement with transculturation as a product of colonial confrontation and violence in *Cuban Counterpoint*. Recognizing the link between transculturation and colonial or neocolonial violence is a step toward reading *mulatez* as a complex poetics that both engages and disengages with the "shallows of Creole nationalist fantasies as they have traditionally exploited the hybrid as the image of desire, appeasement and conciliation" (Buscaglia-Salgado, "Impossible Nations," 10).

VII. REPEATING *Mestizajes*

Any elaboration of *mestizaje* vacillates between two interpretations that seem at times mutually exclusive: one which reads it as a blessing, a form of redeeming elements previously considered inferior; and the other, more recent, which reads it as a failure, as the betrayal of the marginalized community seeking vindication. The poetic works of Guillén, Palés, and others, as well as the critical work of Ortiz and Carpentier, leave us with the tremendous paradox that all Latin American *mestizajes* simultaneously incarnate and dissolve: is *mestizaje* a rallying call for the self-expression of those communities which hegemonic powers would prefer to keep silent, or is it another arm which hegemony uses to insist on its own supremacy and the silence of the racial other(s)? Is it correct, within the project of historical retrieval that *mulatez* supposes, to grant whites and blacks equal recognition for their contributions to national or regional identity, given their distinct positions and their uneven exercise of political and economic power? Is the poetics of *mulatez* yet another abstraction of the problematics of *mestizaje*, in which the contribution of people of color is ennobled and improved by contact with the dominant white culture? Kutzinski has argued that the ideology behind mulatto poetry "en-gendered and de-racialized" Cuba, thus reinforcing, rather than dismantling, existing social hierarchies (*Sugar's Secrets*, 10). Antonio Benítez-Rojo expresses a similar argument (26):

> The high regard for *mestizaje*, the *mestizaje* solution, did not originate in Africa or Indoamerica or with any People of the Sea. It involves a positivistic and logocentric argument, an argument that sees in the biological, economic, and cultural whitening of Caribbean society a series of successive steps toward "progress." And as such it refers to conquest, to slavery, neocolonialism, and dependence. Within the realities of a re-reading, *mestizaje* is nothing more than a concentration of differences, a tangle of dynamics obtained by means of a greater density of the Caribbean object.

This "greater density" is, for Benítez-Rojo, negative; what he both signals and recommends in the configuration of Caribbean identity is the model of chaos, so that even if a trope repeats itself, each repetition will be distinct and localized.

Benítez-Rojo's idea of the repeating (but always unique) island and its phenomena can be extended to a "pluritopic hermeneutics" of Caribbean *mestizaje*. In order to confront the inevitable abstraction of social experience implied within literary projects of *mulatez* that emphasize the metaphorical and the symbolic, readers must approach works within specific contexts—even in the Caribbean—which show the susceptibility of *mestizaje* to local designs and their embeddedness in historical enunciations of race and gender. *Mulatez* has a particular and peculiar encoding in each island and coastal territory.

Still, given these distinctions, what are the traits common to those texts and performances we might consider within a productive or contestatory poetics of *mulatez*? As we have seen, such efforts consistently demonstrate a deliberate (though varied) manipulation of language that employs a multichromatic or multirhythmic repertoire in order to achieve a resemantization of the word, a tactic Walter Mignolo has referred to as "languaging." Mignolo locates this process in the historical displacement of official languages in the context of transculturation, which "subsumes the emphasis placed on borders, migrations, plurilanguaging, and multiculturaling and the increasing need to conceptualize transnational and transimperial languages, literacies, and literatures" ("Linguistic Maps, Literary Geographies, and Cultural Landscapes," 182). Daily contact between peoples, genders, communities, islands, and Caribbean ideologies is still very distant from the ideals proposed by and in the poetics of *mulatez*. Nonetheless, it is amply evident that the projects and poets associated with the aesthetic have successfully prompted compatriots, other West Indians, and Latin Americans throughout the continent to question and reconsider established codes of racial categorization and valorization. Mercedes López Baralt writes of Palés Matos that his work contributed "without doubt to the delayed process of consciousness-raising concerning Puerto Rican cultural identity" (Palés Matos, *Túntun de pasa y grifería*, 42). Despite the failures of Caribbean *mulatez*, it taught and continues to teach readers and listeners, first, that Latin American literature is also African American literature, and, then, that poetry offers specific tools for exposing or challenging racial codes contained in other genres.

The light, the smoke, the stench of flesh in a state of ferment, the
continuous provocation of the bare throats, the spasms of the
arms, the dances of the belly with their varied and cynical
abdominal isolations all drive the black population crazy. It is
an infernal tango . . . Underworldly *they have called it,*
and it is really diabolical. It is the most lascivious dance
known in the choreography of the primitive races.

JOSÉ MARÍA RAMOS MEJÍA, *Rosas y su tiempo* [1]

Caress and aggression, this is the tango.

VICENTE ROSSI, *Cosas de negros*

Sometimes, cradled by a black melody from the United States,
from Cuba, or from Brazil, we are tempted to think that
blacks in Argentina might have left us some local musical
form. But our blacks have hardly left even a memory.

JOSÉ LUIS LANUZA, *Morenada*

The thing is that the rhythm, the timing, one feels.
In the way blacks feel the swing beat, the
Argentinians feel this timing naturally.

MIGUEL ÁNGEL ZOTTO

And here I am, with the tango, attempting to decolonize myself.

MARTA SAVIGLIANO, *Tango and the Political Economy of Passion*

I. PLANET TANGO

Perhaps nothing in the contemporary culturescape is at one and the same
time as specific and ubiquitous,[2] as fiercely national and undeniably transnational, as local and as global, as the tango. A vast musical, literary, cine-

matic, and cybernetic library provides us with a dizzying and contradictory genealogy of tango's parentage and origins—in Argentina or
Uruguay, the two sides of the Río de la Plata, in Cuba or Brazil, in France
or in Spain, in Africa. These multiple images of the tango are further re-
fracted in contemporary settings and frames that are global in nature. It
is not unusual to browse tango web sites in which the "welcome" page appears in as many as six languages; one advises that you can dance tango
any night of the week in Helsinki, and a Tokyo-based site explains that an
entire Japanese subculture is built around "tango aesthetics."

Myriad appropriations of "tango" also demonstrate how the term is at
once employed to claim local or national identity, as in the case of former
Argentinian president Carlos Menem's private jet, named *Tango 01*, and,
simultaneously, to reach vastly dispersed media audiences or *technoscapes*
(Appadurai, *Modernity at Large*, 33), as in the case of a widely used software
program named Tango. A review of electronic and print resources provides a plethora of seemingly contradictory images of tango as the quintessential indicator of Argentinian identity and, concurrently, a fluid, in-
cessantly multiplying sign of postnational global consumption. Given this
symbolic and semantic bombardment, is it reasonable or even possible to
work our way back to the roots or "origins" of the tango? And how do
we proceed, when cultural critics assert, on the one hand, that "if anything is known about Buenos Aires, it is this: Buenos Aires is the home
of the tango" (D. Foster, "Tango, Buenos Aires, Borges," 167), while, on
the other, they describe tango as a fuzzy "impressionist daguerreotype of
profound miscegenation" (Ortiz Nuevo and Núñez, *La rabia del placer*, 13)
with antecedents in Spain, Cuba, and elsewhere?

Setting aside, for the moment, the questions of where it was born or
who its progenitors were, we can examine the processes that coalesced to
produce our contemporary notions of tango as a particular historical engagement with the problematics of Latin American *mestizaje*. An analysis of these complex processes—which concurrently have distilled tango
into its image in the twentieth century as an icon of Argentinian culture
and, at the same time, have offered the tango as a roaming, indeterminate
signifier of Creole Latin American culture, infused with and enhanced
by contact with Europe—reveals a peculiar case of localized resistance to
the ideology of *mestizaje* as a site of cultural and ethnic cooperation and
harmony.

To read the Argentinian tango is, in a variety of senses, to peruse a
document in black and white that reveals a movement from black *to* white.
It is a rhythmic and musical document, both in its performance and in its

musical transcriptions, and it is a document in its dance forms, "rewritten" every time it is danced, the basic steps and gestures composing a code that is in turn scriptable on the printed page. As William McNeill has demonstrated (*Keeping Together in Time*), dance is frequently enlisted as the most important aspect of popular culture in the development of national identity and allegiance, because of its inherently participatory nature. While the history of dance in Latin America is densely interwoven with the discourse of *mestizaje*, this relationship has perhaps been less evident in the case of tango.

Evocations of tango in black and white films made in Argentina and elsewhere during the first half of the twentieth century provide us with an additional library of images to catalogue and study in addressing the relationship between tango and its antecedents and the development of national identity. Of course, the luminous figure that presides over this particular chapter known as the "Golden Age" of tango history is the inimitable Carlos Gardel, whose screen presence helped solidify an international image of tango as an indigenous Argentinian form.[3] While these film versions of tango have perhaps been the most influential in proliferating notions of the causal connection between Buenos Aires and the tango, my study is more directly focused on how written commentary reveals a complex engagement with key problems in nation building, including ethnic or racial difference, immigration, and the relationship of emerging Latin American cultural centers to metropolitan European culture.

In all its forms as rhythm, dance, musical notation, lyrics, performance, script, film, and the histories associated with each, tango provides a complex, voluminous "document" of local engagements with "race" and the negotiation of racial difference, especially within the project of consolidating the national persona.[4] The pervasiveness of tango in postmodernity has allowed many aficionados and bystanders to forget or ignore that "the modernist tango emerged as a product of transculturation between African rhythms and the multiethnicity of 'New World' cultures" (Zavala, *Colonialism and Culture*, 158). The tendency to rewrite the tango as white offers an extreme example of efforts throughout Latin America to domesticate *mestizaje* and its cultural yield and to focus selectively on its European or Euro-American features.

In tango's movement from black to white, that is, between its circum-Atlantic prehistory—clearly a product of triangular and multilevel cultural commerce resulting from the trade in enslaved Africans—and its subsequent sanctification as a national symbol forged from European elements, we find a tangled, complex engagement with notions of "multicultural" or multiethnic phenomena that is characterized by negation. As processes of miscegenation and mixture are purified or simply denied, Argentina is established as a site of whitened and enlightened *mestizaje*. José Vasconcelos, in his mid-century revision of his earlier defense of *mestizaje* in *The Cosmic Race*, offers the Argentine Republic as the shining example of "productive" *mestizaje*, made up of a "mixture of similar races, all of them of European origin" (*La raza cósmica* [1966], 5). A tour of the tango library allows us to contest or question his observations on "productive" Argentinian *mestizaje*; it also alerts us to the specificity with which Vasconcelos-style ideas of fortuitous race *mestizaje* were integrated or rejected in each Latin American setting. As we read through the tango, *mestizaje* is revealed as a complex set of both antagonistic and reciprocal cultural responses to contact between juxtaposed "races," groups, identities, expressive practices, and histories, often presided over by naysayers (particularly historians) who "have trembled with just the thought that this racial interaction might be a factor in their region" (Rossi, 107).

II. BASTARD TANGO

Not surprisingly, some early lyrics personify the tango as a son who doesn't know his birthplace, or, conversely, as a character who variously asserts his black, mulatto, or white identity.[5] "Ensalada criolla" (Creole Collage), a street theater skit composed in 1898, features three male protagonists, a black, a blond, and a "pardo," or mulatto, each of whom claims to have the best tango moves (Ordaz, *Inmigración, escena nacional y figuraciones de la tanguería*, 51–52). "Los disfrazados" (The Costumed Ones), a musical theater number performed at Buenos Aires' Apolo Theater in 1906, similarly featured three male protagonists of varying complexion, all of whom claimed to be the best lover or dancer of the group (Gobello, 22–23). In the following composition, the Argentinian tango speaks as a child of obscure(d) backgrounds, as well as an itinerant musical form in a permanent state of diffusion (Manus, "El tango," 14):

> Con permiso, soy el tango.
> Yo soy el tango que llega
> de las calles del recuerdo.
> Dónde nací ni me acuerdo,
> en una calle cualquiera.
> Una luna arrabalera
> y un bandoneón son testigos.

Yo soy el tango argentino
donde guste y cuando quiera.

Excuse me, I'm the tango.
I'm the tango that comes to you
from the streets of memory.
Where I was born I don't remember
on some street somewhere.
A moon on the outskirts of town
and a *bandoneón* are the witnesses
I am the Argentinian tango
wherever and whenever you like.

As David Foster notes, a reading of tango lyrics like those above "creates, conditions, and imposes problematical meanings every bit as vexed as the social or historical circumstances they pretend to elucidate" ("Tango, Buenos Aires, Borges," 169). The pervasive themes in tango lyrics of love betrayed and of love or desire predestined to fail suggest as well the "fatal" nature of encounters in the racial and cultural contact zones of the dance. "Tango lyrics rarely speak of children: it would seem that love goes awry before the reproductive imperative can take place," Foster notes (170), so that what issues from such encounters is only the illegitimate creature of the tango itself.[6]

In *Así nacieron los tangos* (This Is How the Tangos Were Born), Francisco García Jiménez extends this gesture of personification by writing the "biographies" of sixty-three memorable compositions. The first of these is "El entrerriano" (The Man from Entre Ríos), accepted by many historians as the first written tango of known authorship (Andrews, *The Afro-Argentines of Buenos Aires*, 165). It was composed by Rosendo Mendizábal, a black pianist from the turn of the century whose innovative composition reportedly made the keyboard vibrate, raised the dead, and made even paralytics dance (García Jiménez, *Así nacieron los tangos*, 11–12).[7] This lively description suggests that in its earliest form, the tango was more lively, more raucous, and more "black" than white—an image distant indeed from the consecrated versions later popularized in film and television.

Another colorful tango composer who provides us with a clue to its hidden ancestry is José White, a black musician born in Matanzas, Cuba, in 1836, and famous for his song-writing skills and ability to play sixteen instruments. White traveled widely during the mid-nineteenth century, performing for audiences in both Latin America and Europe that included such figures as Napoleon III and Isabel II. He was also at one time director of the Conservatory of Rio de Janeiro, where he taught the children of Pedro II, emperor of Brazil. In 1875, White was banished from Cuba for participating in the independence movement, and he died in Paris in 1918, just as the tango was achieving "truly international" status (Ortiz Nuevo and Núñez, 52). White's biography parallels many elements in the history of the tango: its diasporic nature; its absorption of myriad musical elements; its ever-shifting delineations and national affiliations; and its rapid evolutionary nature.

We also find a significant challenge to essentialist notions of tango's purebred or thoroughbred background in a broad array of etymological sources, despite the insistent association of the form with national culture.[8] The microhistories that appear in American and European dictionaries from the nineteenth and twentieth centuries are surprisingly wide-ranging and ambivalent about the meanings of "tango." In 1836, an entry appears in a dictionary from Matanzas, Cuba, that not only associates the tango with a geographical site nearly antipodal to its current "birthplace" of Argentina, but also documents the presence of tango in institutionalized discourse almost a century before its so-called Golden Age in the 1920s. This Cuban dictionary defines tango as a meeting of black *bozales*—recently arrived enslaved Africans—for the purpose of dancing to the sound of their drums and other instruments (Ortiz Nuevo and Núñez, 14).[9] Few historians have commented on the fact that, as is true in many other early documents, tango is connected here to the vocabulary and terminology of the slave trade. Other definitions of tango which allude to the trade include (1) the name given the intermediaries in the sale of Africans to the Portuguese, (2) the enclosed areas where these persons were held before embarking on the middle passage, and (3) an African word meaning "closed space" or "circle" (Carretero, 55–56).

Even the definitions of tango as a cultural phenomenon, which focus on its inception principally as a dance form, locate its origins in diverse landscapes that range from Africa north to Andalusia and France, west to Brazil and Cuba, and finally south to Argentina. Given these diasporic wanderings, and the importance of African or African American populations in most of them, we have more reason to take seriously the argument made for tango's linguistic kinship to Changó or Shango, the Yoruba deity of thunder and lightning, variously characterized as a womanizer, a troublemaker, a heavy drinker, or a consummate dancer (Romero, Liner notes, Celia Cruz, *Tributo a los orishas*), who reappears in various New World diasporic religions such as *santería* (Cuba and Puerto Rico), the Shango Baptists (Trinidad), and *candomblé* (Brazil).

In fact, the tango's Euro-Argentinian pedigree is disputed by most etymological and word history sources, which invariably build ambiguity or disparity into the definitions and illustrations provided. As late as 1968, *Webster's New World Dictionary* links word derivation to "a Negro dance from Cuba," but defines the term as "a South American dance with long, gliding steps and intricate movements and poses." Even more recently, the 1992 dictionary of the Real Academia Española, a leading authority for word usage in Spanish, lists a party and dance of blacks or country people in certain American countries as the first definition, and an Argentinian dance of an entwined couple in a binary musical format based on a 2/4 rhythm, internationally disseminated, as the second.

Three things are immediately illustrated by this range of definitions spanning more than 150 years. First, the tango was clearly associated early on with African American dance culture. Second, in tango's standardization and institutionalization, both as a dance form and a specific musical rhythm, racial indicators are displaced or replaced by Euro-American national (in this case, Creole Argentinian) characteristics. Finally, in the national and international cultural consciousness, the definition of tango as a black party or dance form stands in stark contradiction to tango as an Argentinian dance or rhythm. And because we read these two definitions as contradictory, we can recognize how an illegitimate, at times even illegal, form is remade into a nation marker by replacing the passage from Africa with the passage through Europe.

Another important consideration in the complex ontology of the tango and its relation to Argentinian and (Latin) American identity (and *mestizaje* as characteristic of that identity) is the development of the particular language of tango: *lunfardo*, an urban, working-class dialect of Spanish specific to Buenos Aires. Although *lunfardo* is a popular vernacular with many of the same linguistic characteristics of African diasporic Creoles and "pidgins" spoken elsewhere, its clearest influence is from the various dialects of Italian spoken by the millions of immigrants who flooded Buenos Aires at the tail end of the nineteenth century. With the development of *lunfardo*, the tango gradually changes from a discourse that was enunciated principally through rhythm and dance to a vocal and linguistic expression, an expression that was marked by the "polyglossia of the immigrant mixture of languages" as well as a propensity for sexual themes (Zavala, 159). The great tango historian José Gobello marked this moment of departure when he declared that "tango and *lunfardo* are definitely not brothers. The tango has black blood and *lunfardo* has European. I'm not taking part, as concerns the tango, in the polemic between Hispanists and blackologists; I'm just simply saying that there are African as well as Spanish elements to the tango, and in fact the Andalusian tango was Afro-Cuban" (Gobello, "Lunfardo"). Gobello's comments demonstrate the liquid, rather than landlocked, nature of tango's early development, as well as its subsequent disassociation from those early Atlantic circumnavigations through its insertion in and absorption by local vernaculars.

III. *Cosas de Negros*

As these various musical, etymological, and biographical histories suggest, behind or perhaps against the contemporary backdrop of the tango as a Euro-American form, we find substantial evidence of its origins in African rhythms and the colonial slave enterprise. Noteworthy studies of these dark origins include Vicente Rossi's *Cosas de negros: Los oríjenes del tango y otros aportes al folklore ríoplatense. Rectificaciones históricas* (Negro Things: The Origins of the Tango and Other Contributions to Folklore of the Río de la Plata Area. Historical Rectifications), first published in 1926,[10] George Reid Andrews' *The Afro-Argentines of Buenos Aires, 1800–1900* (1980), and Oscar Natale's *Buenos Aires, negros y tangos* (1984).[11] The last establishes four "proofs" of the black roots of the tango (9): the African origin of the term; blacks' key role in the cultural development of Buenos Aires; their participation in the beginning stages of the tango; and, finally, the influence this early involvement exercised on the development of the genre.

Both Rossi and Natale note the link between the word "tango" and the word "tambó" or "tambor," African words for "drums" or "noisy gatherings" that were in common usage in the eighteenth and nineteenth centuries in many areas of the African diaspora, including Brazil, Cuba, and the principal ports of South America. Natale cites an official document from 1788 that warns of the dangers of the free assembly of blacks in a "tango" (17). John Chasteen has studied eighteenth-century bans in Argentina on "indecent" black dances which often accompanied prohibitions against gatherings of blacks with Indians, mulattos, or mestizos ("Patriotic Footwork," 14). A more specific reference appears in 1892, according to Chasteen, when mention is made of a "House and Place of Tango," located in the Concepción neighborhood of Buenos Aires. It is at this point, according to Natale, that meetings of blacks came to be commonly known interchangeably as "tambos" and "tangos," and both terms were also used to refer to the groups or clubs of blacks—concentrated in the Montserrat neighborhood of Buenos Aires—that convened to call for the manumission of their members who were still slaves (18).

The authors (a Cuban and a Spaniard) of the 1999 *La rabia del placer* (The Rage of Pleasure, also the title of a famous tango) argue that, despite the current association of tango with Argentina, any Spaniard from the early twentieth century would have considered the dance part of his or her national patrimony, while a half-century earlier, few would have disputed its Cuban origins (153). Not only that, but even into the early twentieth century, many Argentinians actively *disassociated* its practice from invocations of national traditions or identity. In a telling choice of adjectives, one reviewer called it "repugnant and hybrid" and one of the "lamentable symbols of our denationalization" (cited in Salessi, "Medics, Crooks, and Tango Queens," 166).

José Luis Ortiz Nuevo and Faustino Núñez maintain that after its birth in Havana and its arrival in the theaters of Spain, the tango passed on to Argentina by two main routes: first, the *habanera cubana* rhythm arrived in the ports of the Río de la Plata with marine merchants from Cuba, and was then transformed into the *milonga*, generally considered the parent rhythm of the tango.[12] But since *milonga* and *milonguear* (to dance, to sing) came into Argentinian Spanish via Afro-Brazilian influence, this process was very probably affected by other diasporic influences as well, despite Jorge Luis Borges' contention that the Creole *milonga* was different from the black form of the same name that passed from Brazil to and through Montevideo. Andrews maintains that the development of the tango is, in fact, one more step in the transformation of *candombé* into *milonga*. In the city's *academias de baile*, which were really nothing more than glorified dance halls, "the city's poor whites and poor blacks met to drink and gamble, to fight and dance. Out of this cross-racial contact was born the *milonga*, a dance created by the young white toughs in mocking imitation of the *candombe*" (Andrews, 166).[13] An 1883 document supports this idea, noting that the *milonga*, created by white *compadritos* (show-offs) to make fun of the dances of the blacks, used the same rhythm and movements as the *candombé*. "The steps of the tango form a kinetic memory of the candombe," Andrews writes, "a dance that has died but in dying gave birth to the dance that identifies Buenos Aires, a dance exported around the world" (167).[14]

Like tango, *candombe* or *candombé* signified a variety of practices and events that involved dances and rhythms associated with neo-African performance. In the early nineteenth century, slaves and free blacks—who at that moment constituted a quarter of the population of Buenos Aires—danced publicly to drums and marimbas during the festival of Saint Balthasar or in similar rituals that closely resembled African celebrations. As Chasteen points out, these events, which came to be known as *candombés*, drew a wide mix of participants and spectators ("Patriotic Footwork," 14): "*Candombés* occurred on the edge of town or down by the river shore on Sundays, and they became an important part of the system of black nations and societies that flourished in Buenos Aires during the period in question, but one should not imagine that *candombés* exercised no attraction over *castas* and even whites. One extended explanation of their evils made clear that people of all sorts, including even 'decent' women, thronged to see the *candombés*."

Despite a series of official decrees banning such "dirty dancing" for contributing to the mingling of peoples and sexual promiscuity, *candombés* continued to offer a stage for the enactment of intense tensions around issues of race, class, and citizenship. They also provided a forum for choreographic and gestural changes that ultimately gave rise to the tango (Chasteen, "Patriotic Footwork," 17): "Prohibitions notwithstanding, the dance culture of Buenos Aires continued its fertile gestation. The dances themselves changed, as 'closed couple' dances like waltz, polka, mazurca and habanera replaced the minuet and contradance. As the closed couples of the *academias* tended to slip increasingly into close embraces, combining kinetic elements of their local dance culture with incoming international dance fashions like mazurca and habanera, they produced a distinctive new form that, by the 1880s, increasing[ly] received the name 'tango.'"

The tango has also been connected to the *maxixe*, a Brazilian dance form sometimes called "Brazilian tango" or *tanguinho*, which Chasteen has characterized as "yet another miscegenated tendril of the same twirling choreographical vine" ("African American Choreographical Matrix," 39), a series of movements that could be danced to various rhythms, including polkas, Argentinian tangos, and, ultimately, samba. The neighborhoods of Buenos Aires and Montevideo that provided the backdrop for this complex cultural commerce are obvious examples of what Kevin Mumford has called "interzones" in relation to Chicago and New York in the same time period, spaces that were simultaneously marginal and central, located in lower-class neighborhoods whose transient populations were black and white, areas that allowed for intense cultural, sexual, and social interchange (*Interzones*, 30–31).

IV. THE PARISIAN SURPRISE

Another form in which the tango traveled to Argentina was through the Spanish theater. The authors of *La rabia del placer* note that it begins to appear in popular theater productions in Buenos Aires after a sustained run in the lyric theater of Cádiz, a city with a long tradition of international influence. Still, even for these scholars, whose book is subtitled *The Cuban Origin of the Tango and Its Arrival in Spain, 1823–1923*, the tango crystallizes into its "pristine" form in Paris in the early part of the century, after several years of gestation in Buenos Aires. This paradox of tango's distillation into a "pure" form from impure elements is illustrated in a fragment from a 1913 Spanish newspaper, in which the author concludes that "the tango, like the coarse dance that it is, confuses, mixes, and coarsens. In spite of which, in all the best salons you might visit, you will hear daily, 'tanguez vous?' " (Ortiz Nuevo and Núñez, 153).

Thus, in what at least one critic has called the "Parisian surprise," rich Argentinians who wished to display their wealth at the best addresses in France found that the dance they had denigrated in Buenos Aires had installed itself in the most exclusive salons of Paris and, by 1902, was being studied in more than a hundred dance academies in the City of Light (Carretero, 68). From Paris, the tango traveled "home" to Buenos Aires as a Latin American form that could now pass for white and was reabsorbed into local culture by millions of white European immigrants eager to install themselves in the Argentinian middle class. As a result, "almost no one can relate the tango with anything but the bellows of the *bandoneón* marking the rhythm for the complicated figures of a couple in some small club in Buenos Aires" (Ortiz Nuevo and Núñez, 154).[15]

But this image of the Argentinian tango, or *tango porteño*, danced by an Italianesque couple in a smoky bar on a Buenos Aires back street should be considered an overlay on earlier images that were at one and the same time specific to the local demographics of national and regional identity and reflective of similar scenes of Afro-Atlantic or Afro-American cultural expression in cities such as Havana, Rio de Janeiro, New York, New Orleans, and Chicago. In all of these cases, cultural forms developed amid contacts between blacks, whites, mulattos, and other populations in situations that represented complex mixes of appreciation and depreciation, identification and disdain, appropriation and parody, cooperation and competition. The early history (or, for some, the prehistory) of tango indeed depends on contacts between black and white, and its repackaging in the late twentieth century as an exotic, though whitewashed, Euro-American dance and music form is tied to the circumvention of *mestizaje* in the formative process of Argentinian nation building.[16]

V. ORTIZ THE DANCE CRITIC

At the local level, tango's Argentinian pedigree has been disputed for almost a century by Uruguayans, who, on the other side of the Río de la Plata, typically exhibit less discomfort or incredulity in accepting the African roots of the form. Vicente Rossi's attempts to "rescue" the black origins of the tango can be seen, in some regards, as a parallel project to Fernando Ortiz' multifaceted inquiry into the widespread incorporation of African elements into Cuba's cultural milieu, research which produced the well-known *Contrapunteo cubano* (1940) as well as a host of other texts. Music and dance were privileged sites of this interchange for Ortiz, who wrote that all of Europe had been similarly marked by the influence of African American dances, including jazz, machicha (*maxixe*), samba, tango, rumba, conga, and mambo ("La transculturación blanca de los tambores de los negros," 253). The most important quality of this musical transculturation for Ortiz was rhythm, not as abstract forms, but as the motor behind popular dancing ("La transculturación blanca de los tambores de los negros," 254):

> The music of the black dances first passes into the white lower classes, which is where contacts are established and musical transculturation is initiated. Little by little these exotic dances are transformed, with obvious adjustments, into the customs of the country or poor people, who live alongside the blacks in the lower social levels of the cities; the time comes when, now generalized and common in the populace, among the people, these new exciting and mischievous dances rise by way of popular diversion to the level of the church and the theater, to the higher levels of society. At the beginning the most adamant moralists rant against the new dances as works of the devil, but these continue expanding their realm of influence and finally are incorporated into the music and customs accepted by all. African dances that start by being repudiated for their obscenity end up being the stylish dances of the royal European courts.

Such a dance could still be daring or picaresque, but it was no longer "cosa de negros," black silliness, Ortiz notes. For him, then, transculturation offers a symbol of racial collaboration, if not harmony, because rhythm is a common human experience, and "in every human there is a *tambor* that vibrates" (265).

Vicente Rossi's lengthy study never suggests such a degree of equality or conviviality, however. His discussion of the *candombé*[17] and the African "royal" carnival processions, meetings and parades of costumed and masked blacks in Montevideo and, to some degree, Buenos Aires in the second half of the nineteenth century features "humble people condemned to perpetual poverty" who are "convinced of their human inferiority" (50). Despite the paternalistic tenor of the work, Rossi nevertheless fully demonstrates two notable features of the period: first, in the middle and late nineteenth century, black performers came into physical and cultural contact with members of the middle and upper class—on occasion, even with the president himself; and second, the prehistory of tango on both sides of the Río de la Plata was a site of carnivalesque, identity-questioning encounters. It is in these encounters that we see tango take shape(s) as a mirror of national identity. In both cases, forms of personal and collective expression that were the result of complex connections and confrontations between dissimilar peoples, physiognomies, languages, and histories were reduced to a frame of unitary derivation in which this original complexity and interagency was denied.

It is not coincidental that the progressive whitening of tango in Argentina followed the ouster of Juan Manuel de Rosas, whose dictatorship lasted from 1829 to 1852. Rosas enjoyed a wide base of popular support from both rural populations and the urban black population in Buenos Aires, and he was, on occasion, the patron of the same *candombés* that would later be associated with the tango. A notorious spectator at public dance performances in Buenos Aires, Rosas would attend these events accompanied by his daughter, a young woman with a questionable reputation, and flanked by his two *bufos*, black bodyguards who were known to dance or sing on command. Presented in a central square, these events were accessible to hundreds of high-society *porteños* who could watch safely from their balconies (Carretero, 15). The high regard for locally produced dance forms during the Rosas government—including official acknowledgment of recognizably black forms—"produced a sense of cross-class nativist affiliation" important to the development of nationalist sentiment in the first half of the nineteenth century (Chasteen, "Patriotic Footwork," 19).

But all this took place before tango's transformation into a Parisian import, indeed, before what many believe is the inception of modern tango.

When the leaders of the opposition to the Rosas regime took as their banner the hugely influential slogan of "civilization versus barbarism," thereby associating the dictator with primitivism and barbarity and themselves with civilized Europe (Masiello, *Between Civilization & Barbarism*, 21–22), racist ideology in Argentina prospered. Although blond and blue-eyed, Rosas came to be known as "the mulatto Rosas" (Lanuza, 10). When he finally lost his stronghold on Argentina and was succeeded by Justo Urquiza, the majority of the black population remaining in Buenos Aires, particularly the male population that had served in Rosas' army, was reportedly taken to Entre Ríos, sold as slaves, and sent to Brazil (Carretero, 15–16).[18] This expulsion would partially explain the reduction of a black population in Buenos Aires that numbered 7,235 slaves in 1778—almost half as large as the white population of 16,023—to a sum total of 338 persons who claimed African descent in the black neighborhoods of San Telmo and Monserrat a century later, in 1887, after several epidemics and the arrival of successive waves of Italians, Basques, Arabs, and Spanish immigrants (Carretero, 20, 29). The entanglement of early *candombé* and tango performance with the Rosas regime also explains why tango had to be "rescued" from the brothels, from the lowest economic sectors, and from blacks before it could be incorporated into a doctrine of nationalism that erased African or "primitive" influences from the story of its formation. Lanuza writes that "our common history permits blacks only during the era of Rosas" (8).

VI. BLACKFACE AND RACECHANGE

Two important elements stand out in the myriad shape shifts that tango underwent in its metamorphosis from a radically hybrid, Afro-Atlantic diasporic phenomenon to its "pure" form as an emanation of the (white) Argentinian soul, the *comparsas* (or carnival societies), and the *compadritos*. Rossi writes that beginning in the late 1860s, *comparsas*, or groups of amateur actors formed by blacks for carnival processions in Montevideo, began to be integrated by young whites from middle- and upper-class families, often the "*amitos*," or young masters or bosses, of the black participants. These whites used blackface, imitated the dialect and walk of the *bozales*, carried black instruments, and danced the tango (Rossi, 106). Although blackface already had a long history in Spain and Cuba by this time (Ortiz Nuevo and Núñez, 47), the first groups composed entirely of whites in blackface did not appear in the Río de la Plata until the 1870s. A blackface *comparsa* participated in the carnival of 1874 in Montevideo, dressed, Rossi says, like "the slaves of the Brazilian *fazendas* and the Cuban sugar mills" (109). Within a few years, the popularity of this practice was such that "whites so radically substituted blacks that the people no longer accepted reality in these events" and were disgruntled with the "legitimate blacks" who participated (116–117).

Across the river in Buenos Aires, a similar scene could be witnessed, this time through the intervention of the *compadrito*, an up-and-coming young man, often a European immigrant or a gaucho from the country-side, who gradually came to replace the black dancer as the central figure in the bars and *conventillos* of San Telmo and Monserrat. The initial displace-ment of the principal dancer by the *guapo* or *compadre* was transformed in the displacement of the black by the white, so that as whites began to ac-cept and learn the new rhythms, previously danced almost exclusively by blacks, they progressively came to occupy the place of the central dancer.

Tango's transformation from black to white resulted, then, from an en-tire matrix of social changes that included not only massive European im-migration to Argentina and the dramatic reduction of black populations in the Río de la Plata, but also the subsequent displacement or absorption of black dance forms and rhythms by the white population.[19] It is after this process that tango is exported to the United States and other coun-tries, where, "shorn of crudities which caused it to be criticized," as one Canadian dance instruction manual explained, the tango could be danced "at the most fashionable functions in the cities of Canada and the United States, and also in London and other Old World centres."

To achieve this evacuation of the black body from tango, it appears that whites had to pass through blackness in cultural maneuvers reminiscent of the literary gestures noticed by Toni Morrison in *Playing in the Dark*. In 1869, a group of whites formed a carnival *comparsa* in Buenos Aires known as the Society of Blacks; as the practice flourished, the participants in this type of group came to be known as "soot-blacks" or "burnt-cork blacks" (Carretero, 21). By 1930, the black *comparsas*, which first arose in 1839, and were integrated by whites beginning in 1869, had completely disappeared. But it is during this moment, as Carretero points out, that an "apparent anarchy of two musical and choreographic worlds reigned," and "the dif-ferences were little by little decanted and simplified, allowing for a third [world] which was common to blacks and whites, no longer definitive, but transitory" (55).

In these complex negotiations of carnivalesque inversions and racial otherness, blackface stands out as a practice which encouraged identifica-tion between blacks and whites while at the same time emphasizing racial differentiation. As W. T. Lhamon notes in his study of the phenomenon in the North American context, blackface performance provides "a theatre of interpenetration, sponsored by the dominating culture, in which both the fugitive and the dominant culture agree to understand the motley figure is impossible to seat or resolve. Blackface fascination shows a miscegenated culture becoming aware of itself. It makes theatre out of mingling selves trying to understand their inversions" (*Raising Cain*, 131).[20]

Blackface is at once a sign of recognition of the racial other and the absorption of that otherness into dominant forms of ontology so that its influence can be ultimately deemed only a temporary one. Through parody, blackness is made superficial and thus empty; through blackface, the tango is paradoxically whitewashed. One tango historian writes that "today, when there are so few blacks left, *zambas* and *milongas*, *habaneras* and tangos continue to sound, and it is notable that, for the moment, these last two have become the most furiously Creole music known" (Lara and Roncetti de Panti, *El tema del tango en la literatura argentina*, 35).

Tango dancer and academic historian Marta Savigliano suggests that the suppressed black roots of the tango are at the heart of Argentinian psychological repression (32): "Tango is rooted in long-lasting conflicts over race, class, and gender supremacy. These conflicts are locally performed but globally framed through judgments over sexuality, that obscure question leading into — in Freud's words — a dark continent. Not surprisingly, in tango's case this darkness is associated with its black *rioplatense* roots."

As Eric Lott suggests in his excellent work on the complex appropriations of blackface in the United States during roughly the same period examined here, in nineteenth-century tango we find "contradictory racial impulses at work" that create a "mixed erotic economy of celebration and exploitation" and a simultaneous activity of love and theft (*Love and Theft*, 4–6). And, as happened with blackface in North America, tango in the Río de la Plata created a "shape-shifting middle term in racial conflict which began to disappear . . . once its historical functions had been performed" (6).

The absorption into white culture of the black traditions that inform tango appears to have been so complete that, indeed, tango has lost nearly all connotation of ambivalence (Bhabha, *The Location of Culture*, 181) and has been refashioned as the elite global signifier of white Argentinian ontology. The perplexing riddle of the tango's dual image as both a local and a global aesthetic will be solved, finally, not in a return to unitary origins in a national setting, but in the recognition of a complex array of circumnavigations and counterpromenades in diverse geographies and populations that meet in the nongrammatical logic of performance, but that are subsequently reduced to the national denominator by cultural brokers eager to accentuate certain attributes and obscure others. Perhaps tango has come to stand for what it means to be Argentinian precisely because of the success with which this mestizo form has been dispossessed of its diasporic African character and spirit(s).[21]

Chapter 4

SHOWCASING MIXED RACE IN
NORTHEAST BRAZIL

Brazil is a hell for blacks, a purgatory for whites,
and a paradise for mulattos.

POPULAR BRAZILIAN SAYING

White women are for marrying, black women for working,
and mulatto women for fornicating.

POPULAR BRAZILIAN SAYING

But what if cultural mixings and crossovers become routine
in the context of globalising trends? Does that obviate
the hybrid's transgressive power?

PNINA WERBNER, *Debating Cultural Hybridity*[1]

I. BRAZILIAN *Mestiçagem*

Brazil's fame as a showcase of racial mixing is more than a hundred years old. French traveler Gustave Aimard described the country as a "festival of colors" in 1888, writing that only in Brazil had he observed such a "transformation of the people caused by the blending of races." Later, Sílvio Romero declared Brazil a "society of mingled races" and a "country of mixed blood," noting that "we are mestizos if not in our blood at least in our soul" (both in Schwarcz, *The Spectacle of the Races*, 3–5). In the nineteenth century, this mixture was usually lamented by Brazilians and condemned by foreigners, one of the most famous of them Count Arthur of Gobineau, who, after fifteen months in Rio de Janeiro, wrote, "We're dealing with a totally mulatto population, corrupt of flesh, empty of spirit, and frightfully ugly" (Raeders, *O conde Gobineau no Brasil*, 96). Determinist theorists such as Gobineau and Gustave Le Bon argued that people of mixed race "always inherited the most negative characteristics of the blended races"; thus, hybridization was a phenomenon to be avoided (Schwarcz, 60). In Brazil, as in other parts of Latin America, modernist intellectuals retorted by reinventing *mestiçagem* as a source of pride rather than embarrassment, and then subsequently building it into national identitary constructs.

The characterization of the "mulatto population" as one void of redeeming qualities was to, a substantial degree, overturned in the twentieth century, when certain Brazilian men and women of letters began to exalt the country as a privileged space of physical and cultural contact, mixture and amalgamation.[2] By no means the first, but certainly the best-known, defense of Brazil's privileged experience of miscegenation was Gilberto Freyre's lengthy *Casa-grande e senzala* (1933), later published in English as *The Masters and the Slaves*. In a gesture very similar to Mexican intellectual José Vasconcelos' elaboration of the idea of the "cosmic race," Freyre shifted the focus from miscegenation as racial mixture, from hybridity as a pathology, to *mestiçagem* as productive of a rich, multiaccented culture. Freyre spoke of mestizos as being "plastic mediators" who bisected both opposed physical and aesthetic categories. The gradual progression toward a positive popular conception of race mixture "is being made possible, to a large extent, by mestizo types who are becoming, on the aesthetic level, plastic mediators between extremes. And what is happening on the aesthetic level is happening, to some extent, on the political level."[3] Through a retooling of *mestiçagem* as a principally aesthetic or "plastic" category, Brazil's embarrassing level of "mongrelization" was transformed into multivalent creativity. As Richard Parker has noted, "This shift itself, of course, can be understood at least in part as an attempt to escape or displace the anxiety that [Freyre] shared with other members of the (predominately white) Brazilian intellectual elite when faced with the undeniable empirical reality of miscegenation in the population as a whole" (*Bodies, Pleasures, and Passions*, 21). This progression from *mestiçagem* as, first, a physical, then an aesthetic, and then a political discourse is reflective of larger historical trends in Latin and Latino America throughout the twentieth century.

Freyre claimed that he learned to distinguish between race and culture during his studies with U.S. anthropologist and university professor Franz Boas, who taught him to "discriminate between the effects of purely genetic relations and those resulting from social influences, cultural heritage and milieu" (*The Masters and the Slaves*, 3–4). But this distinction between racial mixture and hybrid culture is still often unclear in Freyre's work. Parker argues that "in Freyre's interpretation, cultural interpenetration was both concretely achieved and metaphorically represented by the miscegenation of races. Once again, then, the question of sexual practice, like that of racial difference, is held up and displayed as definitive of Brazilian civilization as a whole" (22).

To arrive at a modernist moment in which racial mixture is celebrated rather than denigrated, Freyre had to work the idea backward to the time of the conquest, making Indian women the New World counterparts of the brown-skinned, dark-eyed Moorish women who were the idealized agent of male enchantment in fifteenth-century Portugal. In the New World tropics, though, these brown objects of desire become more aggressively sexualized as women who, "for some trinket or other or a bit of broken mirror would give themselves, with legs spread far apart, to the 'caraibas' [Europeans], who were so gluttonous for a woman" (Freyre, *The Masters and the Slaves*, 19). In this citation, the indigenous woman as eager sexual partner serves as an implicit allegory of male exploitation of Brazilian fertility, both of the geography and its inhabitants. The reference to the "gluttonous" European explorers also foreshadows the development of anthropophagy as a key modernist aesthetic appropriation.[4] The land and its women are consumed and reproduced as propitiously, if not providentially, miscegenated.[5] Thus, in Freyre, "the stereotype of sexual abandon is one of the most pernicious and pervasive in the literature, since the sexual appeal of the mulatto woman to the white man is held up as one of the 'proofs' of Brazilian racial democracy," notes Abdias do Nascimento (*Brazil, Mixture or Massacre?* 124). Clearly, the allure of the mulatta and *mestiçagem* in general are for Freyre products of the Portuguese colonial expansion.

While exhibiting this figure of the woman with her "legs spread far apart," Freyre does admit that the licentiousness and sexual laxity so often ascribed to the indigenous and African populations were, in fact, the projection or exercise of Portuguese power and domination, particularly in the development of New World slavery. "There is no slavery without sexual depravity. Depravity is the essence of such a regime," he wrote (*The Masters and the Slaves*, 278). Within the ambiguity that is characteristic of Freyre's writing, this intimate "depravity" is offset, however, by an intimacy between master and slave that is nurturing, affectionate, and familial. The figure of this alter-intimacy is once again the nonwhite woman, but this time she is the wet nurse, the mammy who marks "everything that is a sincere expression of our lives," or the mulatta "who initiated us into physical love, and to the creaking of a canvas cot, gave us our first complete sensation of being a man" (*The Masters and the Slaves*, 256).

By drawing slavery as the milieu in which such sexual abuse and consequent racial mixture took place, Freyre implies that the violent and negative elements of such mixture have been left behind in the period of modernity and its consolidation of national identity. And by incorporating black women and mulattas as the welcoming committee for male desires (as indigenous women were earlier), he legitimates (post)colonial processes of racial and cultural fusion. As should be clear by this point, Freyre ultimately "fell back upon categories of thought initially formulated by those whom he attacked" (Graham, 3) and was unable to extract *mestiçagem* from its racist substructure. Thomas Skidmore summarizes his impact in this way (in Graham, 22): "Freyre was thus furnishing, for those Brazilians who might want to take it that way, a rationale for a multiracial society in which the component 'races'—European, African, and Indigenous—could be seen as equally valuable. The practical effect of his analysis was not, however, to promote such a racial egalitarianism. Rather, it served to reinforce the whitening ideal by showing graphically that the (primarily white) elite had gained valuable cultural traits from its intimate contact with the African (and Indigenous, to a lesser extent) component." Nevertheless, the widespread circulation of ideas such as Freyre's, coupled with the eventual discrediting of various forms of scientific racism, fueled the myth of Brazil's moral superiority and lack of racial discrimination (Graham, 27).

As Parker points out, Freyre's text is ultimately directed at a readership that is more like its author (white, intellectual, economically privileged) than the hybrid and multihued national populace it purports to praise, at "us," rather than at "them" (28). In this regard, Freyre joined company with Vasconcelos and his predecessors, who also presented arguments for Latin American *mestiçagem* to an elite, mostly white reading public.

II. WITHIN THE "HEART OF AFRICA"

Freyre's work reflected an effort to subdue Brazil's fecund *mestiçagem* to tolerable levels within the frame of the sociological essay, and thus within the realm of "science," a task he carried out with some of the same successes and failures Vasconcelos had experienced a few years earlier. Like Ortiz' later *Cuban Counterpoint*, though, *The Master and the Slaves* was a comprehensive (if often chaotic) study of national culture as a product of the colonial infrastructure built around sugar production, and not a defense of *mestiçagem*, per se. A more outspoken and internationally recognized champion and celebrant of Brazilian *mestiçagem* was novelist Jorge Amado (1912–2001), who found in fiction a more welcoming terrain for the affirmation of Brazil's history of intense miscegenation. Among dozens of novels set in the northeastern part of the country, where both Freyre and Amado were born, and where racial mixture was most pronounced, Amado's *Tenda dos Milagres* (Tent of Miracles) stands out as a particularly rich apology for *mestiçagem*. First published in 1969, and set in Bahia, Salvador, that same northeastern port city visited by José Vasconcelos before he wrote *The Cosmic Race*, Amado's text, informed by Freyre's ideas, provides us with a test case for Vasconcelos' contention that Brazil was a "promised land" for the fortuitous fusion of the races.[6]

Like Freyre, Amado saw the Northeast as the hub of Brazil's historical development and the scene where the marked presence of African peoples and practices created a culture that was, to some extent, indelibly Afro-Brazilian. He called Bahia "the heart of Africa" and believed the pulse of the immense country could best be taken in the coastal and port cities of the Northeast, especially Salvador. There, colonial history was still visible in everyday modern life, especially in a place like the Pelourinho, the pillory or square of cobblestone streets framed by colonial architecture where enslaved Africans were once displayed, inspected, bought, sold, and publicly whipped. As one publication triumphantly proclaimed, "No Pelourinho da Bahia a gente se sente mais brasileiro!" [In the Pelourinho neighborhood of Bahia we feel more Brazilian].[7]

The particular relationship to Brazilianness claimed by Bahians is, in large part, a function of its historical and ongoing connections to Africa and African diasporic cultural expression. "There, the racial problem assumes different proportions from what it could assume in other parts of the country," explains Antonio Manzatto. He continues (119):

> Salvador is the Brazilian city where the influences of black culture are most perceptible: in the cuisine, in the music, in the dance, in the religion, in the customs, and in the everyday; there the black population constitutes the majority, since Salvador was the capital of colonial Brazil up to the beginning of the nineteenth century, and was also the principal Brazilian port for slaves arriving from Africa. And it was also there, in the School of Medicine, where racist theories concerning the superiority of the white race and the inferiority of the black population were developed.

And despite Bahia's clearly exceptional present and past in terms of both demographics and a unique racial discourse, the author of *Tent of Miracles* held up the region as representative of the entire Brazilian populace (Manzatto, 94), an idea that, while not new, had perhaps never taken on such a positive light.

The cultural centrality of the Northeast, and particularly Bahia, was emphasized by ethnographers as early as 1890, when a young doctor, Raymundo Nina Rodrigues, made a name for himself in the fields of ethnology and legal medicine. The first researcher to attempt a systematic study of African influence in Brazil, Rodrigues catalogued the precise origins of Africans brought as slaves to the country; identified linguistic groups; studied photographs, drawings, and art pieces of African origin; and analyzed data related to assimilation. Rodrigues believed firmly in the inferiority of blacks, and in his development of medical law, recommended that they be judged and punished much like children (Skidmore, *Black into White*, 58–59). For him, Bahia's people were the living proof of racial degeneracy, Salvador the museum of Africa's pernicious effects on the New World nation.[8]

Following, to some extent, in the footsteps of Freyre, Amado argued that the (mixed) racial presence so apparent in the Northeast was actually generative, rather than degenerate. In fact, he held Brazilian *mestiçagem* to be distinct from and superior to similar manifestations in Spanish America. Many of his contemporaries concurred, including the great plastic artist Carybé, himself the offspring of an Argentinian father and a Brazilian mother. He wrote in 1962, just a few years before the publication of *Tent of Miracles*, "Bahia is not a city of contrasts. It's not. Whoever thinks this is mistaken. Everything here intermixes, melts together, disguises itself and turns back up displaying the most diverse aspects, constituting two or more things at the same time, with another meaning, different clothing, even another face . . . Everything is tied together, everything comes from that magic belly with its deep roots, deep roots which nourish themselves on prayers, litanies, divinities . . . Everything is mixed" (*As sete portas da Bahia*, 23). Carybé, Amado, and others were explicitly responding to entrenched theories of whitening, which consoled an obviously racially "impure" population with the notion that black influence, traits, and even blood would eventually be absorbed and erased by successive contacts with white populations, whether resident or immigrant. In the early twentieth century, João Batista de Lacerda, director of the National Museum in Rio de Janeiro, promised the "disappearance" of black blood by the fifth generation of intermarriage—or sooner—and claimed his prediction had been endorsed by figures as diverse as W. E. B. DuBois and Theodore Roosevelt (Skidmore, *Black into White*, 65–68).[9]

Both thematic and structural elements are enlisted in Amado's renovation of Bahia as the epicenter of Brazilian racial mixture. Perhaps the most striking of these is the incorporation of both historical and fictional elements to produce an upbeat, lyrical text with an unclear dividing line between the imagined and the "real."[10] Pedro Archanjo, Amado's protagonist in *Tent of Miracles*, is based on a composite of several historical figures, including the soothsayer Martiniano do Bonfim; the famed ladies' man and *candomblé* leader Miguel Santana; Luiz Luna, founder of the Pernambuco Black Front; literacy advocate Maj. Cosme da Faria; and, most important, the oft-forgotten Manuel Querino (1851–1923). Querino was a black socioethnographer and labor activist whose work focused on the Bahian region and who once declared Brazil's resources to be "the generosity of its soul and the talent of its *mestiços*" (Stam, *Tropical Multiculturalism*, 300).

Querino is clearly the most alluring of these models for Amado, because of his relationship to Brazilian letters and, especially, to the debate concerning black and mulatto contributions to Brazilian culture. According to E. Bradford Burns, he was a teacher, designer, and painter as well as "the first black to write Brazilian history" ("Introduction," 1).[11] "Querino emerged as the first Brazilian—black or white—to detail, analyze, and do justice to the African contributions to Brazil," Burns writes. He presented his conclusions amid a climate of opinion which was at best indifferent, at worst prejudiced and even hostile, Burns notes (5).

Querino's work focused on several aspects of neo-African life in a port city that saw millions of Africans pass through its harbors in the eighteenth and nineteenth centuries. His areas of research included culinary art, religious syncretism, art, music, and dance.[12] "Bahian cooking, like the ethnic formation of Brazil, represents a fusion of the Portuguese, Indian, and African. It's easy to demonstrate" (24), he wrote in *A arte culinária na Bahia* (Culinary Art in Bahia), first published in 1928 and again in 1951 by the Geographic and Historic Institute of Bahia.[13]

Querino also worked diligently in the abolitionist movement, writing a series of articles favoring manumission that were published in local newspapers. He believed that education would bring about the final, definitive emancipation of the black Brazilian. But Querino, unlike Amado's protagonist, sought to "disassociate himself from the lower classes," an attitude Amado excises from the historical figure and replaces with the populist qualities of his other real-life models (Chamberlain, *Jorge Amado*, 77).

III. INSIDE THE TENT OF MIRACLES

Tent of Miracles draws two time lines, one that follows the life of mulatto scholar, folklorist, and *candomblé* leader Pedro Archanjo, born in the latter part of the nineteenth century, and one that recounts the commemoration of the one hundred-year anniversary of Archanjo's birth in the late 1960s. Amado's novel confronts—and, some might argue, corroborates—deeply internalized notions of positivism, which held that knowledge based on and derived from natural phenomena and their spatiotemporal properties was superior to assumptions derived from theology and metaphysics. The positivists' contention that social and political phenomena could be grouped under and understood by scientific laws and that humanity was ever-evolving is reflected in the words that adorn the Brazilian flag, "Ordem e Progresso"—Order and Progress.[14]

In this provocative overlapping of various levels of the historical and the fictional, Querino is resurrected and displayed in *Tent of Miracles* as a "true child of Bahia," the "learned author of possibly definitive studies on miscegenation" (*Tent of Miracles*, 36) whose *Bahia Cookery—Its Origins and Precepts*, was for one critic the "perfect example of a true anthropophagic essay" (*Tent of Miracles*, 26). Amado's novel gave historical figures such as Querino a central place in the Brazilian literary landscape, but it was also heralded for its innovative incorporation of popular or common characters and speech patterns. "The command that the author revealed of a Brazilian way of speaking that was—and is—right in front of him (and which no one seemed to perceive), created a new Brazilian literature," wrote Antônio Olinto in an enthusiastic review the year *Tent of Miracles* was published (" 'Tenda dos Milagres' ").

As Amado's mulatto, Brazilian Everyman Archanjo's powers of mediation are constantly in evidence, not just between the races, but between numerous other juxtaposed extremes exploited by the story line. With his "powerful tool," which "broke in virgins," "seduced married women," and was "God's gift to whores," he "mediates" the division of women into young and old, good and bad (*Tent of Miracles*, 44).[15] He is intimate with the *orixas*, the Afro-Brazilian deities associated with various Catholic saints, as well as with the heroes of classical antiquity; he reads Greek mythology, the Old Testament, and *Don Quixote*, and his knowledge of poetry, much of which he has memorized, ranges from works by Antonio de Castro Alves, Brazil's best-known abolitionist poet, to certain French masters. In his coffin, he is wrapped in the red cloak of the Catholic Brotherhood and encircled by the seated *mães de santos*, mother spirit guides, of Bahia's *candomblé* community.

But *Tent of Miracles* is more than the story of Pedro Archanjo and his many escapades, which range from the sexual to run-ins with the police and other racist institutions of power in Northeast Brazil. The context in which the novel was published in 1969 must also be taken into account. Archanjo's (Querino's) travails decades earlier serve as an allegory of the abuses being meted out to Bahians and Brazilians elsewhere in the sixties and seventies, a period of particularly severe political repression. Amado thus uses the "history" of his protagonist to point to contemporary ills in a country in the choke hold of a repressive regime installed with a military coup in 1964.[16]

These abuses were all the more apparent in a period when international protest against racist and imperialist systems had reached a zenith: while Amado writes, civil rights leaders challenge racial practices in the United States, citizens of several African countries enjoy the first moments of de-colonization, and Europeans react to the tumultuous effects of the May 1968 uprising in France. Amado's dramatization of Querino's life sheds light on two eras in Brazil in which the established powers rule by force and marginalize large segments of the population.

The theme which eclipses—or perhaps conflates—these two chrono-logical settings, however, is "the confession of love which the author holds for the mestizo people of Bahia and for *candomblé*," claims Antonio Man-zatto, author of a "theological reflection on the anthropology of Amado's novels" (106). "For Amado, the best way of combating racism is race mix-ture; and this happened and still happens in Bahia in such a way that 'a pure white in Bahia is like sugar from the sugar mill: impure through-out'" (Manzatto, 165). Antônio Olinto agrees that the "message" of *Tent of Miracles* is that "we need to defend the mixed culture we have created and which makes us distinct from the majority of countries of our day. And it's within, through, and by this mixture that we will reach our potential as a people and as a nation. And it's within, through, and by this mixture that we become equipped to provide a new contribution to the civilizing forces of mankind, to the humanization of man" (207).

Olinto's review of Amado's novel shows how thoroughly many Brazil-ians had accepted the idea that their unusual level of amalgamation was an advantage, rather than a disadvantage. In some sense, at least, Amado was reaffirming a tradition that included writers such as Mário de Andrade and Oswald de Andrade, who had articulated a "mestiço paradigm, which ex-tolled cultural and racial hybridity as the foundation for a unified national identity," beginning in the late 1920s (Dunn, *Brutality Garden*, 6). Like Fernando Ortiz and Alejo Carpentier in Cuba, Mário de Andrade found important clues to the riddle of national identity in his country's music, music that for him reflected a unified, albeit mixed, race (Dunn, 23).

But the waging of Amado's campaign through the insistence on the mixed-race, mulatto identity of Bahia raises several questions concerning the broader implications of celebratory notions of hybridity. What are the consequences of declaring, explicitly or fictionally, that "in Brazil, the races don't coexist, they've melted together. And it's a happy mixture" (Marras, *América Latina, marca registrada*, 170)? As sociologist Nikos Papastergiadis notes, "Despite its historical association, which bears the dubious traces of colonial and white supremacist ideologies, most of the contemporary discussions on hybridity are preoccupied by its potential for inclusivity. The dark past of hybridity rarely disturbs the more cheerful populist claims" ("Tracing Hybridity in Theory," 258). Gayatri Spivak has commented that the emphasis on hybridity in literary and academic discourse has often tended to obfuscate persistent divisions of class and gender. Her suggestion that a postcolonial model of hybridity, such as Homi Bhabha's, is so "macrological that it cannot account for the micrological texture of power" ("Can the Subaltern Speak?" 74) is relevant to a discussion of Amado's model.

In *Tent of Miracles*, Amado would like to matriculate his readers in an alternative university, which he names the "Popular University of the Pelourinho." It is here where "the whole world teaches and learns" (*Tent of Miracles*, 3) and its rectory is the same Tent of Miracles of the novel's title. The Tent of Miracles is a combination artist's studio, fly-by-night publishing house, and neighborhood hole in the wall whose proprietor, Lídio Corró, commemorates in paint the "miracles" his clients have enjoyed after praying to a variety of Afro-Brazilian saints. Corró spends hours discussing life and love with his friend Pedro Archanjo and presiding over a variety of folk and print mediums (9): "There's Master Lídio Corró painting miracles, casting magic shadows, cutting rough engravings in wood; there's Pedro Archanjo, who might be called the chancellor of the university himself. Bent over the old worn-out type and temperamental printing press in the ancient, poorly furnished shop, the two men are setting type for a book about life in Bahia."

The Tent of Miracles, as well as the nearby School of Medicine, are located in the epicenter of colonial Brazil, where slavery's legacy is still apparent. It is in this setting that Amado showcases the dynamic cultural production of the city's oldest working-class section, a production unmatched and unparalleled in the sanctified echelons of literary refinement. Pedro Archanjo is the hybrid mediator between the two worlds, an avid reader and researcher whose procured knowledge is always auxiliary to what he knows intuitively and experientially. Amado pokes fun at traditional scholarship and apoplectic white scholars by fashioning characters who are caricatures of Bahian sociologists and lawyers famous and infamous for their early-twentieth-century versions of racial profiling.[17] Pedro Archanjo is the thorn in the side of this community of scholars, a savvy messenger not only who intercepts their privileged discourse, but also who ultimately challenges, through example and good research, their contention that "mulatto and criminal are synonymous" (152).

IV. MULATTOS AND MULATTAS

The characterization of the mulatto male as contaminated and criminal stands alongside a long tradition in Brazil of portraying the mulatta as the perfect blend. Amado writes, "It's enough to see a mulatta walk along the beach or down the street to understand the mysteries of *mestiçagem*, cultural syncretism, and a certain national specificity" (Marras, 168). Thus, Amado's mulatto must have his counterpart, and while many of the female characters in *Tent of Miracles* are, in fact, mulattas, the leading role goes to Ana Mercedes, the physical and metaphysical epitome of mixed-race knowledge.[18] With her "very, very sexy" gait "worthy of a flag-bearer in a carnival parade" (*Tent of Miracles*, 18), Amado makes her the object of every man's desire and every woman's envy.

When Ana is introduced to James D. Levenson, the Columbia University professor who has "rediscovered" Archanjo and traveled to Brazil to laud his memory before a crowd of eager Brazilians who had previously ignored the genius in their midst, the North American is equally mesmerized (*Tent of Miracles*, 18): "He had never seen such a dancing walk, such a flexible body, or a face so full of innocence and knowingness, white black mulatta. Ana is mixture personified, a "poetess-reporter" (19) who moves in and out of various pages of text like a "true mestiza from one of Archanjo's books" (73), the "living proof of everything he had written" (74). The narrator provides this footnote to the first encounter between Ana and Levenson (21):

> Archanjo had written in one of his books: "The beauty of the women, the simple women of the lower classes, is an attribute of our mestizo city, of love between the races, of a bright unprejudiced morning." He looked again at the flowering navel, the navel of the world, and said in his hard, correct North American university Spanish:
> "Do you know what I would compare to Pedro Archanjo's work? This young lady standing beside me. She is exactly like a page from Mr. Archanjo, '*igualita*.'"

Thus, in the university of the Pelourinho, and in the expositional space of Bahia, Amado introduces his international readership to two seminal mulatto figures, both endowed with great sexual power and both examples of what he calls the "gift of miscegenation" (*Tent of Miracles*, 131), although, in the case of Ana Mercedes, her function is clearly not to bear children, but to fulfill male fantasies, especially white male fantasies. Both characters personify, to some extent, what Carl Degler has characterized as the "mulatto escape hatch," figures that allow for a mitigated negotiation of racially charged spaces (*Neither Black nor White*, 225).

Despite his lavish display of this "gift" of miscegenation, Amado recognizes the persistent tendency to divide the Brazilian character in two, rather than to unite it. At one point, Pedro Archanjo has a conversation with Prof. Fraga Neto in which the scientist asks him how he manages to reconcile his scientific knowledge with his practice of *candomblé*, how he integrates the rational materialism of his studies with his duties as a spiritual leader. "There seem to be two men inside you: the one who writes those books and the one who dances in the *terreiro*," he points out. Archanjo reacts to the suggestion that he is "two different people, the white man and the black," by saying, "You're mistaken, Professor, if that's what you think. There is only one, a mixture of the two. Just one mulatto" (*Tent of Miracles*, 312–313). He continues (313–315):

> "But Master Pedro, how can you possibly reconcile such enormous differences, be no and yes at one and the same time?"
>
> "Because I'm a mestizo, part black and part white, and so I'm white and black at the same time . . .
>
> "Everything in Bahia is a mixture, Professor. The churchyard of Jesus Christ, the Terreiro of Oxalá, Terreiro de Jesus. I'm a mixture of men and races; I'm a mulatto, a Brazilian. Tomorrow things will be the way you say and hope they will, I'm sure of that; humanity is marching forward. When that day comes, everything will be a part of the total mixture, and what today is a mystery that poor folk have to fight for —meetings of Negroes and mestizos, forbidden music, illegal dances, *candomblé*, samba, and *capoeira*—why all that will be the treasured joy of the Brazilian people. Our music and ballet, our color, our laughter. Do you understand?"

Within a contemporary discussion of Latin American hybridity and *mestiçagem*, Archanjo's words seem prophetic, for Brazil's international fame is, in large part, the product of such manifestations in dance, music, and religious practice. But to emphasize the once-radical nature of such ideas, Amado's novel also cites a brochure published in the 1930s by Nilo Argolo, professor of forensic medicine, which maintained Aryan superiority and named miscegenation Brazil's greatest peril, "a sword hanging over Brazil, a monstrous assault, the creation of a subrace out of the heat of the tropics, a degenerate, incompetent, indolent subrace, predisposed to crime" (*Tent of Miracles*, 316). According to the novel, Argolo also recommended laws that would impose racial segregation and halt the "debased and debasing miscegenation" (317).

Pedro Archanjo's response is to write a book titled *Notes on Miscegenation among the Families of Bahia*, detailing the black ancestry of prominent Brazilian "whites." He includes the history of Bombôxe, who, it turns out, is both his own great-grandfather and the Aryanist professor Nilo Argolo's. In his research for the book, Archanjo discovered that "a pure-blooded white was a thing that did not exist in Bahia. All its white blood had been enriched with that of Indians or Negroes, and usually both. The mixture which began with the shipwrecked Caramurú had never stopped its swift and irresistible flow; it was the very foundation of Brazil" (*Tent of Miracles*, 321). Pedro Archanjo dedicates his book to the racist professor, addressing Nilo Argolo as a relative and cousin throughout the 180 pages. The impact of this action is so radical in the context of the (fictionally re-created) early century, so outrageous, that "the world came to an end" (323). Archanjo is jailed, the Tent of Miracles is destroyed, and the copies of his book are seized by police officers, each of whom takes "a copy home with him, just to have a look at the famous list of Bahia mulattodom" (336).

This scene of Salvador's police officers secretly consulting Archanjo's book, checking, no doubt, for black skeletons in their own family closets as well as in those of their white superiors, provides an appropriate image of the mix of aversion, negation, and fascination which ultimately characterizes official and unofficial encounters with *mestiçagem* in Northeast Brazil. And while the historical record may be purged or destroyed, as occurs with Archanjo's well-researched tome, the living record will remain, both in the people who walk the streets and in the incessant revitalization of cultural activity.

Even as an impoverished and forgotten old man, Pedro Archanjo still manages to make trouble for the right reasons. As a poorly paid proofreader for a morning newspaper, he deliberately alters a reference to Hitler as the "light of the world" to Hitler as the "blight of the world" (*Tent of Miracles*, 349).[19] He is blacklisted and moves on to a job as a transcript copier in the office of a notary public, where business halts as soon as Pedro Archanjo begins to spin tales.

The last chapter of *Tent of Miracles* is titled "The Glory of Bahia," and it is clearly Archanjo who embodies that glory. In the gathering held at the Geographic Institute to honor the millennium that has passed since Archanjo's birth, a series of speakers laud various elements of Brazilian and Bahian life, but spend little time praising the archangel himself. But in the 1969 carnival procession, the Sons of Tororó take to the streets with a theme of "Pedro Archanjo in Four Movements," defending the dead man's memory in song and dance. The other characters of Amado's romance show up on carnival floats as well, and Pedro Archanjo is himself represented by a variety of characters as "old, middle-aged, young, adolescent; vagabond, dancer, fine talker, hard drinker, rebel, radical, striker, street fighter, guitar and *cavaquinho* player, wooer, tender lover, studhorse, writer, sage, sorcerer," every one of them mulatto, indigent, and a native of Bahia (*Tent of Miracles*, 373–374).

When the novel was produced as a film in 1977, famed director Nelson Pereira dos Santos retained Amado's strategy of interweaving alternating time frames and documentary and fictional elements. Amado's highly praised dialogue was enhanced with music by tropicalists Jards Macalé, who also played the young Archanjo, and Gilberto Gil, who in the 1970s had embraced black consciousness after moving to Salvador, but who admitted, "I am the son of a mulatto family in every sense. My parents are mulattos of color, leaning toward whiteness in terms of consciousness and culture" (Dunn, 47). According to Robert Stam, the film version of *Tent of Miracles* "both supports and exposes the myth of 'racial democracy,'" but, more important, "the film suggests that the ideologically explicit and politically violent racism of the past has merely transmuted itself into the subtler mass-mediated racism of today" (*Tropical Multiculturalism*, 305). Elements of that racism would seem to be reified in the film's plot, which "comes perilously close to the official ideology, by which blacks rise socially when they marry mulattos, and mulattos gain status when they infiltrate white families, precisely the formula that continually relegates blacks to the bottom of the hierarchy" (Stam, *Tropical Multiculturalism*, 306). The film version of the novel also participates in the glorification of the mulatta Ana Mercedes, an objectification that "reproduces a tendency within Jorge Amado's work to 'physically exalt mulattas without ever granting them respectability or marriageability'" (Stam, *Tropical Multiculturalism*, 306). While Amado's ebullient, infectious prose had been successfully translated to the silver screen, so also had his celebration of racial mixture, with its myriad paradoxes and contradictions taking on a new visual resonance.

V. BODIES ON DISPLAY

While Amado's principal targets in *Tent of Miracles* are the racist under-pinnings or tendencies in positivism,[20] determinism, and degenerative hy-bridity, another implicit protest is levied against the public institutions which propagated and displayed such ideas. A notable consequence of the popularity of positivism in nineteenth- and early-twentieth-century Latin America, particularly in Brazil, was the growth of ethnographic mu-seums, schools of law and medicine, and institutes of history and geog-raphy, all of which were enlisted in the development of a racial discourse sanctioned by scientific or empirical inquiry.

Through the enactments and narrations of national origin that such institutes and museums produced, "Brazil's intellectual elite not only consumed accounts using racial theories; they made them their own" (Schwarcz, 15). As a result, Brazil's social scientists of the late nineteenth and early twentieth centuries moved "between the acceptance of foreign theories that condemned racial blending, and their adaptation to a na-tion that was already highly interbred" (Schwarcz, 16). Racial theories that seem antiquated and embarrassing from a contemporary perspective not only were widely accepted as a way to address questions of national iden-tity, but also were showcased in buildings and forums constructed and maintained by the intellectual and racial elite. *Tent of Miracles* both ex-poses this history and participates in a conceptualization of racial con-tact that emphasizes uniform hybridity at the expense of the specificity of personal and collective experience enacted within complex discourses of racial difference.[21]

Several local institutions which responded to the mandates of posi-tivism and social Darwinism figure prominently in *Tent of Miracles*. As Schwarcz notes, the growth of these museums and institutes is tied to a logic of new, self-documenting civilization (72). Before the mid-nineteenth century, all scientific research in Brazil was conducted by non-Brazilians, so the opening of such research venues in Bahia, Rio de Janeiro, São Paulo, and elsewhere was deeply significant within the project of as-serting national cultural and intellectual autonomy. "As part of a debate taking place in Brazil's own backyard but extending beyond its borders, the museums helped to disseminate racial theories within Brazil that ques-tioned or puzzled over the future of a 'young mestizo nation' (Lacerda, 1911)" (Schwarcz, 105).

As we soon discover, the city of Salvador even functions in *Tent of Mira-cles* as a kind of museum, or at the very least, as a display case of racial history and practices over which Amado's narrators preside as curators. Bahia was not only the logical choice, but perhaps the only viable option for a story that tries at once to expose Brazilian racism and to advance the case for Brazilian hybridity as the most fully realized form of postcolonial *mestizaje* anywhere on the planet. Amado asserted that the process of race mixture in Brazil produced superior results to those found in Spanish America (Marras, 168): "So [the Portuguese] mixed much more than the Spaniard, and gave rise to a really outstanding mixture which has provided us with an experience in Brazil which is unique, comparable, perhaps, in the best case, with Cuba, which, of all countries of the Americas, is the closest to us; although I believe the antiracist conscience is much deeper in Brazil than in Cuba."

Paradoxically, this exemplary fusion and mixture depends on Bahia's exemplary black population. It was in Bahia, specifically, in its famous School of Medicine, where race and, particularly, racial mixing were linked "scientifically" to criminality, insanity, and degeneracy. Syphilis was offered in an 1894 article as evidence of mestizo degeneracy, and other authors believed race was the causative factor in other maladies; the central tenet of most of their "findings" was that "races are fundamentally different, and their mixing is reprehensible" (Schwarcz, 236, 258). Doctors and lawyers who voiced their opinions in such venues as the *Medical Gazette of Bahia* intimated that "the extreme hybridization found here . . . retards or encumbers the unification of the types, first by upsetting essential traits, and then by reviving among the people atavistic characteristics of individuals deep in the darkness of the ages" (Schwarcz, 256).

Amado's work can, in many ways, be read as a reaction to such ideas, in which the writer exploits the dialogic nature of the novel to counteract a reading of the populace as fragmented or disjointed. His showcasing of racial amalgamation in Bahia and the country at large has drawn much international acclaim, but also significant internal protest. One of his most impassioned critics has been playwright and essayist Abdias do Nascimento, whose *Brazil, Mixture or Massacre?* argues that the myth of racial democracy, perpetuated in part by literary efforts such as Amado's, curbs the growth of African consciousness and the community's political efforts on its own behalf (ix–x). Similarly, Nascimento believes that programs of acculturation, assimilation, miscegenation, and syncretism of black peoples and their cultures into the dominant white population and culture "inherently involve their partial or complete destruction" (88).

Other critics view such models of syncretism as perhaps less pernicious, but no less erroneous. A 1979 report by the Minority Rights Group, which used as its epigraph, "In Brazil, there is no racism: the Negro knows his place," concluded that

> the view of Brazil as the one country in the world where people of dif-
> ferent races live together in harmony and where opportunities are open
> to all irrespective of racial background is definitely a misleading, if not
> a completely inaccurate description of the Brazilian racial situation . . .
> It is necessary to question the validity of another widely-held opinion
> about the Brazilian racial situation, which is, that the successful inter-
> mingling of the races has gone on for so long that it is now impossible to
> say with any degree of certainty who is black and who is white in Brazil.
> (Dzidzienyo, *The Position of Blacks in Brazilian Society*, 5)

Similarly, the author of the report found that the "ostrich-like posture" of this etiquette of race relations "dictates strongly against any discussion, especially in a controversial manner, of the racial situation, and thus it effectively helps to perpetuate the pattern of relationships which has been in existence since the days of slavery" (Dzidzienyo, 5).

Clearly, much discussion has ensued since that report was released, and certain cultural practices increasingly emphasize identification with spe-cific racial groups. For example, the rise of *blocos* such as Ile Ayé and Olo-dum, brotherhoods organized around carnival and musical performances, documents a new focus on the specificity of black cultural heritage in the Northeast and elsewhere. Some of these groups have even limited their membership to blacks, a policy that has drawn substantial criticism in the national and international press. These membership restrictions become most apparent during carnival, when it is assumed that Brazilians of all "races," classes, and backgrounds set aside differences to intermingle and celebrate together.

Contrary to the traditional rhetoric of carnival as an equalizing space of performance and a metonym of the larger matrix of Brazilian cultural practice, the Bahian carnival often emphasizes or dramatizes ethnic alle-giance, thus providing an internal site of popular resistance to the official dogma of racial fraternity. In these practices which run contrary to the traditional rhetoric of carnival as an equalizing space, Bahian carnival can be read as a site of confrontation or "discussion" of the official insistence on racial integration and harmony, and as a counterdisplay to the harmo-nizing narratives presented in museums, histories, and even fiction. This came into stark focus when the Salvadoran *bloco* Olodum adopted "A Nova Tenda dos Milagres" (The New Tent of Miracles) as its theme for the 2002 carnival celebrations. "The idea is to trace the discussion which occurred in the 1930s regarding the struggle against racial prejudice between Pedro Archanjo and Rosa de Oxalá [another character in Amado's novel] and the Faculty of Medicine installed in the Pelourinho, in order to reflect on the role and importance of the black as an element present in the colonization of Bahia and Brazil, where discrimination and intolerance have been the basis of its own development," a spokesman explained on the *bloco*'s Web site.[22] In their retaking of the Pelourinho and the Tent of Miracles, Olodum planned to focus on the cultural significance of such elements as *capoeira angola*, the Brazilian black movement, samba, and their own rehearsals and performances as elements in the "great battle for survival" of the *blocos*.

As Olodum's publicity suggests, the growth of *capoeira angola* is another manifestation of markedly black cultural practices which implicitly question a globalizing national hybridity. Adherents of the martial arts/dance form hold that *capoeira* is an African form brought to Brazil by slaves, rather than a phenomenon born of contact between New World peoples. Other examples also support the portrayal of Bahia as a "Black Rome." Salvador is now a key destination for African American tourists from the United States and advertised as a site where any member of the African diaspora can "connect" and find a part of his or her roots. This emphasis on specific ethnicity implicitly questions the doctrine of national *mestiçagem*. As one observer points out,

> in the case of Salvador, the slow but growing flourishing of black culture in its diverse dimensions—music, dance, carnival associations, religious groups, folk art, etc.—can be understood as a symbolic reinvestment in terms of the image and rescue of ethnicity. Such a statement, when taken alongside the growth in cultural activities promoted by the tourism industry, makes it possible to understand the rapid transformation of the Largo do Pelourinho and the adjacent area as a permanent stage or performance space for cultural practices and competition. (Romano Magnavita, "Quando a história vira espectáculo," 123)

Amado maintained, however, that Brazil was "pure mixture," and that, since no pure black existed in Brazil, "we have the paradox that these black radicals are racists, because in reality they're mestizos; maybe what's at the bottom of this is that the most cherished fantasy of these mulatto Brazilians is to be rich North American blacks" (Marras, 169). After attending the annual dinner of the Academy of Black Arts and Letters in New York in 1971, Amado wrote that "there are antiracist North Americans, millions fighting against discrimination based on race or blood, but the Yankee philosophy of life is racist and present in every moment. Exactly the opposite of Brazil, where there are, without doubt, hundreds of thousands, perhaps millions, of racists, but where the philosophy of life is antiracist, and the Brazilian people are the negation of racism. I say the Brazilian populace, not including the so-called elites" (*Navegação de cabotagem*, 500). In this opinion, Amado clearly follows in the footsteps of Freyre, who was quoted in a 1971 interview with the *Estado de São Paulo* as declaring that negritude (shared consciousness among peoples of African descent) was "a mysticism which has no place in Brazil. Freyre maintained throughout his work that Brazil was a land of mixed-race peoples who lived together on equal terms in a hybrid culture (Dzidzienyo, 14).

The debate highlighted in Amado's work and in current cultural practices in Bahia demonstrates the thorough institutionalization of the ideology of racial amalgamation in Brazil. *Tent of Miracles* marks the high point of Amado's effusive praise of miscegenation, but should be placed in a historical context of similar agendas. The deployment of a racial discourse through a discussion of sexual practice that we see in Freyre is enormously and felicitously expanded in Amado's work, but the invocation of miscegenation as productive of the best elements of national character is virtually identical. In commenting on Dos Santos' production of *Tent of Miracles*, Stam notes that "the film's apparently uncritical advocacy of miscegenation as a solution to Brazil's racial problems echoes a tendency not only within Gilberto Freyre's work but also within Jorge Amado's: the notion that structural political problems can be solved in bed (or in the hammock as the case may be). 'There is only one solution for the racial problem,' Jorge Amado has written, 'the mixture of blood. No other solution exists, only this one which is born from love'" (*Tropical Multiculturalism*, 305).

As Stam points out, this faith in miscegenation as the solution to the country's woes and enmities is itself a product of colonialist ideology, so that the same narrative that would seek to criticize and challenge colonial values, to some extent, at least, reiterates them in a more contemporary setting, and *mestiçagem* proves to be once again complicit with the homogenizing aims of the colonial project.

VI. FOUNDATIONAL MEMORY

The fascination with commemoration and display of key figures in the Bahian debates around race and race mixture takes on another dimension at the Fundação Casa de Jorge Amado, situated in the center of Bahia on the Largo do Pelourinho. The foundation is a combination café, bookstore, library, research center, and, most important, museum of Amado's life, work, and accomplishments. It stands on some of Bahia's hottest tourist property, next to the Museum of the City and down the street from the Afro-Brazilian Institute. Brown- and black-skinned kids roam the plaza in front of it trying to peddle cheap multicolored bracelets that bear the names of Catholic saints, and cars rumble down the cobblestone streets that lead to other parts of the Pelourinho, restored in the late 1990s, thanks to a major UNESCO grant, in a project that also displaced many of the neighborhood's poorest residents.

Tourists enter the building to escape the heat on the street or the vendors in the surrounding shops. They take a few minutes to pore over the dozens and dozens of photographs of Amado that adorn the walls of the exterior display area, or to have an espresso in the interior café, brightly decorated with posters announcing the publication of Amado's novels in an impressive array of world languages. The bookstore/gift shop sells editions of Amado's novels, copies of critical studies of his work, and posters that reproduce photos or other icons, such as the line drawing of Exu, the mischievous and restless Afro-Brazilian messenger deity, Amado's favorite *orixa*. The Casa de Jorge Amado pays permanent homage to the author, ensuring him the ongoing international renown and national affection that his predecessor, Manuel Querino, never enjoyed.

This commemoration and celebration of Amado and his work presents a marked contrast, finally, to the still relative obscurity of Querino, the black historian Amado sought to resurrect in the figure of Pedro Archanjo. In fictionalizing Querino, Amado earned him a much firmer place in history, but his incorporation into the nation's body of fiction modified Querino's biography as it increased Amado's fame. The modifications he underwent as a subject of Amado's pen are perhaps as enlightening as his appearance as Pedro Archanjo within the story line of *Tent of Miracles*. We notice that for Amado, the masterpiece of Archanjo's work is his treatise on miscegenation among the families of Bahia, whereas Manuel Querino's most important text is arguably *A raça africana e o seus costumes na Bahia* (African Race and Customs in Bahia), first published in 1916. In that volume, Querino focused on the distinct ethnic, linguistic, and geographic groups implicated in the slave trade to Brazil, including almost thirty "tribes," with photographic plates of ten of them. Querino detailed the harsh treatment slaves received in the *fazendas*, or plantations, the absolute dependence on African labor for Brazil's economic growth, and the fact that the "dark race hasn't only modified the national character, but has also influenced national institutions, literature, commerce, and science" (43).

Querino also studied the coexistence and interpenetration of *candomblé* and Catholicism, including in his study musical notations, portraits of famous *candomblé* leaders, and photos of sanctuaries and musical instruments common in religious ceremonies in Bahia. The last chapter of *A raça africana e os seus costumes* is dedicated to "Dark-skinned Men in History" and highlights such figures as Dr. Caetano Lopes de Moura, private doctor to Napoleon Bonaparte and a prolific writer, as well as many other doctors, professors, soldiers, politicians, and priests. This last chapter would seem to confirm beyond significant doubt that Querino's focus—unlike Pedro Archanjo's—was the contribution to Bahian culture and history of populations variously defined as African or "dark-skinned," that is, the glorification and vindication of the black rather than the mulatto.

One other element that is missing in Querino's reincarnation as Pedro Archanjo is the fact that he was one of the founders and charter members of the Instituto Geográfico e Histórico da Bahia, a status that, paradoxically, permitted his research on African contributions to Brazilian and especially Bahian society in an intellectual environment that was elite, Europeanized, and, for the most part, white. In reviewing the life of a man virtually unknown, and for whom no biography has been published, the translator of Querino's essay "The African Contribution to Brazilian Civilization" recalls these words of the great African American historian John Hope Franklin: "The world of the Negro scholar is indescribably lonely; and he must, somehow, pursue truth down that lonely path while, at the same time, making certain that his conclusions are sanctioned by universal standards developed and maintained by those who frequently do not even recognize him" (Burns, 10).

Thus, the biggest difference between Manuel Querino and his novelistic reincarnation as Pedro Archanjo may be found in the degree of faith each expresses in the power of *mestiçagem* to create harmony, to correct history, to bridge the gaps. For Querino, hybridity is the end result of the work of hands and minds of many different colors; for Archanjo (or Amado), it is the defining logic of that cultural work. Ella Shohat has noted that "the most generative, hybrid act might be to reclaim and remember and invent specific cultural histories, rather than simply celebrate a hybrid, inchoate identity shorn of all but a nationalist rendering of its history" (Joseph and Fink, *Performing Hybridity*, 250). Natalya Fink warns us that "hybridity may produce a recolonizing multiculturalism that homogenizes the complexity of cultural identities and erases the (already violently erased) historical specificity of narratives of origin," a narrative that in Brazil includes a long-standing appropriation of racial amalgamation that shifts from a focus on its miscontents to its contents and, finally, to its seemingly benign role as the catchall container into which all of Brazil has been deposited.

Indeed, visitors to the Casa de Jorge Amado cannot help but admire and revere the work of Brazil's most widely known and globally translated author, so that the space serves ultimately as a kind of shrine to Amado, Bahia, and Brazilian *mestiçagem*. But the building has also served as a backdrop for decades of police brutality and repression and a showcase for lingering racial conflict. In his 1993 song "Haiti," tropicalist musician Caetano Veloso sings of the space in front of the Casa de Jorge Amado as a place that draws "the eyes of the whole world" to a scene which has been rhapsodically portrayed as a paradise of racial and cultural blend, and where African expression in the New World has triumphed—a situation "opposite" to what one might find in Haiti, usually characterized as impoverished, politically turbulent, and violent. In a brilliant riff on the racial makeup of the crowd gathered in the space in front of the building, Veloso speaks of mulattos and "almost-whites" who are treated like blacks by soldiers who are almost all black themselves, in a space where, formerly, blacks were sold as slaves. Veloso's lyrics show how skin color is a quality always subject to economic status, that class and race remain causes for repression, and that the usual conditions of daily experience do not represent the ideals of Brazil's famed racial democracy:

Se você for a festa do pelô, e se você não for
Pense no Haiti, reze pelo Haiti
O Haiti é aqui
O Haiti não é aqui.

If you go to the party in Pelô, and even if you don't go
think of Haiti, pray for Haiti
Haiti is here, Haiti is not here.[23]

The Casa de Jorge Amado, the Pelourinho, Bahia, Brazil, and Brazilian cultural expression are ultimately sites for both utopian and grim evocations of a pluriracial condition, a condition that Amado celebrated, but about which Veloso and others continue to ask provocative questions.[24]

What will be the fate of Brazil's particular claim to racial mixture and harmony? What has changed since *Tent of Miracles* was written in 1969, or since 1985, when Renato Ortiz published his study on Brazilian culture and national identity? In that essay, Ortiz wrote, "If the myth of *mestiçagem* is ambiguous, it's because concrete difficulties exist which prohibit its full realization. Brazilian society is passing through a period of transition, which means that racialized theories, when applied to Brazil, allow intellectuals to interpret the current reality, but not change it. In anthropological jargon, I would say that the myth of the three races has yet to be realized in daily ritual, because the material conditions of its existence are still entirely symbolic. It is language and not celebration (*Cultura brasileira e identidade nacional*, 38–39). Ortiz also points out that the role of a nationalized doctrine of *mestiçagem* ultimately frustrates, and sometimes silences, the voices of black activists (43–44):

> The propagation of the myth of the three races in society permits individuals from different social classes and different communities of color to interpret, within the proposed frame, the racial relationships which they themselves experience. This poses an interesting problem for black movements. To the degree in which the society appropriates expressions of color and incorporates them into the univocal national discourse, they lose their specificity. Many have insisted on the difficulties of defining the black element of Brazil . . . The construction of a national mestizo identity makes it even more difficult to differentiate the boundaries of color . . . The myth of the three races is in this sense exemplary; it not only covers up racial conflicts, but it also makes it possible for all to recognize themselves as national subjects.

What Amado leaves out of his narrative is the fact that Rodrigues, the intellectual from the School of Medicine who developed a widely disseminated pseudoscientific theory about the inferiority of blacks, was himself a mulatto. Perhaps the real story of the experience and history of racial amalgamation in Bahia, then, is caught in the roily waters that circulate between Rodrigues' condemned view of African ancestry, Manuel Querino's vindication of its place in Bahian culture, and Amado's creation of his most complex and delightful character.[25]

*We are all one in America, and we are, nonetheless,
all of us so distant.*

BENJAMÍN CARRIÓN, *Obras*[1]

I. VASCONCELOS ALONG THE EQUATOR

In 1928, Ecuadorian culture czar Benjamín Carrión (1897–1979) wrote a long essay titled *Los creadores de la nueva América* (The Creators of the New America), in which he proclaimed, "My Ecuador, province of America, will feel powerfully the tonic value of the words of José Vasconcelos, the announcer, the prophet, the poet of the warm territories" (49). Carrión was right: Vasconcelos' ideas had a significant impact in Ecuador, where the discourse of *mestizaje* has enjoyed a long tradition that still can be witnessed in numerous aspects of contemporary cultural and political life. Here and elsewhere in the Andes, indigenous populations may constitute as much as 40 percent of the population. As a result, the rhetoric of *mestizaje* frequently interfaces or clashes with the concerns of *indigenismo*, both as a literary vanguard that seeks the incorporation and valorization of the Indian in national and regional expression, beginning in the 1920s, and as a political posture that recognizes continuing struggles among indigenous communities for political, economic, and cultural autonomy.[2]

While writers, politicians, artists, and other public voices routinely speak of the country's multiethnic and multifaceted cultural character, the attention paid to mestizo populations and to *mestizaje* is read in two very distinct ways. On the one hand, sociopolitical and cultural activities that promote a rhetoric of *mestizaje* are often viewed as efforts in a continuing commitment to the incorporation of indigenous voices and cultural terrain that was first urged by the *indigenista* advocates of the early twentieth century. The same activities are often simultaneously condemned, however, as a negation of indigenous cultural autonomy. The result, more often than not, is a *desencuentro*, or dis/encounter, that is, a disagreement, volatile or unpleasant exchange, frostiness between two parties due to a quarrel or misunderstanding, or simply, a mix-up.[3] A *desencuentro* is, ultimately, a rupture or breach in communication, and in twentieth-century Ecuador, *mestizaje* can be read as a dis/encounter between national agendas and individual and group experiences, between theory and practice.

Two foundational "texts" of *mestizaje* painted against the backdrop of Quito, Ecuador's largest city and a former colonial governmental seat, provide an idea of how such tensions are played out. The first is the novel *El chulla Romero y Flores* (The *chulla* Romero y Flores, 1958), by Jorge Icaza,[4] the second, the architectural and plastic project conceived by the late painter Oswaldo Guayasamín (1919–1999), titled *La capilla del hombre* (The Chapel of Man), inaugurated in 2002.[5] The connection between literary and visual discourses is not accidental. Carrión, who founded the Casa de la Cultura Ecuatoriana (House of Ecuadorian Culture) in Quito in the 1940s, possessed a broadly interdisciplinary vision of national culture that integrated history, folklore, literature, music, and art, "with a particular emphasis on indigenous contributions to the creation of a collective identity" (Balderston, González, and López, *Encyclopedia of Contemporary Latin American and Caribbean Cultures*, 286). Carrión urges Ecuadorians to follow the example of Vasconcelos, who actively supported plastic production in Mexico, particularly the country's famous mural tradition. Under Vasconcelos' watchful eye as minister of education, the Mexican government purchased 150 new paintings a month, contributing to the success and renown of such artists as Diego Rivera, José David Alfaro Siqueiros, and José Clemente Orozco, with whom Guayasamín studied. The huge frescoes in the "Hall of Free Discussions" which Vasconcelos commissioned and to which Orozco dedicated six years' effort were for Carrión the fullest example of governmental homage to freedom of thought. If Mexican muralism was, at least to some degree, the product of Vasconcelos' aesthetic philosophy—a philosophy which early on rested firmly on a celebration of *mestizaje*—it would follow that Ecuadorian visual art, under the tutelage of Carrión, would exhibit a similar foregrounding of a national character that combined and synthesized the country's diverse ethnic or racial characteristics.

Despite the affinity that Carrión found between Vasconcelos' "cosmic race" and his own country's plural constituency, aesthetic engagements with *mestizaje* in Ecuador have never been simple or straightforward. Here, as elsewhere in the Andes, such negotiations stand in complex relationships with everyday experience in which "mestizo" is frequently a label for an Indian who adopts urban, European-modeled values and standards, as a euphemism for metropolitan assimilation. In the 1930s, for example, in a lecture delivered at the University of Guayaquil, medical doctor Rodrigo Chávez González advised his audience that, along with the author of *The Cosmic Race* and Carrión, he himself had addressed *mestizaje* as "the fundamental basis of the present American problem." Like his Andean neighbors, especially those in Peru and Bolivia, the doctor faced a visible indigenous presence that refuted the notion of pervasive absorption or harmonious integration of elements. *Mestizaje* therefore becomes a treatment for this condition, a "cure" which implies minimizing the specifically indigenous presence. "If we help *mestizaje* efficiently with a program of immediate action, in which nutrition, hygiene, and better ways of life among the working class play a central role, the process of hybridization will provide its abundant fruits in the New World," Chávez González admonished (*El mestizaje y su influencia social en América*, 107). He condoned the "new crossings" implied by conquest and looked forward to the progressive evolution of indigenous peoples through further contacts with institutionalized culture that would no doubt distance such communities from their traditional quotidian practices (109). He recalled Vasconcelos' words declaring the future triumph of *mestizaje* as "the only hope of the world"—something to be facilitated rather than feared (122): "Our American soil is still virgin for a new humanity, for a 'new biology.'"

Chávez González' comments demonstrate how twentieth-century appropriations of *mestizaje* could so easily adopt and adapt the language of colonization, conceiving the land as "virgin" and the mestizo as its new inhabitant, once the territory was rid of its indigenous inhabitants. In this way, the contentious encounters between representatives of the Spanish and the Inca empires in the sixteenth century and the ensuing failures of political intercourse in both the colonial and the national periods could be dismissed.

In his 1995 *Los mestizos ecuatorianos*, Manuel Espinosa Apolo urges the rejection of "erroneous" notions of *mestizaje* and mestizos promulgated in the last half of the twentieth century by national ideological organs, particularly the school system. Such ideas, he insists, are remnants of official colonial practices and show little modification in the ensuing five hundred years. Espinosa argues that the conceptualization of *mestizaje* as racial mixture, produced by interethnic relationships, assumes the uninterrupted presence of an indigenous population and subsumes the facts of genocide and reduction of those same indigenous groups. The dominant versions of Ecuadorian *mestizaje* overdraw and overvalue the process of Hispanic-indigenous racial mixture as totally harmonious while, on the other hand, underestimating the participation of the African racial contingent in this same process (44). Such descriptions of national or regional character evoke cultural syncretism or imbrication "only to point to the Western cultural characteristics in them" (44). As a result, the "mestizo" becomes a non-Indian, and the Indian, in turn, becomes a foreigner (45).

Other critics also signal the marked disconnect between theory and practice in the Ecuadorian context. In the introduction to *Ecuador racista* (Racist Ecuador), a collection of essays published in 1999, Emma Cervone writes that while a vocabulary of racial terms still permeates everyday discourse and social interaction, discrimination also appears masked by a euphemistic rhetoric (1):

> In many Latin American countries, Ecuador among them, the contemporary problem goes back to the system of phenotypical classifications established in the colony that situated the Indian and the black on the bottommost social rung, though attributing them the status of "pure race." This type of discrimination has also had an impact in the mestizo population, generating a practice of "endoracism" which is expressed in many forms in daily life. In this sense, one could affirm that racism has not disappeared, but that it now appears in diverse forms, many of them masked by distinct "discursivities" and euphemistic social practices.

Cervone's assessment prompts us to ask several pertinent questions. To what degree is the cult of *mestizaje* in Ecuador a "discursivity" that recuperates or recycles colonialist rhetoric that rationalizes and sanitizes repressive public measures directed at specific racial or ethnic communities in the interest of a unified political subject? To what extent can aesthetic engagements replicate and even stimulate such measures, or, on the other hand, what power do they have to unmask and condemn them? Are the possibilities of this contestation specific to genres or media forms; that is, can a novelist achieve more than a painter, or vice versa? Or do all forms of figuration which take up the mestizo ultimately reveal the same dis/encounter?

II. EQUATORIAL TAXONOMIES

While Ecuador's history of race relations—both colonial and postcolonial—is significantly different from Mexico's, both countries claim privileged histories of *mestizaje*, in which the nation is constructed as an exemplary site of fusion and the coalescence of disparate elements. This mythology circulates freely in public as well as in literary and artistic discourse. One example in Ecuador is the campaign material of politicians such as Freddy Ehlers, a pluralist candidate who, like Jesse Jackson in the United States, adopted the rainbow for his campaign colors. In the late 1990s, Ehlers produced a seven-part film series on Ecuadorian *mestizaje* which aired on national television and emphasized his commitment to a political platform that recognized all of the country's ethnic constituencies. In a piece entitled "Nacimiento de la nación" (Birth of the Nation), written in May of 1995, he defined Ecuadorians as the "separate people" of Bolívar and the "cosmic man" of Vasconcelos, the summary and synthesis of America. His position was that no country better suited Martí's description of "Our America" than Ecuador, where *cholos*, mulattos, blacks, Quechua Indians, Amazonians, Chinese, Jews, and Arabs provided an intensely diverse population, even though the country represented a small percentage of American peoples.

Adapting the Apostle Paul's metaphor for the Christian Church of "one body, but many parts" to claim that Ecuador was a single body composed of "many members," Ehlers provided a taxonomy of the Ecuadorian body, its various limbs and functions represented by different racial, ethnic, and religious groups. Its hands were Indian, its feet, African, its dreams, Amazonian, its voice, Caribbean, and its reason, a legacy from the North.[6] Several things quickly come into focus in this portrayal of the national body. The Indian hands are associated with crafts and agriculture, elements that, before the late twentieth century, did not belong to most definitions of "culture." The overtly physical qualities of the African contribution suggest that even in Ehlers' well-intentioned description of the mestizo national character, this African element is relegated to stereotypical activities such as music, sports, dancing, and manual labor. Ehlers finds that the voice of the nation has a Caribbean timbre, although Ecuador—unlike its northern neighbor Colombia—boasts no Caribbean coast. Given this catalogue of physical characteristics, it is perhaps not surprising that the sense of reason comes from the north in Ehlers' taxonomy, so that Ecuador still owes its rationality to European or Euro-American elements, despite the valorization of indigenous constituencies.

This taxonomy, while attempting to unify Ecuador's diverse elements in one functioning and healthy body, nonetheless suggests an image that is monstrous, in which elements are not synthesized, but, instead, grafted or appended to each other. To visualize this body, the hands one color, the legs and feet another, speaking in Caribbean, dreaming in Amazonian, and thinking like a northerner, is to picture Ecuador's dis/encounter with its own *mestizaje*, even in the imagination of someone like Ehlers, who has declared himself a public servant dedicated to contemporary engagements with his country's obvious pluricultural character. His portrait of multipartite Ecuadorian nationality is both evidence of the continuing attractiveness of the cult of *mestizaje* in formulations of national character and a testament to the failures of the employment of the figure of a mestizo body in the attempt to make the national corpus cohere.

Some of these failures are more pronounced than others. The much less noticeable presence of Afro-Ecuadorian agents in this political engagement is perhaps a symptom of the official definition of multiracial or multicultural identity understood to mean, for the most part, Spanish-Indian mixture. As Michael Handelsman has pointed out, even when the fact of Ecuador's pluralist national identity is intoned, "book after book published in the country by the main publishing houses . . . is characterized by its silence regarding the Afro-Ecuadorian, and thus, the coastal component" (*Lo afro y la plurinacionalidad*, 19). In the Caribbean, the minimal presence of the indigenous population has made it necessary to incorporate black sectors into mestizo aesthetics—even when those same (mixed-race) black inhabitants are resignified as *indios*, as happens in the Dominican Republic. But Ecuadorian mobilizations of *mestizaje* have, for the most part, excluded the citizen of African descent. "In concrete references to racial matters, the official rhetoric of Ecuadorian nonracism was enough to distort the Afro-Ecuadorian, maintaining it in a principally exotic plane, distant from the Afro-American diaspora," Handelsman writes. He notes that certain local authors, particularly Adalberto Ortiz in *Juyungo*, have called attention to the illusory nature of *mestizaje* vis-à-vis the black and mulatto populations in Ecuador (133). Of course, it can also be argued that in Ecuador as elsewhere, the Indian frequently disappears as well in the idea that "we are all mestizos." As Cervone has observed, "This notion of mestizo is revitalized every time indigenous claims question the nationality and integrity of the imagined community . . . On the one hand, the mestizo is presented as a symbol of national identity. On the other hand, in social practice the mestizo is scorned in day-to-day interethnic interactions" (Cervone, "Machos, Mestizos and Ecuadorians," 5–6)

Local engagements also differ from appropriations elsewhere in Latin America in terms of the intersection of an ideology of *mestizaje* with an enunciation of gender. Whereas the quintessential figure of mixture in the Caribbean or Brazil is the mulatta, in Ecuador, this figure is resolutely male,[7] and the role of the female is usually relegated to that of the Indian woman who comes into contact with the white landowner as his employee or dependent. Victim of both sexual and economic violence, she becomes, like La Malinche, the condemned (re)producer of mestizo children, the cause of their "evil *acholamiento*" (Icaza, *El chulla Romero y Flores*, 21). Cervone writes that, "with the exception of the *chola cuencana*, in fact, all representations and discourse of and on mestizos [in Ecuador] refer to male figures," and "in the official discourse of mestizaje, in fact, there is no description of either good or bad qualities of mestizo women" ("Machos, Mestizos and Ecuadorians," 9).

Ecuadorian *mestizaje* also reveals a specific, local relationship with issues of class. In fact, race or ethnicity, family lineage, and socioeconomic rank are so thoroughly intertwined in the Ecuadorian contemporary imaginary that Cervone proposes the use of the term "*claste*," which recognizes a social stratification based on economic and physical characteristics that have remained virtually unchanged since the colonial period ("Machos, Mestizos and Ecuadorians," 4). Thus, aesthetic practices are graphically subject to economic considerations, so that "far from being an all-inclusive ideology, the ideology of mestizaje reaffirms and adapts to modernity the same racial ideology that structured Ecuadorian social hierarchy since colonial times" ("Machos, Mestizos and Ecuadorians," 9). Despite the rhetoric which proclaims and admires the singular and exemplary admixture of the national populace, the praxis of *mestizaje* in Ecuador remains contentious and fractious, qualities we find in ample measure in the work of both Icaza and Guayasamín.

III. ICAZA'S *Chulla*, FRAME(D) FOR ECUADORIAN *Mestizaje*

Like Peruvian author José María Arguedas, Jorge Icaza (1906–1978) spent part of his youth on the latifundio, or country estate, of an uncle, where he witnessed the life of the Indians who worked as *peones* in a situation that differed little from colonial times in the Sierra. But most of his childhood was spent in Quito in a series of prestigious Catholic schools located in the colonial heart of the city. Although he began his creative career as an actor, director, and dramatist, he later turned to realistic fiction. His most famous novel, *Huasipungo* (1934), sold out its first printing in six months, but Icaza was never a writer of great popular reception, and one of his biographers warned that, when read before or after eating, his works could cause indigestion, and when read before sleeping, could provoke insomnia! Nevertheless, Icaza is considered a foundational writer in Ecuador and throughout the Andes, in large part because *Huasipungo* has been a staple text in the *indigenista* canon, providing, as it does, a glimpse of the everyday experience in the Indian highland communities within a frame of stark and often morbid realism.

Huasipungo (the term refers to the small subsistence plots Indians were allowed to live on and farm on the large haciendas left over from the colonial period) and Icaza's other early works portray the miserable conditions of many Indians in the postcolonial period, attest to the lack of political conscience and social progress concerning the representation and public role of the indigenous sector, and document the failures of Christian sentiment and charity in correcting the ills left over from colonial hierarchies. One reader complained that the dark and morose character of these early novels made one wonder if Icaza were somehow afraid of producing a tourist-friendly, postcard version of the Ecuadorian landscape.

Other critics heralded Icaza as the first Ecuadorian novelist to break with standard Spanish speech patterns and fully integrate the language of the people; the glossaries included with some editions of *Huasipungo* and other texts document this integration of a local lexicon. Following precursors such as Juan Montalvo and Gonzalo Zaldumbide,[8] "Icaza appears as the essentially national author, concerned with finding the gilded edge of poetry in the everyday language of the people" (Ojeda, *Cuatro obras de Jorge Icaza*, 30).[9] Icaza reportedly told an interviewer, "We have been able to break with a Spanish way of thinking for the good of our own mental and emotional construction. We speak in Hispano-American, we feel in Hispano-American, we out to construct our written thoughts with expressions from our own world" (Ojeda, 30–31).

Icaza's subject matter changed significantly with the publication of *El chulla Romero y Flores* in 1958. Whereas in *Huasipungo* and other well-known works, he had mined the depths of the Indian experience in the highland villages, in *El chulla Romero y Flores*, the drama that unfolds is the "permanent struggle" of identity for the *cholo*, the Indian of mixed descent, a figure marginalized and frequently rejected by both whites and Indians. Hence, although Icaza is still known chiefly as a writer who defends the place of the Indian, the problem that attracts his attention later in life is arguably the place of the mestizo, who is concentrated and condensed in the dilemma of the *chulla*, an opportunistic, up-and-coming version of the *cholo*, who populates the urban centers and frequently works within the state bureaucracy. Because it takes place in the city and shows the interconnections of the experience of *mestizaje* and questions of class and economic disempowerment, Francisco Fernándiz Alborz (*Jorge Icaza*) judges *El chulla Romero y Flores* to be a much more complex text than *Huasipungo*.

This complexity is incarnated in the figure of the *chulla* Luis Alfonso Romero y Flores.

Chulla is a Quechua or Quichua[10] word that means "one of a pair," as in a single shoe or glove. When applied to persons, it calls attention to their solo status, their aloneness. In Ecuadorian usage, the *chulla* is usually male, mestizo, and a member of the lower middle class. Through scheming, social maneuvering, employment in the public sector, or marriage to a woman in a better economic situation, he hopes to improve his social rank. For those in the lower classes, the *chulla* is a dandy, admired for his access to social sectors off limits to the poor; to the upper classes, he is a shyster, a poseur, an interloper. Postcolonial critics might recognize him as a neocolonial functionary who mediates between the working class, dominated by the historically colonized, and the upper class, represented by the descendants of the *hacendados*, or landowners. The *chulla* is, in many respects, the representative of acquiescence and internalization of colonial values and structures. When used to refer to a woman, *chulla* is derogatory, marking low social class or a suspect reputation.[11]

Romero y Flores is the protagonist Icaza molded during twenty-five years as a novelist, the "ambivalent and complicated fruit of two races" (Ojeda, 112) who abhors all the Indian elements of his makeup and tries to deny or repress the signs of his own racial mixture and cultural syncretism. He is "the point of subjective crystallization of all social contradictions. Trapped between two races, two cultures, two structures, and even two historical periods, he configures a space of rupture and uprooting much more so than a privileged space of fusion," notes Agustín Cueva (*Jorge Icaza*, 25). As with the term *chulla*, itself, the protagonist is the embodiment not of synthesis but of fragmentation and of "the chaotic environment of a society in formation" (Ojeda, 112).

While Icaza's other works provide a detailed study of social conditions related to the indigenous presence, this novel documents "an investigation of the psychological problems which besiege the life of the *cholo*, product of racial mixture" (Vetrano, *La problemática psico-social*, 11). The *chulla*'s internal conflicts, dramatized by Icaza in realistic prose characterized by its pungency, sensitivity, and focus on spiritual and psychological misery, seem to serve a metonymic function; Icaza suggests he is a kind of Everyman, characteristic of *quiteño*, *serrano*, and, ultimately, Ecuadorian identity, an identity that is unavoidably, inharmoniously mestizo. In some sense, the *chulla* embodies the residue ideology of *limpieza de sangre*, or blood purity, left over from the Spanish reconquest. As Manuel Corrales Pascual notes, the novel describes "a mestizo and originally agricultural society that considers its *mestizaje*, or, more correctly, the Indian blood in its veins, as an original sin, which it thus tries to occult and eradicate from itself, substituting a dreamed-of nobility" (*Jorge Icaza*, 202).

The *chulla* is the son of Miguel Romero y Flores, a man with a respectable last name and lineage who has lost his fortune and, with it, his social standing, and of Domitila, the Indian *empleada*, or maid, who worked in his father's home. Known in the neighborhood by the ironic nickname Majestad y Pobreza (Majesty and Poverty), the character of the father is reportedly based on a historical figure who lived in Quito in the early twentieth century named Patas y Orejas (Paws and Ears). In Icaza's reworking, Majestad y Pobreza is a fallen, tragic figure from a landholding, high-born background who shuffles through the streets of Quito as the children run away and the adults laugh derisively at him.

Both parents have in fact died by the time the story starts, but they are present in the narrative as spirits or ghosts. Their son is the transmitter for the running dialogue between the two, as they advise him—usually in contradictory fashion—how to act in given situations (1988, 21): "He was dragged along by that irreconcilable and paradoxical dialogue which had accompanied him since he was a child—clearly defined perennial presence of voices and impulses—which plunged him into desperation and the loneliness of the exile of two nonconforming races, from an illegal home, among people who venerated what they hated and hid what they loved." Icaza's mestizo protagonist, dressed in shame and perpetually conflicted, represents an everyday experience of race mixture in mid-twentieth-century Ecuador that is distant, indeed, from Vasconcelos' ideal portrait.

In a tremendous revelation of the way in which *mestizaje* is alternately integrated into myths of national being and rejected at the personal level, those around the *chulla* who claim economic and racial superiority express disgust at his status as the "fruit of illegal love, mixed with Indian blood" while at the same time recognizing that his is a heritage they also share (1988, 20):

—Nonetheless, there is something in him which is in all of us.
—In all of us.
—Which is ours.
—Ours!

As Renaud Richard notes in the introduction to the 1988 edition, the picture of conflictive national identity presented in the novel suggests an opposition between Indian and Spaniard, but should, by extension, also include the mulatto and any other situation in which "one socioeconomic group exercises traditional domination over another or others" (xx). The *chulla* inhabits the point where these oppositions crystallize, an uneasy mediator between unreconciled and irreconcilable worlds. He is the *indio lavado* (whitewashed Indian) or the *medio blanquito* (semiwhite), an object of external and internal scorn. Obsessed with maintaining the appearance of status and social success, the *chulla* must live above his means, a situation highly dramatized by a scene in which, completely broke, he pays his rent with a painting of his family coat of arms. The scene symbolically portrays his ruin as well as his landlady's greed for the trappings of social standing. Both attempts at self-definition are shown to be inauthentic and ultimately futile.

Not only is the public perception of the *chulla* contemptuous, but the *chulla*'s vision of his own "mestizo" culture and community is suspicious, cynical, and untrusting. When humiliated by his supposed superiors, he responds, "Why was I such a coward? Why didn't I think of a lie, a joke? Why the hell did they open my chest to look inside of me? Why did my tongue stick in my throat? Why? Why did my head feel empty? Why did my legs . . . ? Why? the young man asked, reproaching himself with hatred" (1988, 21).

Icaza's vision of the *chulla* is antiromantic, antiheroic, and crudely realistic, and the actions of the novel convene around the protagonist's frustrated efforts at self-definition and self-determination in a society which still refuses to grant him the possibility of either. Romero y Flores finds himself in constant conflict as both the victim and the agent of imbedded racism that has changed little since the colonial period—or in the four decades between Vasconcelos' essay and Icaza's novel.

Much like Ehlers' national subject constructed from disparate elements, Romero y Flores is a tragicomic figure in a state of constant fragmentation or fracture, reminiscent of the stark, cubist angularity characteristic of many of Guayasamín's large canvases. As Robles has noted, most critics of Icaza have passed over "the grotesque character of the individual and collective protagonist of *El chulla Romero y Flores*" and the "elaboration of a caricaturesque world that refers directly to an old grotesque tradition" with antecedents in Valle-Inclán and other writers. For most critics, the features of this tradition—costumes, incongruence, theatricality, instability, contraband, panic, self-deprecation, and imitation—are produced in Icaza's protagonist as a result of his perception of himself as marked by an ethnic stain. While Robles advises readers to consider Romero y Flores' problems within an economic and a racial context, he believes Icaza's character "points out the aloneness of the American mestizo and the prevailing problematic of the search for identity which still has not been solved in the continent" (73–74).

IV. IN THE LABYRINTHS OF THE CITY

Like its inhabitants, Quito is portrayed as a site of *mezcla chola* (impure or bastard mixture), where colonial domes and tiles are obscured by factory smoke and winds from the bleak plains; where the scent of morning mass mixes with the pungency of the *huasipungo*; where one sees the architecture of the hut alongside a bell tower, hears the cry of the muleteer as well as the screech of the train on its tracks, hears the prayers of the women at church amid the curses of the landowner, and travels along muddy mountain paths as well as cement sidewalks. The close quarters of the urban poor in the city's colonial center are suggestive of the labyrinth in which Romero y Flores finds himself. He is frequently looking for a way out of situations which seem to have no obvious escape. Sackett notes that "Quito, the Ecuadorian capital itself, constitutes a kind of diabolic site. It is a Dantesque labyrinth of sorts in which the pretentious *cholo*, with his original sin well hidden, looks for a way out of hell unsuccessfully . . . But the *chulla* realizes that the city is surrounded with mountains that cut off all routes of escape. And even if he were to miraculously find an escape from this infernal labyrinth, all the paths are the same, leading to nowhere" (*El arte en la novelística de Jorge Icaza*, 407). The synecdoche of this chaos is the bureaucratic world of the city, "a labyrinth without an exit, an illogical and inexplicable system" (Sackett, 409) that, in turn, represents the oppressive nature of official codes and doctrines.

What is remarkable about Icaza's portrayal of the *chulla* is the degree to which his protagonist internalizes the prejudices and contradictions of his social milieu. At one point, ashamed of the public disapprobation of his father, he responds with "tears in his throat," a metonymy for a pain so intimate that it must be swallowed symbolically, rather than appear on the surface of the body (Sackett, 402). In his professional life and, later, in his love life, the *chulla* is shown to be a man of poses (and thus a wearer of masks and disguises) who continuously strives to live in a half-light that favors his Spanish side and obscures his Indian background. As Cueva notes, he lives in such social ambiguity that he never really integrates any single social group and is perpetually trapped among false attitudes and behaviors, venerating that which he hates and hiding that which he loves (52). He is, finally, only "a centrifugal force which cannot locate itself in a social system which is characterized by the polar positions of the colonial castes of its origin" (Cueva, 53). The discord and stark inequality that existed between the Spanish father and the Indian mother pervade the *chulla*'s subconscious, and, as a result, he lacks an authentic personality and stable social identity and feels toward the Indian contradictory impulses of violence, hatred, love, and tenderness. The *chulla* Romero y Flores is a brilliant example of Manuel Zapata Olivella's contention that the hybrid Latin American is both "the affirmation and the negation of his progenitors" (*La rebelión de los genes*, 241).

Product of the unsanctioned union between unlike parents, Romero y Flores is doomed to continue the tradition of ill-fated matches. When he seduces Rosario, a young woman from an even less respectable social sector whom he initially considers only a temporary conquest, the scene is drawn this way (1988, 48): "Plaything of that diabolic impulse which stretched his father out next to Mama Domitila, and many gentlemen of the conquest and colony alongside Indian women—without thinking about scandal, sin, or the future—Romero y Flores joined himself once more to his lover. Intensity of possession and surrender that eclipsed the ghosts of the *chulla*." The narrative thus connects colonial and contemporary moments with a reference to the impulse of sexual contact that produces the mestizo. Icaza's portrayal of the scene as "diabolic" is an implicit rejection of the notion of racial *mestizaje* as a site productive of harmony, and an explicit attempt to question and supersede official discourses that ignore the difficulties of everyday life for mestizo persons. He repeatedly represents *mestizaje* as grim, even torturous.

Learning that Rosario is pregnant produces another set of highly conflictive emotional responses for Romero y Flores. At first, he wants to get rid of the baby, calling it a child of adultery, a child without a name. When Rosario protests, he realizes that the scene reenacts his own history. "I also was born thanks to the timid but stubborn Indian presence in the face of the tragicomic pride of Majesty and Poverty," he reflects. He hears his mother's voice telling him that his own father was cruel and uncompassionate, a *taita blanco* (white daddy) who wanted to bury him along with the other orphaned children (1988, 65), a euphemism for abortion or abandonment. Understanding finally the situation of his own birth, Romero y Flores converts his shame into tenderness toward his child. But this tenderness is ultimately impotent. Caught in an illegal scheme to raise money for the new mother and child, he is hunted down by the police, who stake out his one-room home and prevent him from witnessing the birth of the baby or Rosario's death during childbirth.

In the final scene, Romero y Flores recognizes the cowardice of his arrogance, supported only by blood ties to his father, "a man of adventure, of conquest, of the *encomienda*, of nobility, of pride, of the cross, of the sword." He also acknowledges the generosity and nobility of his neighbors, whose value he has typically measured according to their lack of material wealth, rather than by their wealth of character. He must admit that any hope he maintains for himself and his son is intimately tied to this community. For Corrales Pascual, the novel constitutes a charge to no longer talk of *mestizaje* as a defect or blemish, or of *indigenismo* as Indian nonsense ("Introduction," 28). That is, it reveals a history of depreciation of the mestizo to prompt a reevaluation and reaffirmation of a condition that is inevitable and characteristic. Icaza's *chulla* frames the *cholo ecuatoriano* as the representative protagonist of the Latin American condition.

IV. OTHER PICTURES IN THE EXHIBITION

The correlation between the work of Icaza and that of Oswaldo Guayasamín has received little attention, even within Ecuador, although the latter was commissioned to illustrate a cover for a 1988 critical edition of *El chulla Romero y Flores* (Robles, 71). The entry pertaining to Guayasamín in the *Encyclopedia of Contemporary Latin American and Caribbean Cultures* (Balderston, González, and López), however, makes this connection explicit (688): "The most prominent feature of his work, however, is the depiction of a world of anxiety, constrained suffering, wrath about to explode, and human beings subjected to extreme pain and sorrow. Guayasamín's expressionistic brush moves quickly on the canvas, capturing the essential. Visually he recalls Jorge Icaza's prose with its abrupt and almost angry juxtaposition of quick images; he also echoes that writer's social and political concerns in his use of his art to depict an unacceptable social and historical reality." Enrique Ojeda also notes that, "like Guayasamín, Icaza is essentially a national poet" (25), and in his essay on Icaza, repeatedly refers to the novelist as a "painter." He concludes that "one must study the characters that complement the picture displayed by Icaza. The truth of the painting and the depth of the philosophy are admirable"; the novelist has provided readers with "shadows of dusk, rain, and suffering over the face of the beloved city to a degree that no one until now has been able to paint" (120). These comments tempt us to view Guayasamín's paintings, as well as his elaborate plans for the completion of the monumental Chapel of Man, well under way when he passed away in 1999, as a pictographic narrative of Ecuadorian identity that provides a counterpoint to Icaza's painterly text.

Expelled from various schools for painting caricatures of teachers and classmates, Guayasamín began his career as an artist by selling small paintings to tourists. After studying in the School of Fine Arts in Quito, he spent seven months in the United Sates during 1942–1943 at the invitation of the State Department. In the mid-forties, he worked alongside Orozco in Mexico and became friends with the Chilean poet Pablo Neruda. Between 1944 and 1945, he traveled widely in Peru, Chile, Argentina, and Bolivia, doing research for the project *Huacayñán*, a collection of 103 paintings whose title translates from Quichua as "trail of tears." *Huacayñán*, divided into three thematic sections titled "Tema Negro," "Tema Mestizo," and "Tema Indio" (Black Theme, Mestizo Theme, Indian Theme), was shown in the Museum of Colonial Art in Quito in 1952. Guayasamín did not travel to Europe until 1956, choosing instead to focus on the Americas. In the late fifties, he began to gain international renown and won prizes and formed friendships with a number of important cultural figures.

Invited to Cuba by Fidel Castro in 1959, he witnessed the aftermath of the Revolution and formulated the project *La edad de la ira* (The Age of Anger). This collection of 250 paintings, perhaps Guayasamín's signature work, would later form the core collection for the Museo Guayasamín, one of Ecuador's most extensive and valuable museums, housing, as it does, substantial collections of pre-Columbian, colonial, and contemporary art. In 1962, he traveled back to Cuba and became friends with Salvador Allende, who would later become president of Chile. These contacts with famous Latin American leaders continued until Guayasamín's death and were often reflected in his many large-scale portraits and other documentary-style works.

Guayasamín's oeuvre, like Icaza's, emphasizes the pervasiveness of colonial structures and repressive social practices in the contemporary period while simultaneously insisting on the centrality of indigenous expression. His views on the supposed mestizo national character would seem to represent a wide spectrum of responses ranging from scorn to respect. Publicity materials for the Chapel of Man refer repeatedly to the project as a memorial to the American man, "from his pre-Columbian ancestral world and his evolution to contemporary *mestizaje*." The idea of the project was to "evoke the destiny of all Latin America" from the preconquest moment to the present, when "*mestizaje* begins to offer its best fruits: Beginning with the great independence leaders, America now has great literary, artistic, scientific, and political figures, equal to those in other continents." [12]

Guayasamín was already planning the Chapel of Man in the 1980s, hoping to inaugurate the structure in 1992 for the quincentenary of Columbus' appearance in the Americas. But the monumental task would take several more years to come together and would require the support of a number of key figures and organizations. In the mid-1990s, the Guayasamín Foundation received the stamp of approval and seed money from UNESCO, which, according to the artist, had judged the Chapel of Man the most important artistic endeavor in Latin America at that moment. In June of 1996, eighteen musicians and singers from throughout Latin America, including well-known figures such as Mercedes Sosa, Silvio Rodríguez, Fito Páez, and Víctor Heredia, as well as the Chilean folkloric ensemble Inti-Illimani, convened for a three-day concert in Quito titled "Todas las voces, todas" (All Voices, All). The musicians had agreed to donate their efforts and a portion of the royalties from the quadruple CD recorded at the event to construction efforts for the Chapel of Man.

Guayasamín appeared again in the entertainment pages in 1997, after a much-publicized dinner at the Tropicana Club in Havana, where Castro himself took the stage to admire and sign a cigar box built and decorated by the artist. The item was auctioned for $135,000 to help fund the building of the Chapel of Man (Rice, "Fidel Wows Smokers at the Tropicana"). As of 2002, web sites for the Chapel of Man were still soliciting donations, and a flask of *ron chota*, Cuban rum packaged in a bottle designed by the artist, could be also be purchased electronically to help fund the effort. [13] This multimedia artistic and commercial collaboration of well-known figures from a wide range of aesthetic and political aspirations in the service of a single museum project is perhaps unprecedented, confirming that Guayasamín—perhaps more than any artist before him—succeeded in representing, both symbolically and on the canvas, a continental Latin American identity.

The thematic centrality of *mestizaje* in Guayasamín's art is by no means unidimensional. In an interview published in *Nuestra América frente al V centenario* (Our America at the Quincentenary), Guayasamín referred to the "encounter of two worlds" as "phraseologies to justify disastrous events in the continent" (Benedetti et al., 232). When asked if he believed the Spanish conquest initiated five hundred years earlier had ended, he insisted on the persistence of discrimination: "Do you know that the worst insult one can make to another person is to call him 'indio de mierda' [shitty Indian], that is, the mestizo continues to hate the Indian, who as I said before, is the true owner and proprietor of this continent" (236). The reason for this hatred, the painter added, was the mestizo's "shame of having Indian blood" (237).

This ambivalent, seemingly contradictory, stance toward processes of *mestizaje* was also in evidence in a 1996 interview with the painter sandwiched between a portrait session with Guatemalan indigenous leader Rigoberta Menchú and Guayasamín's trip to Cuba the following morning with an entourage of some two hundred friends and family members. Along with writer and journalist María Gabriela Alemán,[14] I was invited into Guayasamín's home in the exclusive neighborhood of Bellavista and offered a place at a dining table that appeared to seat some thirty people. Before taking us on a tour of his studio and remarkable collections of precolonial, colonial, and contemporary art from Latin America, Europe, and Asia, Guayasamín smoked Chestertons nonstop and spoke of his troubled boyhood, when he was frequently ridiculed and ostracized for being an Indian. When the maestro began to address questions about the role of *mestizaje* in his current work and future projects, including the Chapel of Man, his mixed feelings quickly become apparent.

Guayasamín acknowledged that *mestizaje* was a principal theme of his last, still unfinished project and would categorize, in fact, an entire section of the chapel. An initial section would feature an homage to the three great cultures of the Aztecs, the Mayas, and the Incas, and a second would represent the moments of "discovery" and conquest. The final section was devoted to *mestizaje* and would include fifteen portraits of "positive men" such as Bolívar, Carlos Gardel, and Che Guevara, and fifteen negative characters, such as Augusto Pinochet and other "evil dictators."

Unlike Vasconcelos, whose glorification of the cosmic race (at least in his early work) left little room for multivalence, Guayasamín conceived of *mestizaje* as contradictory and two-faced. What the two innovators seemingly shared was the association of a mestizo aesthetic with a kind of Latin American spiritual essentialism. Guayasamín, nevertheless, posited this spiritualized notion against a concrete everyday reality in which *mestizaje* was assumed in a variety of forms that ranged from complete negation to an exclusive identification with Indianness.

At some level, all these versions were suspect for the artist. Although *mestizaje* obviously existed and could not be denied, especially in its linguistic and religious forms, it also represented cruelty, violence, and loss.

Not only were mestizos frequently avid collaborators with the projects of conquest and colonization, but in many cases, they proved to be as cruel or crueler than their Spanish colleagues.

This contentious engagement with the problematics of mestizo identity is visible in much of the artist's prolific plastic production. Certain techniques, particularly the pronounced use of geometrization, the emphasis on angles and the broken or pronounced line, and the use of flat colors—especially black, white, red, yellow, and brown—are clear links between pre-Columbian and postcolonial mestizo plastic art, notes Barney Cabrera (*La transculturación en el arte colombiano*, 47). Frequently, Guayasamín's somber subject matter, allusions to pain and suffering, and emphasis on a fragmented or fractured human form have been associated with the plight of indigenous populations, just as Icaza's narrative techniques were considered starkly revelatory of the same conditions.

As had been the case with Icaza, some viewers found Guayasamín's social content overwhelming. A 1943 review of Guayasamín in the *St. Louis Star-Times*, recalling a disgruntled reader's complaint that Icaza's texts produced indigestion, suggested a strong stomach was needed to view his work. But Guayasamín argued that such techniques were not mere aesthetic affectations. Despite comparisons to European expressionists and cubists, the painter claimed his greatest influences were in the Americas, many of them indigenous religious sites. When he was twenty-three, he visited Sechín, a pre-Columbian architectural complex in Peru and the scene of important preconquest battles. "When I arrived there, I felt that I had already been there, that I had already worked in that land, and had molded the tears of the faces of the women . . . All the expressionism that I have in my painting was born in Sechín and is not from the German expressionists, or the Europeans, it's born of Sechín, of that history, of that battle."[15] Guayasamín spoke of painting "for the last three or five thousand years, more or less," and this panoramic and multitemporal conception of his work is one shared by many critics, who have called him not only "the painter god of Ecuador" but also the "Picasso of Ibero-America"—a term Guayasamín disliked—and "one of the most transcendental painters of our day." José Camón Aznar linked him to an earlier tradition, calling him the "Michelangelo of the vanquished race."[16]

The need to respond to the destruction of indigenous material culture, temples, images, and sacred spaces is also strongly felt in Guayasamín's tendency toward oversized or monolithic projects, such as the huge murals in the Chapel of Man and the structure itself. The cultural retrieval and revalorization of indigenous expression fundamental to his oeuvre is most

FIGURE I.   Mural de Baraja de Huacayñán, *by Oswaldo Guayasamín, 1952.*
Courtesy of the Fundación Guayasamín, Quito.

vividly exemplified, perhaps, in the construction of the Chapel of Man as
a corollary to the Temple of the Sun, a preconquest Inca place of worship
located across the city on a hill now known as the Panecillo.[17] Both sites
are located at approximately 3,050 meters above sea level, and Guayasamín's intention was to architecturally re-create the Temple of the Sun,
including its 40-meter-square space without any sustaining column.

Alongside the highly metaphysical concerns of the Chapel of Man, we
find a marked predilection in Guayasamín's earlier work for the material,
particularly evident in the emphasis on the human body or face in its many
forms, ages, and hues (see Figure 1). In the tripartite collection *Huacayñán*,
catalogued in a bilingual edition by the Casa de la Cultura Ecuatoriana in
1953 and dedicated to Benjamín Carrión, Guayasamín displays an obvious
commitment to a multiracial, multicultural visualization of the Ecuadorian and Latin American character. The paintings cost him seven years'
effort and were undertaken following a two-year tour of Latin America.
In the presentation of the text, Carrión writes, "The three great human
stocks of Ecuador, the mestizo, the Indian, the black, have been interpreted in this great plastic poem of Guayasamín. Such are the vigor, richness, and grandeur of the achievement that in commenting on it, musical
thoughts and terms come to mind more readily: symphony, orchestra-
tion, counterpoint, rhythm" (20). On few occasions, however, do these
distinct elements appear to coalesce harmoniously; it is much more com-

FIGURE 2. Los amantes, *by Oswaldo Guayasamín, 1957. Courtesy of the Fundación Guayasamín, Quito.*

mon to see them in juxtaposition, as evidenced in the cover illustration for the collection, which portrays two figures intertwined in a contorted concert of black against white (Figure 2). This cover illustration is typical of other works in *Huacayñán* (Ribadeneira in Guayasamín, *Algunas claves para Guayasamín,* 5): "The color used by Guayasamín with the objective of fully interpreting the mestizo was white and black. Expressionism served as a well-suited element for highlighting what results from an unstable psyche, still unformed, of a new man born of a conflictive biology. Black and white offered the painter the sole plastic form capable of placing in relief the contrasting psychology of the mestizo."

As this comment illustrates, art critics were not immune to equating an "unstable psyche" with a "conflictive biology." Guayasamín's work was considered successful in its evocation precisely because of this disjunctive, fractious portrayal. "The mestizo theme is interpreted in lines and colors of transition and indecision, since hybridization is still an uncertain condition in the process of fixing the features and characteristics within the scope of what is Ecuadorian," explained Carrión (Guayasamín, *Huacayñán,* 20).

The exaggeration of opposed values is prevalent in both *Huacayñán* and *La edad de la ira,* Guayasamín's subsequent collection. *Se volvió noche al mediodía* (It Became Night in the Middle of the Day), from 1950, features, instead of a twilight landscape, a human figure separated in two halves, one light and one dark. Rather than a sumptuous fusion of these elements, the skeletal body represents want and imminent death. Guayasamín repeats the gesture of the divided face or body in several other canvases from the same series. In the collage triptych *Cabezas* (Heads), from the collection *La edad de la ira*, features torn from their implied whole are arranged in a melange of colors and sizes, emphasizing the disparity of elements in each face. The huge Venetian crystal mosaic *Homenaje al hombre americano* (Homage to the American Man, 1952), at the Centro Bolívar in Caracas, features another face and body, divided in two between light and dark halves, contorted, with the head seeming to turn backward to look at the viewer across his back.

From *Los amantes* (The Lovers, 1954) to *El grito* (The Scream, painted two decades later, in 1973), the painter offers several visions of these same pronounced internal oppositions. In fact, one of the very few paintings that does not represent some form of rupture or fragmentation is the portrait of his daughter Verenice, painted in 1967. Even in the works from the 1980s which deal with "warmer" more intimate subjects, such as *Madre y niño* (Mother and Child) and *Maternidad* (Maternity), the constitutive elements more often produce a sensation of dissonance than a notion of integration.

V. MONSTROUS DIMENSIONS

The *Enciclopedia El Ateneo* notes that Guayasamín "translates America, from the point of the Ecuadorian reality, as something virgin, strong, dawning, and overflowing, marked by those hot coals and those monsters that populate the world of the artist from Ecuador" (Guayasamín, *Oswaldo Guayasamín*, 93). The focus on the monstrous, already considered in relation to Ehlers and Icaza, finds a place here as well. Guayasamín's employment of chiaroscuro in the portrayal of the American face recalls a portrait of the great mestizo historian El Inca Garcilaso de la Vega done by Peruvian artist José Sabogal. In that painting, Sabogal "establishes graphically the fallacy of the discourse on 'cultural mestizaje' " (Lienhard, *La voz y su huella*, 133) by representing the Inca "with his face divided in two sections: one side Spanish and light-colored, and the other Indian, copper-colored. Strangely, this solution repeats the superimposition of styles in Cuzqueño architecture and is, for the most part, a negation of *mestizaje*. Two distinct half faces do not create the human face" (Stastny, " ¿Un arte mestizo?" 156). Although this "negation" may be less explicit in Guayasamín's commentary, both oral and visual, the quality of unresolvedness in his work is nevertheless unavoidable.

The confrontations that we see in specific paintings, collages, and mosaics, as well as in the juxtaposition of "bad" and "good" figures in a neo-sacred space dedicated to a summary of *mestizaje*'s impact on the Latin American character, may be viewed, perhaps, as a parallelogram of daily experience in Ecuador and other parts of the continent. The artistic opposition that Guayasamín developed seems to reflect two competing visions of the phenomenon, one which sees it as the enriching inheritance of the contact of two worlds, the other as the terrain of degradation and destruction, especially in the enactment of social interactions. Guayasamín's art, instead of clarifying this contradiction, accentuates it. In the forty years that passed between the publication of Icaza's *El chulla Romero y Flores* and Guayasamín's death, the figure of Ecuadorian *mestizaje* remained unreconciled, caught in the half-light of the city's labyrinths, twists, and turns, its monstrous dimensions never fully tamed by the purveyors of official discourse.

*I see a whole generation
freefalling toward a borderless future
incredible mixtures beyond sci-fi
cholo-punks, pachuco krishnas
Irish concheros, high-tech mariachis
Indian rockers and Anglosandinistas
I see them all
wandering around
a continent without a name*

GUILLERMO GÓMEZ-PEÑA, *Warrior for Gringostroika*[1]

I. STILL WAITING TO BE COSMIC

Buried deep in a long list of "187 Reasons Why Mexicanos Can't Cross the Border," part of the 1996 collaborative text *Temple of Confessions: Mexican Beasts and Living Santos* by Guillermo Gómez-Peña and Roberto Sifuentes, the reader finds the item "CAN'T CROSS because we're still waiting to be cosmic" (104). At the turn of the twenty-first century, Gómez-Peña and Sifuentes "confess," tongue-in-cheek (and sometimes in less-demure positions), what should by now be abundantly clear: Vasconcelos' grand ideas for an ultimate, harmonious, fifth "cosmic" race that would bring together the best of its constituent members in Mexico and elsewhere in Latin America remain a utopian dream with sometimes nightmarish results. And yet, in the same text, in an essay titled "Los Techno-Subversivos," poet and essayist Ed Morales writes, "The sweet tropical fruit of the mestizaje [miscegenation] phenomenon of Latin America—once described by Mexican philosopher Jose Vasconcelos as 'La Raza Cosmica'—is now 'infecting' the Information World, just as said world was taking itself for granted as a suburban oasis in the middle of late capitalism's virtual metropolis" (136).[2]

The space of Latin Americanness in *Temple of Confessions* is variously characterized, then, as both "waiting to be cosmic" or recognizing the failures of the cult of *mestizaje*, and as a new force with viruslike power that is "infecting" and altering the matrix of information systems that inform and are informed by cultural practice.

Where does this seemingly contradictory multipositioning leave the discussion of Latin America's privileged claim to hybrid cultures at the turn of the twenty-first century? *Mestizaje* has repeatedly proven to be a flawed doctrine of Latin American identity that nonetheless continues to distinguish Latin Americans from their northern neighbors. At the same time, it is newly mobilized and empowered through electronic diffusion that renders it ever more ubiquitous, so that its ideology is now pervasively felt in the United States, that same national and cultural power it was fashioned to repel. This turn of events is strikingly apparent in Morales' allusion to Vasconcelos-style *mestizaje* as the common ground he finds between his own work as a Puerto Rican and member of the Nuyorican Poets Café—an urban, bilingual, performance-based group in New York City—and that of Gómez-Peña and Sifuentes, performance artists whose background and experiences in Mexico and the southwestern United States are arguably remote from his own. A strange twist has occurred in the cult of *mestizaje*, one that would likely have made Vasconcelos cringe. His "raza cósmica," so stubbornly antipathetic to cultural intervention from North America, now becomes a synonym for all Latino expression *in* the United States. In fact, "Latino" cultural production becomes the new, quintessential site of *mestizaje*, epitomized in the performance-based genres practiced by Gómez-Peña and Sifuentes. In an essay included in *Temple of Confessions*, Morales notes that

> while the presence of La Raza Cosmica is felt through the efforts of almost every political/academic/advocacy think tank/community organization /university club that has anything to do with Latinos, its most palpable manifestation can be found in the recent "performance art" of Guillermo Gómez-Peña and his collaborator Roberto Sifuentes. The *Temple of Confessions* is a multimedia art project that uses high technology and lowbrow kitsch; it encourages well-intentioned dialogue between different ethnic groups and *razas* as well as exposes some of the trashiest jokes and ethnic slurs found on mid-America's minds. (136)

The association of Gómez-Peña's work with *mestizaje* is at once related to and distinct from a late-twentieth-century tradition of the appropriation of Vasconcelos' ideas by Chicano and Chicana writers, artists, and activists, briefly discussed in Chapter 1. Whereas Gloria Anzaldúa and many of her contemporaries found the notions helpful for addressing the bicultural experience of people of Mexican descent living in the United States, Gómez-Peña's relationship to the idea places it in the context of a postnational, globalized, and globalizing moment in which people, ideas, and cultural production are marked by constant movement, flux, and de-territorialization. In his early work, the border may be a concrete site which is nonetheless permeable; in his later work, the border dissolves into a condition.

The text "Biconception," part prose, part poetry, and part script, demonstrates how in his early textual production, Gómez-Peña was already hypothesizing the possibilities of a transnational, subversive *mestizaje* (*Warrior for Gringostroika*, 160):

BICONCEPTION
(TIJUANA/SAN DIEGO, 1985)
[PRE-PROJECT OF EROTIC-ARTISTIC-POLITICAL ACTIVISM]

A. A Mexican man (preferably a cholo) and a North American woman (preferably a punk) meet at midnight at the border fence, each on his/her respective side. She is in her most fertile state. They undress, and proceed to fondle each other through the barbed wire with their fingertips. With extreme care and a clear historical consciousness, they begin the binational coitus. She gets pregnant despite the border.
B. The baby is born nine months later at the intersection of Playas de Tijuana and Border Field State Park (the end of the border and the beginning of the Pacific Ocean/the end of Western civilization, and the northern-most point of Latin America). Two doctors, a Mexican and an Anglo-Saxon, assist the birth.
C. The parents demand dual citizenship for the child.
D. The child is educated at the best schools in both countries, and spends time with cultural and political leaders from both Americas. One day, she/he will become the most important leader of the new transcontinental culture.

A mixed "race," bicultural child is conceived, delivered, accorded civil status, and educated in a liminal, double-coded contact zone; it is from there that he or she emerges as the leader of a "new transcontinental culture." While many of the elements in this encounter are reminiscent of ideas that appeared in Vasconcelos' work and that were honed in Paz, there is one notable new characteristic: the "clear historical consciousness" of both participants, evident in their insistence on access to the resources and custody of both of their communities for their border-straddling offspring.

Gómez-Peña's "poem" is optimistic, perhaps, but it also recognizes the dangers which must be navigated in this new, conscious waging of "bi-conception." It graphically suggests that the ideal site for *mestizaje* in the twenty-first century will not be a specific nation or even region of Latin America, but the myriad contact zones *between* Latin America and the United States.

Homi Bhabha mentions Gómez-Peña twice in *The Location of Culture*, which has become something of a desk companion for critics working out the relationships between hybridity, postcoloniality, and moribund notions of modernity. In the first reference, the performance artist serves as an example of a postcolonial critique that is "otherwise than modernity" (6; original emphasis): "Such cultures of a postcolonial *contra-modernity* may be contingent to modernity, discontinuous or in contention with it, resistant to its oppressive, assimilationist technologies; but they also deploy the cultural hybridity of their borderline conditions to 'translate,' and therefore reinscribe, the social imaginary of both metropolis and modernity." Bhabha situates Gómez-Peña in an "intervening space" in which he creates insurgent acts of cultural translation that resonate with a "hybrid chicano aesthetic." In his chapter "How Newness Enters the World: Postmodern Space, Postcolonial Times and the Trials of Cultural Translation," he is again inspired by Gómez-Peña's work, including this fragment from "The New World (B)Order," published in *Third Text* in 1993 (74):

> This new society is characterized by mass migrations and bizarre interracial relations. As a result new hybrid and transitional identities are emerging . . . Such is the case of the crazy *Chica-riricuas*, who are the products of the Puertorican-mulatto and Chicano-mestizo parents . . . When a *Chica-riricua* marries a Hassidic Jew their child is called *Hassidic vato loco* . . .
>
> The bankrupt notion of the melting pot has been replaced by a model that is more germane to the times, that of the *menudo chowder.* According to this model, most of the ingredients do melt, but some stubborn chunks are condemned merely to float. Vergi-gratia!

Bhabha finds that these "fantastic renamings" and "hybrid hyphenations" of the subjects of cultural difference "expose the limits of any claim to a singular or autonomous sign of difference—be it class, gender or race," creating, instead, an "in-between" and an interstitial future (219). The notion of intermediacy is compelling and retrieves, to some extent, the creative, innovative potential for reconfigured identity and expression suggested by earlier terms such as "transculturation" and the "contact zone."

In the introduction to Gómez-Peña's *Warrior for Gringostroika*, anthropologist Roger Bartra writes that the movement of thousands of people back and forth across the border between the United States and Mexico "generates a sociocultural process of mestizaje and symbiosis that no nationalist discourse can stop" (11). Gómez-Peña has defined this new *mestizaje* as "the borderization of the world" (*Warrior for Gringostroika*, 11), thus extending the phenomenon far beyond the Americas. Not only is the liminal space of the border, literal or otherwise, a place where transculturation necessarily occurs, but attempts to impede these processes themselves become utopian, Bartra says (12). This New World (b)order recalls the shared colonial history of Latin America and the United States as frontiers of European expansion, provides for fluid demographics that challenge both national frontiers and ideologies, and insists on working out questions of agency and subjectivity in a "jagged terrain of transnational cultural exchange and hybrid identities" (Gómez-Peña, *Dangerous Border Crossers*, 72).

II. HYBRID SAINTS AND CYBERIMMIGRANTS

How do Gómez-Peña and his collaborators situate themselves in this strange landscape of failed/renovated *mestizaje* that seems most present in the United States, but may include the entire continent, if not the world? Their chief strategy is insistently to address issues of identity, particularly the identity of the United States' most populous cultural others—Latin American immigrants—with exaggerated irony and exponential hybridity. *Temple of Confessions*, for example, took several forms. It was at the same time a museum installation and a research project collecting "confessions" submitted vocally or in writing by museum visitors or by people on the streets surrounding the museum as well as by both regular and electronic mail during and after the exhibit. This material was, in turn, formatted in a book and audio CD set that offered selections from the gathered research. The web site the authors created to process these "confessions" received over twenty thousand hits the first year, and the electronic questionnaire that many of the visitors filled out provided material for later composite creations which Gómez-Peña classified as "projections of people's own psychological and cultural monsters" (*Dangerous Border Crossers*, 49).[3] "After reading thousands of pages of internet submissions, my colleagues and I concluded that a perverse dialectic of inter-cultural violence and interracial desire was central to America's percep-tion/projection of cultural otherness," he notes (50).

These confessions show how cultural otherness becomes the object of desire and gratification as it is produced in the cultural marketplace. Be-cause of the sheer breadth of the responses, however, they also provide testimony of the wide range of experiences and enormous degree of dif-ference among the throngs of "adherents" to the temple. As the clerics of a pseudoreligious sanctuary, the authors thus mediate and reveal a vast sample of behaviors that cluster around various understandings of cul-tural and racial otherness. These they exploit for their own creative pur-poses, fashioning a new pantheon of "hybrid saints" such as "Santa Frida of Detroit," a portrayal of the renowned twentieth-century Mexican artist Frida Kahlo with a Uniroyal tire "halo" framing her head (Gómez-Peña and Sifuentes, *Temple of Confessions*, 37) and "El Azteca de East L.A.," who sports a feather headdress and hieroglyphics on his face, wears a plaid shirt and blue jeans, and uses a red bandanna as a tourniquet on his arm while handcuffs dangle from the hand he prepares to shoot up with (34). A final empty gold frame in the series asks the viewer or reader to "place your favorite Cultural Other here" (41).

The performance personae that Gómez-Peña and Sifuentes create in this exhibit and elsewhere, such as "El Pre-Colombian Vato," "Cyber-Vato," "Supernintendo Ranchero," "El Mariachi Liberachi," "El Web-back," and "El Aztec High-Tech," relentlessly conflate features that are culturally, ethnically, temporally, economically, ideologically, geographi-cally, and technologically disparate. The alliances between high tech-nology and the "lower" cultural registers of the migrant worker, the im-migrant, or the barrio *"vato"* challenge the sanctity and unity of all "pure" identities.[4]

In a similar move, Gómez-Peña has adopted a resolutely multivoiced position of enunciation in a political environment punctuated by English-only and Spanish-only campaigns that claim monolingualism as a tool for "protecting national culture."[5] In "Criminal Identity Profile," which ap-pears in *Dangerous Border Crossers*, Gómez-Peña lists "Spanglish, Grin-goñol, Franglais, Robo-esperanto and fake Nahuatl" as the languages he is fluent in, besides Spanish and English. In the same document, he lists his race as "non-specific, probably mestizo" (21). Of course, the ambigui-ties of "non-specific" and "probably" are as important or more important than the identification as mestizo.

"Ethno-cyborgs" and "cyber-immigrants" are two other experimental identities Gómez-Peña and his collaborators developed in the 1990s as a response, first, to discussions of the capacity of cyberspace to render the body obsolete, and, then, to a subsequent backlash from members of the arts community who attempted to reclaim the "body primitive" from its erasure by and in technology (*Dangerous Border Crossers*, 45–46). Again, multivoicedness, both between languages and between *technes*, was key (*Dangerous Border Crossers*, 46): "Our original goals were to politicize the debates around digital technologies and to infect virtual space with Chicano humor and *linguas polutas* (such as Spanglish). We also wanted to employ new technologies to enhance mytho-poetical interactivity between performer and live audience, and as a tool for researching fundamental expressions of inter-cultural fear and desire."

In the interactive exhibit "The Ethno-Cyberpunk Trading Post & Curio Shop On the Electronic Frontier," "computer screens, video monitors, neon signs and digital bars flashing taxonomic descriptions of the 'ethnographic specimens' (ourselves), added a sci-fi flavor to our techno-tribal environment" (*Dangerous Border Crossers*, 46). The responses to this exhibit prompted significant changes in the direction of Gómez-Peña and Sifuentes' work; as a result of public response, the two then set up the "techno-confessional" web site discussed above, which allowed visitors "to discuss sensitive matters of race, sexuality, and identity in an artificially safe environment," including their "interracial desires and sexual fantasies" (47).

III. FIRST WORLD *Mestizaje*, FIFTH WORLD TECHNOLOGY

This revelation of (North) America's fascination with the "perverse dialectic" of the intercultural and the interracial must be seen, I think, as documentation of the United States' latent devotion to the cult of *mestizaje*. As this America takes a turn confronting cultural dis/encounters and otherness within its own national imaginary, *mestizaje* becomes a kind of dangerous, edgy version of a melting pot in which certain elements refuse to dissolve or adhere. Marked by both a desire for cultural specificity and expression that produces "alternative" lifestyles endorsed by the mainstream and by fears that constitute what Gómez-Peña calls "neo-puritanism," U.S. culture takes up the question of hybridity not in the tradition of Vasconcelos, that is, as a consensus on national or regional identity, but as a global project of codification, commodification, and conglomeration of otherness in culturally attractive but politically diluted categories such as "Latino." The end result of each strategy, the rejection

or disabling of those voices extraneous to the homogenizing or hegemo-
nizing project—whether national or global, seems strikingly similar. In
a postnational environment in which geographic borders are rendered
merely symbolic by pervasive physical and electronic movement, this response can be seen as a way to manage the "alien" both inside and outside
national borders.

Of course, one strategy of this management is to refuse this "alien"
element access to the technological tools of cultural dissemination, either
by insisting on its primitive, premodern character, or by domesticating its
production for one's own purposes. These tactics are repeatedly addressed
by Gómez-Peña, in terms of both content and the multilevel integration
of technology into his performances, exhibits, and other productions. A
series of four "highly diverse" collaborative performances were "unified
primarily by a goal of destabilizing and subverting problematic notions of
'racial' and cultural authenticity" (*Dangerous Border Crossers*, 79).

Gómez-Peña's many inventions of the "artificial savage" often use high
technology, but have also highlighted the complicity of other media forms
in the United States' negotiation of its relationship to Mexico and the rest
of Latin America. A memorable example of the latter is *The Couple in the
Cage*, a traveling exhibit that coincided with quincentenary events in the
Americas and in Spain in the early 1990s. The film version of that exhibit
documents a variety of audience reactions to Gómez-Peña and his collaborator, Coco Fusco, who caged themselves as representatives of an un-
discovered South American tribe. Despite the exaggerated use of pop culture and kitsch in the exhibits (their "habitat" included a television, boom
box, sunglasses, Pepto-Bismol, etc.), visitors at museums throughout the
world reacted with varying degrees of anger, horror, ingenuousness, and
fascination, many of them convinced the two were, indeed, "real Indians"
instead of performance artists.

In an article published in 2002 ("Cyber-Aztecs and Cholo-Punks,"
45), Thomas Foster traces the connection between Gómez-Peña's notion
of positive hybridity and his development of a theory of five worlds, as
well as the relationship of both to new communications technologies.
While Gómez-Peña, for the most part, maintains the standard meanings
of "First," "Second," and "Third" World in his concluding piece in *The
New World Border*, "End-of-the-Century Topography Review," these delineations are rendered inadequate by a focus on the "Fourth" and "Fifth"
Worlds. The Fourth World, which combines "portions of all the previous worlds" (*The New World Border*, 245), provides a conceptual plane
in which "the indigenous inhabitants of the Americas meet with the de-

territorialized peoples, the immigrants and the exiles" (17) in a common, postnational or non-national cause.[6] The Fifth World, then, extends this notion of deterritorialization into the realm of the virtual, into cyberspace, the mass media, and global commercial culture.

As Thomas Foster points out, whereas all of these worlds are finally conceptual, whether they adhere to or supersede nationalist ideologies, "the Fourth and Fifth Worlds embody a concept of spatial relations defined in terms of motion, flux, and relationality" that allow for the semantic borders of both (and their relationship to each other) to remain open (46–47). A hybrid figure such as "El Aztec High-Tech" references Fourth World indigenous culture in tension, confrontation, and perhaps even collaboration with Fifth World high technology. But as a fictional character, it still leaves unanswered the question of whether or to what extent Native Americans, immigrants, and exiles have been able to create the kind of Fourth World common-cause coalition enhanced by Fifth World media that Gómez-Peña envisions.

IV. "LA CHINGADA"

One of the complex "sites" in Gómez-Peña's Fifth World matrix is "La Chingada," also known as Doña Marina or La Malinche, the "screwed" indigenous collaborator and consort of the conquistador Hernando Cortés. Her history of collaboration has become an allegory for Mexican contact with external powers and influences. To better capture what Gómez-Peña's resurrection of the figure might represent, it is useful to return to the landmark essay by Octavio Paz, *The Labyrinth of Solitude*, in which the Mexican poet and critic describes La Chingada (86):

> If the *Chingada* is a representation of the violated Mother, it is appropriate to associate her with the Conquest, which was also a violation, not only in the historical sense but also in the very flesh of Indian women. The symbol of this violation is doña Malinche, the mistress of Cortés . . . This explains the success of the contemptuous adjective *malinchista* recently put into circulation by the newspapers to denounce all those who have been corrupted by foreign influences. The *malinchistas* are those who want Mexico to open itself to the outside world: the true sons of la Malinche, who is the *Chingada* in person. Once again we see the opposition of the closed and the open.

In Paz, the interpenetration of Europe and America at the moment of New World conquest (or the penetration of America *by* Europe) establishes a precedent for viewing internal contradictions in Mexico as betrayal, as instances in which local integrity has been sacrificed to external exploitation. In the historical instance, the key players were La Malinche and Cortés, but in a second act of this drama, the protagonists are the *malinchistas* and the "outside world," a world in which the United States has now become dominant. As a result, the contact zone between Latin America and the First World has been characterized as a danger zone, a space in which Mexico is repeatedly violated, *chingado*. *Lo mestizo* is therefore marked as a complex national trait that attests to and explains repeated victimization.[7] Because La Malinche has been consistently read as raped (*violada*), as La Chingada, Mexicans have condemned their origins and denied inherent possibilities for productive hybridity, according to Paz (87): "The Mexican does not want to be either an Indian or a Spaniard. Nor does he want to be descended from them. He denies them. And he does not affirm himself as a mixture, but rather as an abstraction: he is a man. He becomes the son of Nothingness. His beginnings are in his own self." Paz attests to the many fissures in the national identity that Vasconcelos sought to build, and a falling-away, as it were, from faith in the recognition of disparate ancestors and their consolidation in *la raza*, in an advantageous mixture of the best and purest elements of each constituency. We are not surprised to discover, then, that *The Labyrinth of Solitude* was published only two years after Vasconcelos' 1948 retraction of his earlier adherence to the dogma of *mestizaje*. In the portrait of the Mexican that Paz paints, the "agnostic" has now become a disbeliever, one who has successfully distanced himself from determinist notions of identity, but who has simultaneously inured himself to discomfiting engagements with his "Others" and with Otherness.

What Paz proposes, then, is a return to the notion of a dialectic, a dialectic which he draws not in class terms, but in terms of ethnic and national categories—a hint that the legacy of Vasconcelos has not been wholly abandoned. In a 1969 essay entitled "The Other Mexico" (in *The Labyrinth of Solitude*), he insists on the pursuit of self-understanding, whether personal or collective, through attention to the interrelated experiences of Mexico, Latin America, and the Americas (218): "I repeat that we are nothing except a relationship: something that can be defined only as a part of a history. The question of Mexico is inseparable from the question of Latin America's future, and this, in turn, is included in another: that of the future relations between Latin America and the United States. The question of ourselves always turns out to be a question of others." These comments notably prefigure a much more sustained engagement with a poetics of relation in the work of Édouard Glissant, but, more important, they set the stage for a reworking of Vasconcelos that incorporates *mestizaje* not as a defense of Latinization in the face of U.S. cultural imperialism, not as the prized characteristic of *Latin* Americanness in counterdistinction to the United States, but as a discourse of engagement with competing notions of American identity.

Paz concludes by suggesting that a dialogue could ensue between Mexico and the United States, "on condition that first they learn to speak with themselves, with their own otherness: their Blacks, their Chicanos, their young people" (220). First, he recognizes that Mexico and other Latin American nations that claimed to be people of the cosmic race had failed to incorporate their "Others" or even to provide a forum for their full expression. And second, he sees that this failure has, in turn, produced an inability for Latin Americans to significantly contest U.S. cultural norms, either from within Mexico or from within immigrant or migrant positions inside the United States.

Clearly, Gómez-Peña's work can be viewed and read as a(n) (ad)venture into this dialogue, as a recognition that "La Chingada" has herself been deterritorialized, that she now occupies a terrain of ethnic, cultural, and linguistic interaction that supersedes the sites of conquest or the nation. Besides alluding to the violence inherent in the contemporary encounters between the United States and "Our America," this new border-defying mode reveals that the United States now stands in the same relationship *to* Latin America, in some senses, as national centers stood to their ethnic or cultural others in colonial and republican epochs *in* Latin America. The United States is the latest agent to attempt the absorption of its mestizo offspring into institutionalized culture or, alternately, their relegation to peripheries where their cultural power is suppressed.

According to Thomas Foster, "La Chingada" represents for Gómez-Peña "a crossing of racial categories into the virtual, and his use of the term moves toward Donna Haraway's definition of the cyborg as figuring a 'monstrous and illegitimate' unity and as having 'no origin story in the Western sense'" (47). By placing La Chingada in the Fifth World, "Gómez Peña intends to highlight the danger of generalizing specific experiences of dislocation and hybridity" (48) and to alert his viewers and readers to a new, transnational institutionalization of the mestizo or the hybrid in which the only "others" left will be those in monocultural communities. While Foster's reading is perceptive, he underestimates, I think, the degree to which irony and hyperbole are activated in Gómez-Peña's later work to show how such an accentuated Fifth World *mestizaje* remains absurdly funny and, thus, provisional.

In his performance "The New World Border," for example, Gómez-Peña lays out a futuristic "official transculture" with a "Spanglish Only Initiative," new hybrid identities of "mesti-mulatas" and other peoples who are "the product of at least four racial mixtures," new ultrasyncretic religious figures, and commercial markets that employ "multicultural consumer training." But while transnational global commerce clearly has recognized the opportunities for commodifying the multicultural,[8] and U.S. cultural norms increasingly allow for the integration of hybrid models of identity (evidenced perhaps by the inclusion of a multiracial category in the U.S. national census for the first time in 2000),[9] Gómez-Peña's "Spanglish Only" scenario and prophecy of the future veneration of Funkahuatl, the Aztec divinity of funk (*The New World Border,* 41), are funny because they still seem patently absurd. Such configurations ultimately accentuate, then, the degree to which monolingual, monocultural, and neonational practices and policies remain firmly entrenched.

V. FIFTH ~~RACE~~ WORLD *Mestizaje*

Fifth World *mestizaje* is resolutely ambivalent, because it signifies both aperture and mass access to the realities of cultural contact, cultural exchange, and resident difference, but also registers the exploitation and institutional appropriation of these conditions across national boundaries. The possibilities are thus promising and dangerous, subversive and repressive. And what about the connection of such ideas to racial discourses, whether national, regional, or global? Gómez-Peña's inclusion of high technology and pseudotechnology in his performances and exhibits, which often call for audience participation as well, highlights the fact that the virtual world is ultimately bound by the social conventions of everyday experience. Gómez-Peña notes that when he and Sifuentes "arrived late at the technological debate," they were "shocked by the unexamined ethnocentrism permeating the discussions around art and digital technology," even in a place as culturally "diverse" as California (*Dangerous Border Crossers,* 255). They found that, despite the purported disembodiment of cyberspace (and the possible similarities between La Malinche and a cyborg), "racialized modes of perception are inevitably imported to cyberspace, and racial fantasies are restaged there" (T. Foster, 62).

This waking up to the pervasiveness of "race" in the new globalized "technoscapes" of the twenty-first century is important, especially when most recent discussions of hybridity, transculturation, and the like have veered away from any analysis of the vestiges of race-based discrimination, profiling, repression, marginalization, and exclusionary practices in the contemporary moment. Néstor García Canclini's *Hybrid Cultures*, for example, is symptomatic of the way *mestizaje* has been increasingly disassociated from questions of race in the transition from the twentieth to the twenty-first century. In a frequently cited note in the introduction, García Canclini notes that "occasional mention will be made of the terms *syncretism, mestizaje*, and others used to designate processes of *hybridization*. I prefer this last term because it includes diverse intercultural mixtures—not only the racial ones to which mestizaje tends to be limited—and because it permits the inclusion of modern forms of hybridization better than does 'syncretism,' a term that almost always refers to religious fusions or traditional symbolic movements" (11). But, in fact, these are the only mentions of *"mestizaje"* in the entire text, and in his elaboration of hybridizing processes, García Canclini makes it clear that he believes the relationship of these processes to specific localized racial discourses is of secondary, if not negligible, importance. His hybridity is resolutely "intercultural," not interracial.

In a chapter titled "Hybrid Cultures, Oblique Powers," he locates three key processes inherent in the production of hybridity: the "breakup and mixing of the collections that used to organize cultural systems, the deterritorialization of symbolic processes, and the expansion of impure genres" (207). It is easy to see all three of these processes at work in colonial processes of *mestizaje*, in which "collections" of peoples were broken up and mixed, in which symbolic processes that previously belonged to these "collections" were reconfigured in new formats and settings, and in which only one letter need be dropped to recognize the "expansion of impure genes." Nonetheless, due to the density, complexity, and acceleration of these hybridizing processes, García Canclini defines them as postmodern (243) and, in fact, concludes that, based on the evidence of the hybridizations he examines, "today all cultures are border cultures" (261).

This *neomestizaje*, synonymous with hybridity, but, for the most part, divorced from notions of race, is apparent in a number of other turn-of-the-new-century texts by prominent Latin Americanists. In Francine Masiello's *The Art of Transition*, for example, *mestizaje* seems to blur into a vague register of either theme or form. She comments on the ability of Chilean poet and visual artist Cecilia Vicuña to "remind her listeners and viewers of the mestizaje of cultural expression throughout the Americas"

(275), and on *mestizaje* as an "inaugural voice" in the poetry of Elvira Hernández (278). She notes that, "for the woman poet, entry into the scene of writing can only be described as a bid for self-deformation; it is confusion, hybridity, the mestizaje of American culture" (282). Here, *mestizaje* is reduced to a low-tech attempt to ascertain the self through writing; it is taken for granted that the found self assumes her voice through a recognition and employment of "mestizaje," whatever that has come to mean.

Serge Gruzinski's *El pensamiento mestizo* (Mestizo Thought, first published in French in 1999) is a more ambitious project that similarly distances the notion of *mestizaje* from "race." Gruzinski's contention that *mestizaje* is an integral phenomenon of occidental culture from at least as far back as ancient Greece, accentuated and accelerated by the growth of world capital, for the most part ignores the ways in which ideas about the clash and mix of cultures and "races" were transformed into legitimizing narratives of national and regional identity in the Americas, narratives that frequently excluded or distorted nonoccidental contributions. His idea of a "planetary mestizaje," while provocative, ultimately seems to provide a study of the way Europe and the West incorporated and suffused otherness through the use of capitalism and, more recently, technology, rather than a testament to the ways in which the cult of *mestizaje* affected specific populations and experiences.

Together, these deracialized notions of *mestizaje* suggest a welcome departure from the association of specific physical characteristics with cultural manifestations and a recognition of the ways in which the aesthetic response to *mestizaje* has profoundly affected both "high" and "low" cultural production in Latin America. On the positive side, they also reveal how hybrid constructions can weaken many of the ramparts and barriers of social categorization and hierarchies in a wide range of terrains. Paul Gilroy notes that "transcultural mixture alerts us not only to the syncretic complexities of language, culture, and everyday modern life in the torrid areas where racial slavery was practiced, but also to the purity-defying metamorphoses of individual identity in the 'contact-zones' of an imperial metropolis" (*Against Race*, 117). Yet, these recent uses also suggest a disturbing trend of overlooking historical and contemporary processes in which "race" continues to figure, and in which *mestizaje* had a starring role. Even in his highly controversial suggestion that inhabitants of the twenty-first century move beyond "raciological reasoning," Gilroy repeatedly acknowledges that new conceptualizations of hybridity carry with them laden histories in which mixture, both racial and cultural, has typically been associated with catastrophe and jeopardy (216).[10]

Despite the distastefulness of *mestizaje*'s lingering racial connotations for some critics, the historical processes of corporeal contact cannot be extricated from remnant cultural practices in postcolonial territories. Robert Young points out that "the historical links between language and sex were, however, fundamental. Both produced what were regarded as 'hybrid' forms (creole, pidgin and miscegenated children), which were seen to embody threatening forms of perversion and degeneration and became the basis for endless metaphoric extension in the racial discourse of social commentary" (*Colonial Desire*, 5). Young has complained that what is often missing in literary and cultural studies is attention to the "mechanics of the intricate processes of cultural contact, intrusion, fusion and disjunction," critical work that has already been done in fields such as religious studies, archeology, medicine, and economics. By taking a closer look at the nascence, decline, and ever-present absence of Vasconcelos' cosmic race, both in national appropriations and in the specific apertures of some of Latin America's noted writers, artists, and performers, such intricate processes come into clear and kaleidoscopic view.

NOTES

INTRODUCTION

1. "Ha ocurrido que la palabra mestizaje se ha convertido en objeto de un verdadero culto y en símbolo de la nacionalidad." All translations, unless otherwise noted, are mine.

2. "En lo que concierne a América, la observación nos demuestra que lo único invariable en el mosaico de sus etnias ha sido su constante y rico mestizaje."

3. See, for example, Fisher ("Mestizaje and the Cuadros de Castas") and García Saiz (*Las castas mexicanas*) for an analysis of the *cuadros de castas* in Mexico. An excellent full-color reproduction is available in *Artes de México*, no. 8, published in Mexico City with the title *La pintura de castas* (no date).

4. As Vera Kutzinski points out in *Sugar's Secrets* (4–5), *mestizaje* simultaneously invokes miscegenation and racial mixture as well as *blanqueamiento*, or whitening.

5. The citation refers to a discussion of hybridity rather than *mestizaje*, but the problem appears to be identical.

6. An important application of Bakhtin to theories of *mestizaje* can be found in Françoise Lionnet's "The Politics and Aesthetics of *Métissage*," the introductory essay to her *Autobiographical Voices*. Lionnet shows how the efforts of certain Francophone Caribbean authors who value Creole dialects constitute a particular contribution "to the development of heteroglossia and the dialogic imagination" (2). Borrowing from Martinican poet and essayist Édouard Glissant the notion of *métissage* as a "braiding of cultural forms," she cites contemporary postcolonial narrative as a specific form of heteroglossia characterized by "egalitarian interrelations in which binary impasses are deconstructed" (5). Lionnet offers *métissage* as a political and aesthetic posture, as a strategy of writing and a way of reading, and as a theoretical concept that, due to its transformative nature, can never be fully explained or contained (8): "*Métissage* is a praxis and cannot be subsumed under a fully elaborated theoretical system. *Métissage* is a form of *bricolage* in the sense used by Claude Lévi-Strauss, but as an aesthetic concept it encompasses far more: it brings together biology and history, anthropology and philosophy, linguistics and literature. Above all, it is a reading practice that allows me to bring out the interreferential nature of a particular set of texts." For her, *métissage*, or

mestizaje, is not, then, a category that would bring us back to the fixity of forms that Bakhtin rejected, but "a concept of solidarity which demystifies all essentialist glorifications of unitary origins, be they racial, sexual, geographic, or cultural" (9). As such, Lionnet points out, it is subversive both biologically and culturally.

7. Despite Mignolo's squeamishness with the terms "*mestizaje*" and "transculturation" in *Local Histories/Global Designs* (and previous texts) because of their association with race, he seems to have few qualms about "creolization," a term that became popular, in part, because of the English translation of Édouard Glissant's elaboration of both *creolité* and *métissage* as "creolization." Dash's translation choices reveal both the unavailability of an English corollary to *métissage* and the close etymological ties between *métissage* (creolization) and *mestizaje*; see Glissant, *Caribbean Discourse*. Mignolo is also unperturbed by the reification of race implicit in the appropriation of *mestizaje* by Anzaldúa and others as the "new mestiza consciousness." See, for example, Saldaña-Portillo, who argues that the reliance on *mestizaje* as the dominant trope of Chicano/a identity formation "fetishizes a residual Indian identity to the detriment of contemporary Indians in the United States and Mexico" ("Who's the Indian in Aztlán?" 403).

8. Of course, these two "moments" often cross-contaminate each other as well. Antonio Benítez-Rojo argues that in the case of the Caribbean, for example, the premodern, modern, and postmodern coexist (see Chapter 2 here).

9. Aline Helg writes, for example, that "racism—as a 'rationalized pseudoscientific theory positing the innate and permanent inferiority of nonwhites'—accompanied European colonialism and U.S. imperialism" (Graham, 37–38).

10. The colonial period also boasts an important, though less extensive, textual history of *mestizaje*. The most exemplary document in this history is arguably the *Comentarios reales* (Royal Commentaries), written by the mestizo historiographer El Inca Garcilaso de la Vega at the turn of the seventeenth century. Several anecdotal moments in the colonial history of *mestizaje* have arguably had more impact on twentieth-century literary critics. Two particularly noteworthy figures are Gonzalo Guerrero, a Spaniard who arrived in Mexico before Cortés, formed a relationship with an indigenous woman, became a protagonist in local indigenous politics, and refused to leave his new life to accompany Cortés on his campaign; and Doña Marina, or La Malinche, interpreter and consort to Cortés. Both have been repeatedly invoked in Mexican and Chicano appropriations of *mestizaje*. On the former, see, for example, Mario Aguirre Rosas, *Gonzalo de Guerrero, padre del mestizaje iberomexicano*. La Malinche is discussed further in the last section of this chapter.

11. "Creole" is used following its traditional employment in Latin America to mean persons or cultural phenomena of "purely" European stock or origins, but born in the Americas.

12. There is an inherent contradiction in the passage, since Bolívar implies that the "same mother" that all share is the Indian mother, but he has previously stated that most of the native inhabitants have been annihilated.

13. See Bolívar's "On the Reasons for Abolishing Slavery," (*The Hope of the Universe*, 171–172) and "A Further Appeal for the Emancipation of Slaves" (*The Hope of the Universe*, 184). In the first document, Bolívar clarifies, "I have ordered that all useful slaves shall be called to arms. This must be construed as relating only to those whom the forces need, since too many such recruits would do more harm than good" (172).

14. José Martí and other Cubans such as Fernando Ortiz and contemporary writers Roberto Fernández Retamar and Antonio Benítez-Rojo have left valuable commentary in this regard in Spanish; Martinicans Frantz Fanon and Édouard Glissant have contributed immensely important perspectives in French; and Wilson Harris and Derek Walcott have elaborated ideas in English. The impact of Francophone theorists has been recognized in a number of texts by Latin Americanists, including Fernández Retamar's *Caliban and Other Essays* and Mignolo's *Local Histories/Global Designs*.

15. Bolívar did not exploit the terms "mestizo" and "*mestizaje*," though his "género aparte," or separate people, is clearly the product of racial and cultural contact. Thus, the argument has been made that a more explicit bibliography of Latin American *mestizaje* should begin with Francisco Bilbao, a nineteenth-century Chilean dissident who took up questions of "race" and the impact of racial contact in *El evangelio americano*, published in 1864. Bilbao's text is relatively unknown, however, and he at best represents a minor figure in the "cult" of *mestizaje*.

16. I have substituted "mestizo" for "half-breed" in the translation cited. English translations of Martí invariably still use the term "half-breed" for mestizo, despite its archaism and negative connotations.

17. The sacred status of "Our America" is confirmed by the publication of *José Martí's "Our America": From National to Hemispheric Cultural Studies* (Jeffrey Belnap and Raúl Fernández, eds.) by Duke University Press in 1998. Several of the chapter authors had previously published extensively on the topic, particularly José David Saldívar (*The Dialectics of Our America*).

18. Ortega y Medina suggests that Sarmiento's rejection of *mestizaje*, or the "bastard amalgam" of Indians, Spaniards, and blacks, was based on Bolívar's loss of faith in the ideas he espoused in the Discourse of Angostura and the Letter from Jamaica (*Reflexiones históricas*, 279). Sarmiento diverged, however, from Bolivaran principles in his fondness for solutions to racial problems endorsed by the United States. The idea of depopulating the land of blacks and repopulating it with white European immigrants had already been extensively discussed in the late eighteenth century by Thomas Jefferson and other North American leaders.

19. The translation of Fernández Retamar's essay demonstrates that nearly a century after Martí, an English equivalent to *mestizaje* still could not be found, and indigenous peoples were still being referred to with the depreciative "aborigines."

20. Robert Young notes that "hybridity" was chiefly used in the nineteenth century as a linguistic term. Contemporary theorists have found the term preferable to *mestizaje* because of its connotation of forced, rather than natural, union,

thus allowing for the inclusion of violence in a particular usage. See Young's enlightening discussions in *White Mythologies* and, in particular, *Colonial Desire*.

21. De la Campa argues that the traditional reading of transculturation as developed by both Ortiz and his successors, including Rama, has been one of positive synthesis, which provides for a kind of cultural cohesion in the face of postmodern dispersion. He suggests further that "deconstructive" readings of transculturation (Benítez-Rojo, Pérez Firmat, Moreiras) have come from the context of an entrenched academicism distant from everyday experience in Latin America ("Hibridez posmoderna y transculturación," 7). Certainly, there is much truth in his assertion that, as has been the case with other terms such as "magic realism" and "lo real maravilloso" (the marvelous real), "transculturation" has come to be an imprecise, generalized term used to refer to the autonomous and authentic nature of Latin American cultural expression ("Hibridez posmoderna y transculturación," 13–14). I argue for a reading and employment of "transculturation" and "transculture" that accent their inherent violence, as both a response to and a reconfiguration of the colonial (dis)encounter. Particularly in relation to the colonial period, transculturation is very often presented, not as a felicitous process, but as a horrific one. Ortiz writes, "The contact between the two cultures was terrible . . . failed transculturation for the Indians and radical and cruel transculturation for the newcomers" (*Contrapunteo cubano del tabaco y azúcar*, 88).

22. De la Campa ("Hibridez posmoderna y transculturación," 13–18) judges Rama's achievement to be the bringing of structuralist criticism into the terrain of hybridity previously defined more in scientific terms by Ortiz.

23. See the discussion of Richard and issues of hybridity in Mabardi ("Encounters of a Heterogeneous Kind").

24. This "extreme ambiguity" is very frequently missing in employments of the term. For example, in their revisionist essay on Mexico's colonial history, *The Forging of the Cosmic Race*, MacLachlan and Rodríguez argue that the colonial era was not principally a story of tragedy and exploitation, but of a "complex, balanced, and integrated economy that transformed the area into the most important and dynamic part of the Spanish empire" (1). Miscegenation "facilitated the formation of a hybrid, or mestizo, people in a biological as well as a cultural sense," and "aspects of native culture blended easily with Spanish traditions and provided the foundations for the new colonial society" (2).

25. De la Campa argues that the traditional reading of transculturation as developed by both Ortiz and his successors, including Rama, has been one of positive synthesis, which provides for a kind of cultural cohesion in the face of postmodern dispersion. He suggests further that "deconstructive" readings of transculturation (by Benítez-Rojo, Pérez Firmat, and Moreiras) have come from the context of an entrenched academicism distant from everyday experience in Latin America (7).

26. See also Catherine Poupeney-Hart, "Mestizaje: 'I Understand the Reality, I Just Do Not Like the Word.'"

27. For an overview of Bakhtin's impact on Latin American criticism, see Rita

de Grandis, "Pursuing Hybridity: From the Linguistic to the Symbolic" (*Unforeseeable Americas*, 208–225).

28. La Malinche, despite her very momentary appearance in colonial historiography, has been a subject of intense study for scholars interested in questions of Mexican and Chicano identity and gender issues. See Margo Glantz, *La malinche, sus padres y sus hijos;* Sandra Messinger Cypess, *La Malinche in Mexican Literature from History to Myth;* and Mary Louise Pratt, "'Yo Soy la Malinche': Chicana Writers and the Poetics of Ethnonationalism." Octavio Paz' well-known characterization of La Malinche as the mother of Mexican *mestizaje* and illegitimacy is taken up briefly in Chapter 1 here.

29. For example, Alejo Carpentier refers to America's "fecund mestizaje" in his essay "On the Marvelous Real in America" in the prologue to his novel *El reino de este mundo* (The Kingdom of This World), and he refers to the term again in a lecture entitled "The Baroque and the Marvelous Real," delivered in 1975. In "Derek Walcott and Alejo Carpentier: Nature, History, and the Caribbean Writer," David Mikics argues that in the work of Walcott, Carpentier, and others, "magical realism forms one aspect of a much larger strategy of cultural mixing— a creolizing or transculturation—that is central to much of what Vera Kutzinski has called 'New World writing'" (372). All three texts are also quoted in Zamora and Faris, *Magical Realism.*

CHAPTER 1

1. Although Vasconcelos' providential reading of *mestizaje* was related to the revolutionary struggle, as was the case with Bolívar and Martí, his participation was less that of *un hombre de armas y letras,* a man of arms and letters, than it was of an outspoken politician reacting to the volatile and frequently violent period following the Mexican Revolution. For a lengthy discussion of the period that includes Vasconcelos' response in several different moments, see Alan Knight's *La revolución mexicana.*

2. In his capacity as "maestro de América," Vasconcelos was one of the first intellectuals to initiate a pedagogical project that exceeded national concerns and resources. For example, he invited the celebrated Chilean poet Gabriela Mistral to participate in Mexico's educational reform (long before she was to win the Nobel Prize in Literature). Mistral used the occasion to focus on the intellectual needs of women, composing her *Lecturas para mujeres* (Readings for Women) while in Mexico. She also directed severe criticism at economic interests she deemed to be complicit with Yankee imperialism (Skirius, *José Vasconcelos,* 19).

3. For a detailed discussion of the historical context of Vasconcelos' bid for the presidency, see Skirius, *José Vasconcelos.*

4. This seems especially true, given that Anzaldúa's ideas have been included in a volume titled *Feminisms: An Anthology of Literary Theory and Criticism* (edited by Warhol and Herndl).

5. Despite comments on women in *The Cosmic Race* which seem demeaning or derogatory by contemporary standards, Vasconcelos enjoyed a loyal following among Mexican women, who applauded his educational reforms and participated in the political life of the nation in unprecedented numbers during the period he was secretary of education. Women suffragists also supported Vasconcelos' candidacy for president, prompting some analysts to speak of "Vasconcelian feminism" (Skirius, 124–125).

6. Jonathan Brennan takes up the problem of mestizo identity for Native Americans in the United States in his introduction to the essay collection *Mixed Race Literature* (2–3):

> In fact, for many mixed race members of marginalized communities, their attempts to assert a mixed race identity are often met with concern or derision because the marginalized community believes (often rightly) that it cannot afford to lose additional members in the face of centuries of sustained genocide (or allow unknown potential members to join), and that because the majority of the members of Native American and African American communities are of mixed race, such an assertion might lead to the disintegration of their communities (and/or nations), and to a disruption or dissolution of their cultural traditions, social fabric, and political power.

7. I attempt to read *Ceremony*, Leslie Marmon Silko's novel of mixed-blood experience alongside Latin American elaborations of *mestizaje* in Marilyn Miller, "Mixedblood Mediation and Territorial Re-Inscription in *Ceremony*."

8. In his autobiography, Vasconcelos acknowledges having abandoned the idea of an ideal *mestizaje* as early as 1927; see *El desastre*. Skirius discusses this change of heart as part of a larger process of Vasconcelos' distancing himself from the Left (21–22).

9. See Gobineau's comments on race mixture in relation to Brazil in Chapter 4.

CHAPTER 2

1. "So this, my green island, is you/an are too, am not over race/a not this, not that your pedigree/that makes you so Caribbean . . ./To drum rhythms you dance/your pretty not this, not that,/half of you Spanish,/the other African" (Palés Matos, *Selected Poems*, 73).

2. "Here we're all coffee with cream; some more coffee, others more cream."

3. Interestingly, Vasconcelos' comment valorizing mulatto identity was written in response to meeting Pedro Albízu Campos, the great Puerto Rican politician of the early twentieth century. Tremendously impressed with Albízu Campos, Vasconcelos noted that when he would comment on the leader's passionate vision and admirable work ethic, certain Puerto Ricans would respond, "Yes, but he's a mulatto . . . as if being mulatto weren't the most illustrious document of citizen-

ship in America" (Díaz Quiñones, *El arte de bregar,* 93). For a recent discussion of Albízu Campos, see Díaz Quiñones, "La Pasión, según Albízu," in *El arte de Bregar* (89-95).

4. I use "counterpoint" here as a broad translation of both *contrapunto* and *contrapunteo.* While both can refer in the musical sense to the "harmonious concordance of counterposed voices," the second term also implies the idea of confrontation, wrangling, friction (*Diccionario de las Américas,* 1973). I believe it is important to rescue this connotation in our reading of the English translation of Fernando Ortiz' *Contrapunteo cubano,* as well as in an understanding of the complex processes that exemplify transculturation and Caribbean *mestizaje.*

5. All these racial signifiers should be read in the context of Vasconcelos' simplification of each and their subsequent assimilation into his homogenizing fifth race, not as essential or essentializing categories.

6. "The dying-off of pre-Columbian populations because of contact with European disease was far more severe in the tropical lowlands than in any other part of the Americas. For all practical purposes it was complete for the Caribbean islands and coasts by the end of the sixteenth century, under the dual impact of African tropical diseases such as malaria and yellow fever and the endemic diseases of the Afro-Eurasian land mass such as measles, typhoid fever and smallpox. The correlation between places with this most serious mortality and those with the most intense slave regimes is close" (Curtin, "Slavery and Empire," 8).

7. As I discuss later in the chapter, "Sóngoro cosongo" is an untranslatable title, though clearly neo-African in tonality and rhythm. The explanation of this "African" term in the subtitle—"Mulatto Verses"—calls attention to the persistent slippage between notions of *negritud* and *mulatez* in works from the period.

8. "No ignoro, desde luego, que estos versos les repugnan a muchas personas, porque ellos tratan asuntos de los negros y del pueblo. No me importa. O mejor dicho: me alegra. Eso quiere decir que espíritus tan puntiagudos no están incluidos en mi temario lírico . . .

"Diré finalmente que éstos son unos versos mulatos. Participan acaso de los mismos elementos que entran en la composición étnica de Cuba, donde todos somos un poco níspero. ¿Duele? No lo creo. En todo caso, precisa decirlo antes de que lo vayamos a olvidar. La inyección africana en esta tierra es tan profunda, y se cruzan y entrecruzan en nuestra bien regada hidrografía social tantas corrientes capilares, que sería trabajo de miniaturista desenredar el jeroglífico.

"Opino por tanto que una poesía criolla entre nosotros no lo será de un modo cabal con olvido del negro. El negro—a mi juicio—aporta esencias muy firmes a nuestro cóctel."

9. "Palés never insisted on presenting himself as white, because he preferred to position himself as Puerto Rican, as Antillean, and as Caribbean. Nor did he ever present himself as black" (Ríos Ávila, *La raza cómica,* 147).

10. Ríos Ávila makes a similar argument for the close connection between a mulatto or black aesthetic and a focus on the body in relation to Luis Palés Matos'

Tuntún de pasa y grifería: "We can see in *Tun Tun* that founding a poetics of black-ness in a certain way is equivalent to founding a poetics of the body. What's inter-esting is to see how this legacy, this acquired prejudice, is transformed into an in-strument of rhetorical and, ultimately, ideological mobilization in Palés" (*La raza cómica*, 128).

11. The other version of Latin American *mestizaje* which is routinely written on the body of the mulatta concerns Brazil (see Chapter 4). Not surprisingly, Bra-zil is also the parallel case in terms of the need to incorporate a highly visible black population.

12. This investigation finds a kind of echo in the discussion of Ecuadorian *mes-tizaje* in Chapter 5, in which Freddy Ehlers associates the head of the Ecuadorian body with reason and the "North," that is, with whiteness.

13. Political events in Cuba may very well have played a role in this shift in Ortiz' thinking. In 1908, Afro-Cubans formed the Independent Party of Color and, within two years, boasted some sixty thousand members. An alarmed gov-ernment reacted to the armed protest of 1912 by massacring some three thousand to four thousand Afro-Cubans and imposing other severely repressive measures. Ortiz' works were used as reference works in further efforts to quash Afro-Cuban political expression in 1910 and 1920 by imprisonment and even lynching (Graham, 56). This Ortiz is clearly much less known or studied than Ortiz as the architect of transculturation.

14. Ortiz' *ajiaco* is reminiscent of the notion of the "melting pot theory" in the United States, the difference being that in the Caribbean example, the constitutive ingredients maintain their specific character and properties within the national composition, instead of "melting," or being absorbed.

15. For Salvador Bueno, this statistic calls for a definition of Cuba as Afro-American rather than Indo-American ("'La canción del bongó,'" 100).

16. Ada Ferrer argues that Martí's elaboration of "our mestizo America" did not use Cuba as a model: "Martí wrote of a mestizo America, but not quite of a mestizo Cuba. For him, as for others, racial union in Cuba was less the product of miscegenation than of masculine heroism and will" (*Insurgent Cuba*, 126). This distinction is relevant to a discussion of *mulatez*, since in this version of Cuban fusion defined by fraternity and masculinity, the contribution of women is more explicitly disregarded and excluded.

17. For a discussion of Hughes' influence on Guillén's early poetic project, see Miller, "(Gypsy) Rhythm and (Cuban) Blues."

18. While Cabrera Infante clearly wants to suggest that Guillén had distanced himself from overt association with Cuba's black community, other anecdotes sug-gest otherwise. Guillén told the group of authors assembled for the Second Inter-national Congress of Writers for the Defense of Culture, held in Madrid in 1937, "I come . . . as one exploited and persecuted, but also as a man who cares for his freedom and knows, like his racial brothers, that only by breaking down the walls

that exist between the present and the future, can he achieve it completely. I come as a black man" (Sardinha, 39).

19. The section title refers to Puerto Rico's nickname as the "Isla del Encanto," emblazoned—with multilevel irony—on the island's license plates.

20. For a more in-depth reading of Lloréns Torres, see the first section of Arcadio Díaz Quiñones' *El almuerzo en la hierba* (Lunch on the Grass), in which he comments on the unevenness of the poet's oeuvre, his influence on Palés Matos and other Puerto Rican poets, his insistence on poetry as a form of resistance and cultural retention in the face of the North American invasion, and his association of the national subject with the *jíbaro* (white country homesteader or farmer) as the "bastion of cultural and political resistance in the face of colonial power" (63). He does not study Lloréns Torres as a precursor of the development of *mulatez.*

21. Palés' poetry is extraordinarily difficult to translate, apparent in the English rendering of the title of his 1937 collection. That translation loses not only the rhythmic intensity of the original, but also the semantic density of *grifería*, which suggests more a mulatto aesthetic or identity, comparable, say, to *cubanía*, that is, *mulattoness* or perhaps *blackness*, more than "black things." *Grifería* is also a specifically Puerto Rican voicing of the idea, although the term *"grifo"* shows up in eighteenth-century Mexican caste paintings. Dictionaries define *grifo* variously as "fabulous animal, an eagle from the waist up, and a lion from the waist down" (*Diccionario de las Américas*), "curly, kinky hair," "griffin or griffon (mythical animal)," "offspring of a black and an Indian" (*Simon & Schuster's International Spanish Dictionary*), or "person with curly hair that indicates a mix of white and black" (*Real Academia Española*). The Real Academia lists specific meanings for Costa Rica, El Salvador, Honduras, Colombia, Mexico, Peru, and Cuba, but not for Puerto Rico.

22. In his introduction to the 1937 edition, Ángel Valbuena Prat notes that during the period in which he wrote the poems for this collection, Palés was also reading works by Vachel Lindsay and Langston Hughes, listening to work songs and Negro spirituals, and adapting forms he found in the work of Federico García Lorca. He also compares Pales' poems to the *plena*, a Puerto Rican rhythm built on African elements.

23. An overview of the reception of Palés Matos' early work can be found in López-Baralt's comprehensive introduction to the poet in the 1993 edition of *Túntun de pasa y grifería*. Unfortunately, many of the sources she cites are unavailable to the general researcher.

24. The second section of Ríos Ávila's 2002 text, "Hacia Palés," offers an excellent summary of key moments in the reading of Palés within his contemporary context as well as by later figures such as José Luis González.

25. Ríos Ávila expands on the relationship between Palés' poetry and dance in "El secreto de la danza" (*La raza cómica*, 163–172). Despite a comparison between minuet and metaphor which might seem an allusion to classical dance, he makes

clear that his reference is to popular, diasporic forms and notes that "in Palés, dance seems to emigrate from the head and establish its power in the *culo* [ass]. The dance is the dance of the *culo*, of the *culipandeo* [ass shaking]" (171).

26. Palés Matos defines "ten con ten" as a phenomenon "which supports itself, first in one thing, then in another; which is not firm, which maintains itself in pendular motion" (*La poesía de Luis Palés Matos*, 563).

27. These anxieties, revealed in *Insularismo*, are also portrayed, perhaps even more graphically, in the famous essay by Tomás Blanco, "Elogio de la plena" (In Praise of the *Plena*). A critic who lauded Palés' poetry and was himself the author of a book on racial prejudice in Puerto Rico, Blanco nevertheless felt it necessary to sustain that "Puerto Rico is the whitest of all the Antilles; we hardly have any pure blacks" (*Antología de ensayos*, 43).

28. Cotto performed in a November 9, 2002, event titled "¡Palés, Plena y Tapices!" at the Convento de los Dominicos in Old San Juan in a concert funded by the Instituto de Cultura Puertorriqueña.

29. My translation unavoidably erases many of the rich nuances of Ríos Ávila's original, particularly the play between *estar* and *ser* as distinct forms of being: "Un mundo cómico sería precisamente un mundo que se resiste a ser gobernado por los reclamos de la coherencia, un mundo abierto en el presente del indicativo, abocado al ahora abierto e incompleto del estar, no la futuridad utópica del ser."

30. The relatively early date of abolition in the Dominican Republic points to the relationship between historical events there and in neighboring Haiti, as well as important differences between the Dominican Republic and the other Spanish island colonies, where abolition was not declared until 1873 (Puerto Rico) and 1886 (Cuba).

31. Peter Roberts explores the relationship of the *indio* to the idea of the *raza latina* in Hostos and other Caribbean writers of the early twentieth century. See "The (Re)construction of the Concept of 'Indio' in the National Identities of Cuba, the Dominican Republic and Puerto Rico." In Puerto Rico, the Taínos are still hailed as a fundamental contributor to "national" culture, despite their virtual disappearance in the sixteenth century. When José Luis González suggested in his landmark essay *El país de cuatro pisos* (The Four-Story Country) that the African dimension constituted the ground floor of Puerto Rican "national" or cultural identity, many intellectuals countered with criticisms of the displacement of the "residual" Taíno element. Juan Flores has written, for example, that "the evidence is abundant in the literary, musical and pictorial arts of the nineteenth and twentieth centuries in the naming of children, places and events, and in the growing body of critical scholarship on Puerto Rican indigenous culture . . . Rather than 'archaic,' Taíno culture harbors an enduring 'residual' significance in the national history. In this sense, the indigenous culture may be considered the footing or foundation of the whole cultural construct" (*Divided Borders*, 66–67).

32. For an explanation of how *indigenismo* was tailored to the needs of a society

loathe to accept its African component, see Sagás, 34-35. He also provides an illuminating account (105-112) of how antiblack and anti-Haitian ideology were enlisted at the national level during the 1994 elections, when front-runner José Francisco Peña Gómez was accused of having Haitian ancestry, practicing voodoo and other "Satanic" acts, and harboring plans for unifying the Dominican Republic and Haiti. After his defeat, which came amid allegations of massive vote fraud, Peña Gómez reportedly stated that "Dominican society is not yet ready for a black president."

33. In Haiti, center of the most successful black resistance against colonial powers and a cultural environment in which the neo-African and the diasporic have remained constant despite cultural imperialisms, *mulatez* has been nuanced in a very particular manner. It is significant that Haiti becomes the stage on which foundational Caribbean concepts such as Alejo Carpentier's "marvelous real" have been played out. Anthony Maingot notes that, "in Haiti, strength against the white enemy from outside was found in organizing around race, even when internal struggles were organized according to color . . . Haitians, like all Caribbean peoples, have a capacity for underlining or silencing divisions of race and color, in search of a desired goal" ("Race, Color and Class in the Caribbean," 213).

34. Ortiz suggests that the African American church in the United States functioned similarly to the *cabildos de nación*, or politicoreligious societies, that different African ethnic and linguistic groups established in colonial Cuba (*Estudios etnosociológicos*, 146). He argues that, for a variety of reasons, including a lax attitude toward integration of blacks into the Catholic Church, neo-African religious practices and their reflection in literature had remained much more "uncontaminated" in Cuba than in North America. In the Caribbean, he notes, many slaveholders considered religious instruction both superfluous and dangerous, particularly the evangelical notions of human equality and redemption, which "signified a ferment of social justice which they hoped to avoid" (147), and not only were black churches unknown, but so also were black or mulatto priests (150).

35. Ortiz continues with a study of verses which focus on this topic, beginning with Guillén's "Sensemayá," which he considers mulatto poetry of "the most religious primitivism" ("La religión en la poesía mulata," 159). The rite of *sensemayá* is an individual spell from African witchcraft which is aesthetically renewed in the verse of Guillén, he explains. Since other critics have emphasized the African elements of a poem such as "Sensemayá" (Kutzinski, *Against the American Grain*), it is worth asking whether it is a valid example of "mulatto poetry," as Ortiz maintains, and whether "black poetry" and "mulatto poetry" can or should be distinguished from each other in early-twentieth-century Caribbean texts. The three essays show that for the self-proclaimed founder of Afro-Cuban studies, black and mulatto poetry were very nearly one and the same.

CHAPTER 3

1. The citation is from vol. 3 of Ramos Mejía's dense 1907 profile *Rosas y su tiempo* (Rosas and His Time), which discusses tango as a criminal activity associated with the Rosas era in Buenos Aires (Juan Manuel Rosas was named governor of Buenos Aires in 1829, and exerted substantial influence in Argentina for some three decades). In Ramos Mejía's portrayal, tango is primarily a dance associated almost exclusively with blacks. The original Spanish of the epigraph reads, "La luz, el humo y el hedor de la carne en ebullición, el continuo provocar de la desnudez torácica, el espasmo de los brazos, las danzas de vientre con sus variadas y cínicas localizaciones abdominales, acaban de enloquecer a la negrada. Es un tango infernal y peculiar . . . Hampa lo ha descripto y es realmente diabólico. Es el baile más lascivo que conoce la coreografía de las razas primitivas" (33–34).

2. "Culturescape" and "technoscape" are terms suggested by Appadurai in *Modernity at Large*.

3. Works focused on Gardel's role in the international growth of the tango include Grünewald, *Carlos Gardel, lunfardo e tango*); Bayardo, *Tango: De la mala vida a Gardel*; various texts by Gobello, including *Crónica general del tango*; and Zubillaga, *Carlos Gardel*, with a prologue by Jorge Luis Borges. Borges is studied as the only literary critic to seriously consider the tango phenomenon in the early twentieth century in Paoletti's "Borges y Gardel," published in the collection *El tango nómade* (2000), edited by Ramón Pelinski.

4. For an analysis of tango as a "cherished symbol of national identity," see John Chasteen's "Patriotic Footwork."

5. Tango's fundamental "illegitimacy" is noted by many critics. Carretero, for example, writes that the *conventillo* (flophouse or boardinghouse) and the brothel were for the tango what orphanages were for children who didn't know who their fathers were (*Tango*, 45).

6. David Foster's 1998 article focuses on the tango as a space which celebrates the cult of masculinity rather than the cult of *mestizaje*, masculinity that is "constantly under siege, continually threatened by often futile efforts to maintain its integrity" ("Tango, Buenos Aires, Borges," 179). In this environment, the tango functions as "an opportunity to play sexual monitor" (183). Tango "is both a highly complex conjunction of music, poetry, and dance while being at the same time a not particularly subtle enactment of masculinist violence," he writes (191–192).

7. Tomás de Lara and Inés Leonilda Roncetti de Panti, in *El tema del tango en la literatura argentina*, claim that the first tangos in verse appeared about 1917, after the musical and dance forms had circulated for a century or more.

8. Iris Zavala writes that the tango was understood to be "properly national" by 1903 (159), but Chasteen's work suggests that this identification was in process much earlier.

9. "*Bozal*" was also the name of the language spoken among Afro-Brazilian slaves, according to Rossi. The term was also generally used in the Spanish Carib-

bean during the colonial period to refer to recently arrived slaves who still had not mastered linguistic and other Creole cultural codes.

10. The phrase "cosas de negros" was a depreciative idiomatic expression used during this period to mean "nonsense" or "silliness."

11. Juan Carlos Cáceres provides his own interdisciplinary "study" of the black origins of tango in a 1999 recording titled "El tango, cosas de negros. Un argentino en París." Also a painter, Cáceres concurrently exhibited a series of forty paintings that "develop[ed] the topic of the presumed African root of the tango" in a gallery in the Latin Quarter in Paris (Nudler, "El tango," http://www.todotango.com /spanish/biblioteca/cronicas/negros.html).

12. To complicate matters, *milonga* is recognized by several tango historians as an Afro-Brazilian, or *bunda*, term which means words, discourse, or "hot air" (Rossi, 126, 139).

13. Chasteen provides another anecdote corroborating the interracial nature of such zones ("Patriotic Footwork," 16):

> The neighbors of one *academia* wrote angrily to the newspaper in 1855 that the dances kept them awake all night and that the two police officials on duty there were too distracted by dark-skinned señoritas to prevent the dances from ending with bloodshed. After one such skirmish, in which the guards themselves got into a fight over one of the dancers, bringing on a general mélee that spilled out into the street, one of the neighbors claimed to have found a woman's garter inscribed "For el Señor Comisario, with Thanks."

14. Zavala suggests a different, Europe-originated, trajectory for the tango, based on "well-known and documented facts (156–157): that the English country dance migrated to France at the end of the seventeenth century, and from there to America in the eighteenth, giving rise to its polemical counterpart, the Cuban *contradanza*, in the nineteenth, which, transformed into the *habanera*, remigrated to Europe and returned to the Platine area, and is at least, if not the mother, the cousin of the tango."

15. In 1943, a Boston publisher offered the Bernard Whitefield beginner's guide to playing the tango, conga, rumba, and samba for seventy-five cents (*Beginner's Book on the Tango, Conga, Rumba and Samba*). The introduction to the tango provides this history (iii; my emphasis): "The Tango of Argentina first became popular *in Europe* where it acquired various characteristics of Spanish Tangos and came to the United States a few years before World War I." The rumba "also came to us by way *of Europe*." All these rhythms are based on a 2/4 tempo, converted to 4/4 in U.S. transcription.

16. Carretero notes that public opinion toward mestizos in preindependence Argentina was generally negative, with abundant reference to mixed-blood persons as "vagabundos," "peste," "perdidos" (drifters, trash, losers), etc. (12).

17. Linguistic similarities between *candombé* and *candomblé*, the Afro-Brazilian corollary to Cuban *santería*, are obvious. The name for the same Yoruba deity

previously mentioned appears in Brazilian Portuguese as Xangô. A neo-African religion practiced by slaves and their descendants in the Pernambuco and Alagoas regions of Northeast Brazil is also known as Xangô ("Resources," http://project drum.com/news/article_35.html).

18. Slave traffic had been prohibited in 1812, and "libertad de vientres" (freedom of the womb) declared in 1813, but the slaves were not freed until 1843 (Rossi, 70).

19. This change is best demonstrated, perhaps, by the substitution in the early twentieth century of the drum, or *tambó*, with the European *bandoneón*, thus rendering a principally rhythmic form into a melodic one. According to Carretero, there are two main theories about the arrival of the *bandoneón*, a small concertina or accordion-like instrument, in the Río de la Plata: (1) it was introduced in 1870 by Bartolo, a Brazilian; or (2) it was introduced by Domingo Santa Cruz in the War of Paraguay between 1864 and 1870. In 1911, Albert Arnold began to produce *bandoneones* specifically for markets in Argentina and Uruguay, both home to new populations of German immigrants. In 1930 alone, twenty-five thousand instruments were exported to Argentina. See Mensing, Christian's bandoneon Web site.

20. For a discussion of blackface as one form of "racechange," or the complex negotiation of racial otherness within mainstream media, see Gubar.

21. Most historians view syncretic New World religious and cultural forms such as *candomblé*, *santería*, and *voudou* (spellings vary) as amalgamations that also incorporated, to a lesser degree, local indigenous beliefs and rituals.

CHAPTER 4

1. Werbner, "Introduction," 1.

2. Robert Stam has noticed this "jujitsu trait of turning strategic weakness into tactical strength" in several other aesthetic projects in Latin America, such as those developed around the notions of *lo real maravilloso*, *santería*, *tropicália*, and magic realism ("Palimpsestic Aesthetics," 59).

3. These comments are from a talk Freyre gave at the University of Sussex in June 1965 titled "The Racial Factor in Contemporary Politics." In the same speech, he noted that

> if a new Marx were to appear now, he might address himself to the increasing number of mestizos, dynamically cultural as well as dynamically racial, in the world telling them: "Mestizos of the world, unite yourself!" This hypothetical union would possibly mean, if it would grow from a more sociological fiction into something else, a new anti-racist presence in international politics. This presence might express itself as a correction of extremes of racial conflict in contemporary politics, and as a broad sociological substitute for a Pax Romana or for a Pax Britannica — classical forms of international political equilibrium based on the rule of a single, pure, or apparently pure, race, or of a single, or appar-

ently single, type of civilization, also emphatic about its purity, over all the other races of men and over their different cultures regarded as inferior by this or that imperial one. It would mean interpenetration—sociological and biological. And possibly the results of this double interpenetration, far from being uniformity, would be, for many of us, a most desirable combination of diversity with unity.

A transcript of the lecture is available at http://prossiga.bvgf.fgf.org.br/portugues /obra/opusculos/racial_factor.htm.

4. For a definition and literary history of anthropophagy, see Haroldo de Campos, "The Rule of Anthropophagy" (originally published in Portuguese as "Da razão antropofágica"; also appeared in Spanish in *Vuelta*, "De la razón antropofágica: Diálogo y deferencia en la cultura brasileña." I am grateful to Camilo Gomides for providing me with a range of bibliographic sources on anthropophagy.

5. It is not surprising that a common name for the phallus in Brazil is *pão*, stick, which conflates the idea of sexual domination with the term *pão brazil*, the wood exploited by the early explorers and the source of the country's name. Other terms, such as *caralho* (small stick), *madeira* (wood), *cacete* (club, cudgel), *vara* (pole, shaft, stick), and *arma* (weapon), emphasize the relationship between male sexuality and violence. Richard Parker writes in his perceptive study that "in the play of words, the phallus becomes, figuratively if not literally, an *arma*--a weapon, an instrument of metaphoric aggression, or . . . an extension of Pierre Bourdieu's expression of symbolic violence" (37).

6. The story has been adapted to both film and television (Manzatto, *Teologia e literatura*, 115). Amado notes that *Tent of Miracles, Dona Flor and Her Two Husbands*, and *Shepherds of the Night* were all filmed in Bahia in the same time period (*Navegação de cabotagem*, 360).

7. This is the concluding sentence of Cerqueira, *Pelourinho, centro histórico de Salvador, Bahia*, a book commemorating the restoration of the Pelourinho historical area in 1994 with grant money from UNESCO.

8. Rodrigues and other Brazilian intellectuals were generally cautious about comparing their country's situation to the "Negro problem" in the United States, but Manuel de Oliveira Lima, a career diplomat who lived in Washington, DC, in the 1890s, published a book in which he discussed this "problem" and compared the American South to the Brazilian North (Skidmore, *Black into White*, 71). Literary critic José Verísimo praised the work and consoled readers that

> there is no danger, as Sr. Oliveira Lima implies, that the Negro problem will arise in Brazil. Before it could arise it was already resolved by love. Miscegenation has robbed the Negro element of its numerical importance, thinning it down into the white population. Here the mulatto, beginning with the second generation, wants to be white and the white man, harboring no illusions and with some insignificant exceptions, welcomes, esteems, and joins with him. As ethnographers assure us, and as can be confirmed at first glance, race mixture is facilitating the

prevalence of the superior element. Sooner or later it will perforce eliminate the Negro race here. (*Jornal do Comercio* [Dec. 4, 1899])

9. After a trip into the interior of Mato Grosso, Roosevelt wrote that "the Brazilian of the future will be in blood more European than in the past, and he will differ in culture [from the European] only as the American of the North differs" (Skidmore, *Black into White*, 68–69).

10. Besides forging two temporally disparate moments, Amado also presents several "fused" characters. One of the minor characters in *Tent of Miracles* is Caetano Gil, a figure composed of poet-musicians Caetano Veloso and Gilberto Gil, both of whom have paid homage to Amado in various projects, including a collaborative album produced in 2000 that incorporates citations from Amado's works. Amado places Caetano Gil in a historical moment previous to the birth of either musician.

11. Certain other details are also true to life: Manuel's mother died of cholera, as did Pedro's, but is was Querino, and not his father, who served in the War of the Triple Alliance at the age of seventeen.

12. For a more complete bibliography, see Querino, *A raça africana e os seus costumes*, 13–16.

13. In the preface, the institute's director, Bernardino Souza, notes that he believes Querino to be the first scholar in Brazil to undertake a serious "historio-geographic" study of Bahia (19).

14. Writings by Auguste Compte were particularly influential in Brazil, and his name is also invoked in the novel.

15. Amado's celebration of Archanjo's sexual prowess is, of course, very reminiscent of Freyre's portrayal of the Portuguese explorers and conquistadors as sexually ravenous and the indigenous (and, later, black and mulatta) women as eager accomplices in this exercise of desire.

16. Skidmore notes that the period from 1969 to 1974 produced the "national security state" in its purest form (*The Politics of Military Rule in Brazil, 1964–85*, v; see especially Chapter 1).

17. Of course, there is also a serious side to such evocations. Amado took particular liberties with the character of Raymundo Rodrigues, the model for the arch-racist professor Nilo Argolo de Araújo. Amado attributes the titles of Rodrigues' works, such as *Os africanos no Brasil* (1945), to Araújo, but Amado develops their content "along much more exaggeratedly racist lines than Rodrigues ever wrote," according to Skidmore (*Black into White*, 240).

18. For a somewhat limited discussion of the mulatta in *Tent of Miracles*, see Steven V. Hunsaker, "Representing the Mulata."

19. *Tent of Miracles*' translator, Barbara Shelby, deserves praise for this rhymed rendering of Archanjo's replacement of "Hitler, luz do mundo" with "Hitler, puz do mundo" (*Tenda dos milagres*, 301), although she loses the element of repugnance in Amado's text.

20. Amado's novel makes specific reference to Lombrosian positivism, which holds that criminals represent a distinct anthropological type, are marked by physical and mental stigmata, and are the product of heredity. Such a formula was frequently applied to the mulatto as the epitome of these factors.

21. Of course, this characteristic "hybridity" was always subject to negotiations of economic and social power, just as "whiteness" was enmeshed in such negotiations in earlier periods of Brazil's history. Kátia M. de Queirós Mattoso, for example, writes that

> miscegenation and manumission—both aspects of social mobility—began early in Brazil and continued to be common throughout the seventeenth, eighteenth, and nineteenth centuries. It was common, moreover, for a slave without legal status to own one or more slaves. Actual practice was, in this respect at least, totally in contradiction with the law. Thus masters were found in every class of society. There were white masters, masters of mixed race, and black masters. Their behavior did not depend on their color or social position but on their quality as individuals. But for the slave the master—whether rich or poor, white or black—was always a "white" master, because to be "white" in Brazilian society meant to adopt certain superior attitudes, to wield a certain power. (*To Be a Slave in Brazil, 1550–1888,* 115)

22. Olodum also referred to Bahia as "Black Rome" and the religious retaking of the Tent of Miracles as a "return to life like the Phoenix, emerging out of the ashes to challenge the public with the spear of equality and the same passion" (http://www.uol.com.br/olodum/carnaval.htm).

23. For a more lengthy discussion of "Haiti" in the context of the 1993 annual musical festival Femadum, see Dunn, 193–194. I am grateful to Christopher Dunn for providing a transcript and sound file of the song.

24. See also Dunn's discussion of Veloso's "Sugarcane Fields Forever," in which he "alludes to an embodied history of miscegenation and cultural hybridity that constitutes his own identity." Dunn writes that "referring to racial, political, and regional identities, Veloso's self-affirmation as a 'democratic mulatto' from the Bahian coast implicitly called into question the pretensions of the military regime that disingenuously claimed to be democratic, while also alluding to the racial dimensions of any struggle for democracy in Brazil" (169).

25. Amado called *Tent of Miracles* his favorite book, and Pedro Archanjo his most complete character (Manzatto, 121).

CHAPTER 5

1. "Somos unos en América, y estamos, sin embargo, tan lejanos todos" (Carrión, *Obras,* 15). The citation is from the first page of Carrión's essay "Los creadores de la Nueva América," in which he highlights the contributions of José

Vasconcelos, Manuel Ugarte, F. García Calderón, and Alcides Arguedas. Vasconcelos is arguably the only figure of the four whose influence is still widely felt.

2. The collection *Siete ensayos de interpretación de la realidad peruana* (Seven Interpretive Essays of the Peruvian Reality), by José Carlos Mariátegui, first published in the 1920s, is considered a founding text in the establishment of the indigenist vanguard. For a contemporary summary of important events and documents related to *indigenismo*, see Alcina Franch, *Indianismo e indigenismo en América*.

3. I am deeply indebted to Julio Ramos, whose landmark *Desencuentros de la modernidad en América Latina: Literatura y política en el siglo XIX* (published as *Divergent Modernities* in 2001), provides a rich study of the use of *desencuentro* as a critical tool; and to Guillermo Bustos, who suggested, on a busy Quito street corner, that *desencuentro* was perhaps the only way to think about Ecuador's specific adherence to the cult of *mestizaje*.

4. The novel has not, to my knowledge, been translated.

5. Opening activities were originally scheduled for January of 2000. Due to the untimely death of Guayasamín in 1999 and subsequent delays, they were postponed; the event was celebrated in late November 2002, and guests included Ecuadorian president Gustavo Noboa, Venezuelan president Hugo Chávez, and Cuban president Fidel Castro, whose portrait Guayasamín painted on three occasions.

6. Ehlers' description suggests a certain intertextuality with Juan Montalvo's "Tercera lección al pueblo" (Third Lesson for the People), published in 1876. Ehlers' text is a parable of sorts, in which various parts of the body rebel: the arms weary of doing what the head ordered; the feet tire of being so low to the ground; the ears enjoy a superior position; and so on. The head secretly convenes with the heart and stomach, which together convince the other members and limbs of the importance of their specific functions, so that, ultimately, all submit, "humbly recognizing their error; and from that day they lived in harmony, cultivating peace, happy and content" ("Nacimiento de la nación," 219). Montalvo had extended the metaphor to the community, reminding the people that each member, priest, soldier, man of letters, artist, artisan, laborer, and the like, together make up civilization, and such stations are ultimately permanently fixed. For example, "The thoughts of the slave are as low as his fortune; his ordinary soul cannot be bettered; neither the best artist nor a divine magician could make of it the shadow of God" (in Roig, *El pensamiento social de Juan Montalvo*, 220).

7. Several critics have argued that this association of *mestizaje* with the male subject is also the case, to a certain extent, in Mexico, where celebration of an overwhelmingly male *mestizaje* stands in contrast to denigration of the female contribution to *mestizaje*, epitomized by La Malinche. Cervone recommends Melhuus' work on Mexico as an aid to reading the male construction of *mestizaje* in Ecuador.

8. Robles also considers Icaza a literary heir to José de la Cuadra, whose *Los monos enloquecidos* treats a similar problem of internal racial conflict among a cast

of characters in Guayaquil who deny or denigrate their own mestizo or mulatto character, "thus signaling a fundamental excision and crisis of identity" ("Review of Jorge Icaza, *El Chulla Romero y Flores*," 72).

9. Ojeda notes further, "For the first time in the literature of Ecuador, literary language forgets the model in order to hear only its own accent, to rock itself to the rhythm of the native passion, rough or primitive, but equally expressive and fecund and ready to receive the mark of poetry" (31).

10. Quichua is a highland Ecuadorian variant of Quechua, the lingua franca of the Inca empire. See Jaramillo de Lubensky, *Diccionario de ecuatorianismos en la literatura*, 174–175.

11. The *Diccionario de la Real Academia* lists Bolivia, Colombia, Ecuador, and Peru as areas in which the term refers to an object—"Dícese del objeto que usándose en número par, se queda solo"—and Bolivia, Ecuador, and Peru for the second meaning, "a middle-class person" (1992, 655). The *Diccionario de ecuatorianismos en la literatura* lists both usages as variants of Ecuadorian Quechua and offers several examples in the works of contemporary authors Jorge Enrique Adoum and Iván Egüez (50).

12. See, for example, Capilla del hombre Web site, http://www.capilladel hombre.com/index.html.

13. The bottle was sculpted in the shape of a woman from Chota, an Ecuadorian highland community with a significant population of African descent. A Web site advertising the rum described the women of the region as "statuesque, shapely, and sensual" (http://www.chiribogainvest.com/ronchota/english/botella.htm; accessed May 30, 2001; site discontinued). The site advertised a retail price of $1,200 per bottle.

14. I am indebted to Alemán for arranging this interview and for sharing her perspectives on Guayasamín and other elements of cultural life in Quito. Much of her fiction focuses on similar themes of fracture. See, for example, *Maldito corazón* and *Zoom*.

15. These comments are included in an essay titled "Como nací hace tres mil años . . ." (How I Was Born Three Thousand Years Ago . . .), in which Guayasamín speaks of his painting as a way of discovering who he is. He also claims to have carved the great door of the Compañía de San Francisco, a treasured building from Quito's colonial period,

> because in the three thousand years that I lived, while Rumiñahuy is persecuted by the Spaniards and I was helping him, I was in Mexico in those moments, five hundred years ago, and so I come to help him in Quito; of course, then they burned the city, and Rumiñahuy died, they hid the treasures and I stayed here, and of course everything changed and I went to work on the Compañía de San Francisco, to carve many of the altars that are in the temples, all of those made by us, who stayed here mixed, a little screwed [un poco jodidos], we stayed here to make things of the new civilization, but we did not forget ourselves.

The essay, with an audio link, was published at Vásquez Rubiños and Soca Pascual, "80 años de vida" (http://www.guegue.net/guayasamin/bloque.htm).

16. Camón Aznar's comment (*Oswaldo Guayasamín*, 159) is representative of the critical characterization of Guayasamín as an *indigenista* painter. It is doubly ironic, then, that Camón Aznar uses Michelangelo as the European model for the painter's success.

17. The structure that now adorns the site, La Virgen de Quito, is an embarrassment to many *quiteños*, especially artists, who consider it a baroque monstrosity. In some sense, the Chapel of Man represents a challenge to the artistic traditions embodied in the structure, traditions heavily influenced by European models.

EPILOGUE

1. The fragment comes from the end of a 1987 performance script titled "Califas," reprinted in *Warrior for Gringostroika*, 74.

2. Once again, the use of the word *mestizaje* and its poor bracketed translation, "miscegenation" demonstrate how the word's meaning still remains problematic in an English-language context.

3. The comment provides a nice intertextual interface with the connection between *mestizaje* and monstrosity taken up in Chapter 5 here.

4. The frequency of "*vato*" is interesting in these formations, given its older connotations of seer or wise man, alongside its contemporary range of meanings, which might include "greaser" or "thug."

5. For a discussion of the Spanish-only campaign in Puerto Rico as a version of the English-only position in the United States, see Carlos Pabón, *Nación postmortem*, especially "La imposible lengua apropiada," pages 89–103.

6. Despite its conceptual attractions, the reference to a Fourth World seems ultimately problematic in this engagement, precisely because the condition shared by its unified indigenous and migrant populations would seem to be landlessness, whether as a result of geographic dispersion due to economic pressures or to a lack of political and legal autonomy within the communities that harbor their own land-based livelihood and daily experience. Both communities experience landlessness, but in radically distinct ways. Bugajski defines "Fourth World" as follows (*Fourth World Conflicts*, 1):

> The term Fourth World has been employed by political scientists, sociologists, and economists to refer to the poorest and most powerless underdeveloped states or to the most underprivileged sectors of such countries. For the purposes of this study Fourth World will signify a whole range of tribal and peasant societies that often form the bulk of the population in Third World nations. In this context, a society is generally characterized as "indigenous" according to the following criteria: traditional rural habitation, a reliance on subsistence pur-

suits and local trading networks, together with extensive preservation of native social organization, culture, language, and religious life. Despite their great diversity, Fourth World societies share a number of attributes, including a low level of political and economic integration in the state system, an inferior political status, and an underprivileged economic position. Indigenous tribal groups may constitute minorities inhabiting peripheral or thinly populated areas, but the peasantry often forms the majority of the populace in developing agrarian countries.

7. In an essay included in *América Latina en su literatura*, Augusto Tamayo Vargas judges La Chingada and her relationship to Mexico's mestizo character to be the principal idea of *The Labyrinth of Solitude* ("Interpretaciones de América Latina," 446).

8. A hilarious and harrowing response to the phenomenon of postnational multicultural marketing can be found in Edgardo Bermejo Mora's *Marcos' fashion*, in which the United Colors of Benetton Company decides to use Zapatista resistance leader Subcommander Marcos as a model for its latest clothing line. Although the work is fictional, advertising executives, in fact, seriously considered using Marcos for at least one international publicity campaign.

9. The inclusion of a multiracial category on the 2000 U.S. Census was extremely controversial, perhaps most so for so-called ethnic and racial interest groups, who worried that citizens and legal residents who claimed multiracial identity would shrink the numbers and political power of their already marginalized "minority" constituencies. Although the inclusion of the multiracial category represents the first large-scale official attempt to recognize a phenomenon parallel to *mestizaje*, the resulting anxieties in both the "majority" and the "minority" sectors are evidence of continuing difficulties with integration of such a concept into the U.S. cultural consciousness.

10. While Gilroy's frame here is arguably Europe and the United States, or the English Atlantic, where *mestizaje* clearly suffered a different fate from that in Latin America, many of the conditions he describes were, in fact, products of European colonization in the Spanish colonies as well.

BIBLIOGRAPHY

Aguirre Rosas, Mario. *Gonzalo de Guerrero, padre del mestizaje iberomexicano.* Mexico City: Editorial Jus, 1975.

Alcina Franch, José, et al. *Indianismo e indigenismo en América.* Madrid: Alianza, 1990.

Alemán Salvador, María Gabriela. *Maldito corazón.* Quito: Editorial El Conejo; Banco del Progreso, 1996.

———. *Zoom: Cuentos.* Quito: Eskeletra Editorial, 1997.

Alleyne, Mervyn. *The Roots of Jamaican Culture.* London: Pluto Press, 1988.

Amado, Jorge. *Navegação de cabotagem.* Rio de Janeiro: Record, 1992.

———. *Tenda dos milagres.* Rio de Janeiro: Record, [1969] 1998.

———. *Tent of Miracles.* Trans. Barbara Shelby. New York: Alfred A. Knopf, 1971.

Andrews, George Reid. *The Afro-Argentines of Buenos Aires, 1800–1900.* Madison: University of Wisconsin Press, 1980.

Anzaldúa, Gloria. *Borderlands: The New Mestiza = La Frontera.* San Francisco: Spinsters/Aunt Lute, 1987.

———. "La Conciencia de la Mestiza: Towards a New Consciousness." In Robyn R. Warhol and Diane Price Herndl, eds., *Feminisms: An Anthology of Literary Theory and Criticism,* 765–775. New Brunswick, NJ: Rutgers University Press, 1997.

Appadurai, Arjun. *Modernity at Large: Cultural Dimensions of Globalization.* Minneapolis: University of Minnesota Press, 1996.

Arguedas, José María. *Canto Kechwa: Con un ensayo sobre la capacidad de creación artística del pueblo indio y mestizo.* Lima: Editorial Horizonte, 1989.

Avendaño de Vargas, Ernestina, and Elva Liliana Patiño. *Mestizaje en la literatura iberoamericana a partir de la raíz aborigen.* San Juan, Arg.: Universidad Nacional de San Juan, 1989.

Ayestarán, Lauro. *El folklore musical uruguayo.* Montevideo: Arca Editorial, 1968.

Bakhtin, M. M. *The Dialogic Imagination.* Ed. Michael Holquist, trans. Caryl Emerson and Michael Holquist. Austin: University of Texas Press, 1988.

Balderston, Daniel, Mike González, and Ana M. López, eds. *Encyclopedia of Contemporary Latin American and Caribbean Cultures.* New York: Routledge, 2000.

Ballagas, Emilio. *Obra poética.* Havana: Editorial Letras Cubanas, 1984.

Barney Cabrera, Eugenio. *La transculturación en el arte colombiano.* Bogotá: Escuela de Bellas Artes, Universidad Nacional de Colombia, 1962.

Basave Benítez, Agustín. *México mestizo: Análisis del nacionalismo mexicano en torno a la mestizofilia de Andrés Molina Enríquez*. Mexico City: Fondo de Cultura Económica, 1992.

Bayardo, Nelson. *Tango: De la mala vida a Gardel*. Montevideo: AGUILAR: Fundación Bank Boston, 2002.

Belnap, Jeffrey, and Raúl Fernández, eds. *José Martí's "Our America": From National to Hemispheric Cultural Studies*. Durham, NC: Duke University Press, 1998.

Benedetti, Mario. *Letras del continente mestizo*. Montevideo: Arca, 1967.

———, et al. *Nuestra América frente al V centenario: Emancipación e identidad de América Latina, 1492–1992*. Mexico City: J. Mortiz/Planeta, 1989.

Benítez-Rojo, Antonio. *The Repeating Island: The Caribbean and the Postmodern Perspective*. Durham, NC: Duke University Press, 1992.

Bermejo Mora, Edgardo. *Marcos' fashion: O de cómo sobrevivir al derrumbe de las ideologías sin perder el estilo*. Mexico City: Océano, 1996.

Berry, Brewton. "America's Mestizos." In Noel P. Gist and Anthony Gary Dworkin, eds., *The Blending of Races: Marginality and Identity in World Perspective*, 191–212. New York: Wiley-Interscience, 1972.

Bhabha, Homi K. *The Location of Culture*. London: Routledge, 1994.

Bilbao, Francisco. *El evangelio americano*. Caracas: Biblioteca Ayacucho, [1864] 1988.

Blanco, Tomás. *Antología de ensayos*. Mexico City: Editorial Orion, 1974.

———. *Sobre Palés Matos*. San Juan, PR: Biblioteca de Autores Puertorriqueños, 1950.

Bolívar, Simón. *The Hope of the Universe*. Paris: UNESCO, 1983.

———. *Selected Writings of Bolivar*. Comp. Vicente Lecuna; ed. Harold A. Bierck, Jr.; trans. Lewis Bertrand. Vol. 1: 1810–1822. New York: Colonial Press, 1951.

Brennan, Jonathan, ed. *Mixed Race Literature*. Stanford, CA: Stanford University Press, 2002.

Brindis de Salas, Virginia. *Pregón de Marimorena: Poemas*. Montevideo: Sociedad Cultural Editora Indoamericana, 1946.

Browning, Barbara. "The Daughters of Gandhi." In May Joseph and Jennifer Natalya Fink, eds., *Performing Hybridity*, 79–95. Minneapolis: University of Minnesota Press, 1999.

Bueno, Eva P., ed. *Imagination beyond Nation*. Pittsburgh: University of Pittsburgh Press, 1998.

Bueno, Salvador. " 'La canción del bongó': Sobre la cultura mulata de Cuba." *Cuadernos Americanos* 24 (Nov. 1975–Jan. 1976): 89–106.

Bugajski, Janusz. *Fourth World Conflicts: Communism and Rural Societies*. Boulder, CO: Westview Press, 1991.

Burgos, Julia de. *Song of the Simple Truth: The Complete Poems of Julia de Burgos*. Trans. Jack Agüeros. Willimantic, CT: Curbstone Press, 1997.

Burns, E. Bradford. "Introduction." In Manuel Raimondo Querino, *The African Contribution to Brazilian Civilization*, 1–11. Tempe, AZ: Center for Latin American Studies, 1978.

Buscaglia-Salgado, José F. "Impossible Nations: Body and Ideal in the Mulatto World of the Caribbean." PhD diss., State University of New York, Buffalo, 1998.

Caamaño de Fernández, Vicenta. *El negro en la poesía dominicana*. Santo Juan: Centro de Estudios Avanzados de Puerto Rico y el Caribe, 1989.

Cabral, Manuel del. *Obra poética completa*. Santo Domingo: Alfa y Omega, 1976.

Cabrera Infante, Guillermo. "Nicolás Guillén: Poet and Partisan." *Review: Latin American Literature and Arts* 42 (1990): 31–33.

Cámara, Madeline. "¿Dónde está la hija de Cecilia?" *Revista Hispano Cubana HC* (1998). http://www.hispanocubana.org/revistahc/paginas/revista8910/REVISTA6/ensayos/dondeesta.html (accessed Dec. 23, 2003).

Camón Aznar, José. *Oswaldo Guayasamín*. Barcelona: Ediciones Polígrafa, 1973.

Campos, Haroldo de. "Da razão antropofágica: A Europa sob o signo da devoração." *Colóquio-Letras* 62 (July 1981): 10–25.

———. "De la razón antropofágica: Diálogo y diferencia en la cultura brasileña." *Vuelta* 6 (July 1982): 12–19.

———. "The Rule of Anthropophagy: Europe under the Sign of Devoration." *Latin American Literary Review* 14, no. 27 (Jan.–June 1986): 42–60.

Candelier, Bruno Rosario. "Historia y mito en *Compadre Mon*." *Revista Iberoamericana* 142 (Jan.–Mar. 1988): 229–256.

Capilla del hombre Web site. http://www.capilladelhombre.com/index.html (accessed Jan. 6, 2004).

Cardoza y Aragón, Luis. *Poesías completas y algunas prosas*. Mexico City: Fondo de Cultura Económica, 1977.

Carpentier, Alejo. *Écue-yamba-ó!* Madrid: Editorial España, 1933.

———. *The Kingdom of This World*. Trans. Harriet de Onís. New York: Knopf, 1957.

———. *El reino de este mundo*. Barcelona: Seix Barral, [1946] 1988.

Carretero, Andrés M. *Tango: Testigo social*. Buenos Aires: Editorial J. A. Roca, 1996.

Carrión, Benjamín. *Obras*. Quito: Editorial Casa de la Cultura Ecuatoriana, 1981.

Carybé. *As sete portas da Bahia*. São Paulo: Martins, 1962.

Castro, Donald S. *The Argentine Tango as Social History, 1880–1955: The Soul of the People*. Lewiston, NY: Edwin Mellen Press, 1991.

Cerqueira, Nelson, ed. *Pelourinho, centro histórico de Salvador, Bahia: A grandeza restaurada*. Salvador, Brazil: Fundação Cultural do Estado da Bahia, 1995.

Cervone, Emma. "Machos, Mestizos and Ecuadorians: The Ideology of Mestizaje and the Construction of Ecuadorian National Identity." Paper delivered at the Latin American Studies Association conference, Mar. 16–18, 2000, Miami.

———, and Fredy Rivera Vélez. *Ecuador racista*. Quito: FLACSO, 1999.

Chamberlain, Bobby J. *Jorge Amado*. Boston: Twayne Publishers, 1990.

Chanady, Amaryll. "Latin American Discourses of Identity and the Appropriation of the Amerindian Other." *Sociocriticism* 6, nos. 11–22 (1990): 33–48.

Chasteen, John. "African American Choreographical Matrix." *Journal of Latin American Studies* 28 (Feb. 1996): 29–47.

———. "Patriotic Footwork: Social Dance, Popular Culture and the Watershed of Independence in Buenos Aires." *Journal of Latin American Cultural Studies* 5, no. 1 (1996): 11–24.

Chávez González, Rodrigo A. *El mestizaje y su influencia social en América*. Guayaquil: Imprenta y Talleres Municipales, 1937.

Clark, Vèvè A. "Developing Diaspora Literacy and Marasa Consciousness." In Hortense J. Spillers, ed., *Comparative American Identities: Race, Sex, and Nationality in the Modern Text*, 40–61. New York: Routledge, 1991.

Cornejo-Polar, Antonio. *Escribir en el aire: Ensayo sobre la heterogeneidad sociocultural en las literaturas andinas*. Lima: Editorial Horizonte, 1994.

———. *The Multiple Voices of Latin American Literature*. Berkeley: Doe Library, University of California, 1994.

———. "A Non-Dialectic Heterogeneity: The Subject and Discourse of Urban Migration in Modern Peru." In Rita De Grandis and Zilà Bernd, eds., *Unforeseeable Americas: Questioning Cultural Hybridity in the Americas*, 112–123. Critical Studies 13. Amsterdam: Rodopi, 2000.

Corrales Pascual, Manuel. "Introduction." In Jorge Icaza, *El chulla Romero y Flores*, ed. Manuel Corrales Pascual, 13–29. Quito: Libresa, 1985.

———. *Jorge Icaza: Frontera del relato indigenista*. Quito: Centro de Publicaciones de la Pontificia Universidad Católica del Ecuador, 1974.

Cueva, Agustín. *Jorge Icaza*. Buenos Aires: Centro Editor de América Latina, 1968.

Curtin, Philip D. "Slavery and Empire." In Vera Rubin and Arthur Tuden, eds., *Comparative Perspectives on Slavery in New World Plantation Societies*, 4–11. New York: New York Academy of Sciences, 1977.

Cypess, Sandra Messinger. *La Malinche in Mexican Literature from History to Myth*. Austin: University of Texas Press, 1991.

De Beer, Gabriella. *José Vasconcelos and His World*. New York: Las Américas Publishing, 1966.

De Castro, Juan E. *Mestizo Nations: Culture, Race, and Conformity in Latin American Literature*. Tucson: University of Arizona Press, 2002.

Degler, Carl N. *Neither Black nor White: Slavery and Race Relations in Brazil and the United States*. New York: Macmillan, 1971

De Grandis, Rita, and Zilà Bernd, eds. *Unforeseeable Americas: Questioning Cultural Hybridity in the Americas*. Critical Studies 13. Amsterdam: Rodopi, 2000.

De la Campa, Román. "Hibridez posmoderna y transculturación: Políticas de montaje en torno a Latinoamérica." *Hispamérica* 69 (1994): 3–22.

Díaz Quiñones, Arcadio. *El almuerzo en la hierba*. San Juan, PR: Ediciones Huracán, 1982.

————. *El arte de bregar.* San Juan, PR: Ediciones Callejón, 2000.

Domínguez, Jorge I., ed. *Race and Ethnicity in Latin America.* New York: Garland Publishing, 1994.

Domínguez Michael, Christopher. "Estudio preliminar, selección, notas, cronología y bibliografía." In José Vasconcelos, *Obra selecta,* 9–47. Caracas: Biblioteca Ayacucho, 1992.

Dunn, Christopher. *Brutality Garden: Tropicália and the Emergence of a Brazilian Counterculture.* Chapel Hill: University of North Carolina Press, 2001.

Dworkin, Anthony Gary. "The Peoples of La Raza: The Mexican-Americans of Los Angeles." In Noel P. Gist and Anthony Gary Dworkin, eds., *The Blending of Races: Marginality and Identity in World Perspective,* 167–190. New York: Wiley-Interscience, 1972.

Dzidzienyo, Anani. *The Position of Blacks in Brazilian Society.* London: Minority Rights Group, 1971.

Earle, Peter G. "Utopía, Universópolis, Macondo." *Hispanic Review* 50 (1982): 143–157.

Ehlers, Freddy. "Nacimiento de la nación." Unpublished, Quito, 1995.

Espinosa Apolo, Manuel. *Los mestizos ecuatorianos.* Quito: Centro de Estudios Felipe Guamán Poma de Ayala, 1995.

Esteva-Fábregat, Claudio. *El mestizaje en Iberoamérica.* Madrid: Revista de Indias, 1964.

Fajardo Estrada, Ramón. *Rita Montaner: Testimonio de una época.* Havana: Casa de las Américas, 1997.

Faulkner, William. *Absalom, Absalom!* New York: Random House, [1936] 1986.

Fernández MacGrégor, Genaro, ed. *Vasconcelos.* Mexico City: Ediciones de la Secretaría de Educación Pública, 1942.

Fernández Retamar, Roberto. *Caliban and Other Essays.* Trans. Edward Baker. Minneapolis: University of Minnesota Press, 1989.

Fernándiz Alborz, Francisco. "El novelista hispanoamericano Jorge Icaza." In *Jorge Icaza: Obras escogidas,* 9–71. Mexico City: Aguilar, 1961.

Ferrer, Ada. *Insurgent Cuba: Race, Nation, and Revolution, 1868–1898.* Chapel Hill: University of North Carolina Press, 1999.

Fink, Jennifer Natalya. "Conclusion. Pushing through the Surface: Notes on Hybridity and Writing." In May Joseph and Jennifer Natalya Fink, eds., *Performing Hybridity,* Minneapolis: University of Minnesota Press, 1999.

Fisher, Abby Sue. "Mestizaje and the Cuadros de Castas: Visual Representations of Race, Status, and Dress in Eighteenth Century Mexico." PhD diss., University of Minnesota, 1992.

Flores, Juan. *Divided Borders: Essays on Puerto Rican Identity.* Houston: Arte Público Press, 1993.

Foster, David William. *Para una lectura semiótica del ensayo latinoamericano: Textos representativos.* Madrid: Studia Humanitatis, 1983.

————. "Tango, Buenos Aires, Borges: Cultural Production and Urban Sexual

Regulation." In Eva P. Bueno and Terry Caesar, eds., *Imagination beyond Nation: Latin American Popular Culture*, 167–192. Pittsburgh: University of Pittsburgh Press, 1998.

Foster, Thomas. "Cyber-Aztecs and Cholo-Punks: Guillermo Gómez-Peña's Five-Worlds Theory." *PMLA* 117, no. 1 (Jan. 2002): 43–67.

Franco Pichardo, Franklin. *Sobre racismo y antihaitianismo (y otros ensayos)*. Santo Domingo: Impresora Vidal, 1997.

Fraser Delgado, Celeste, and José Esteban Muñoz, eds. *Everynight Life: Culture and Dance in Latin/o America*. Durham, NC: Duke University Press, 1997.

Freyre, Gilberto. *Casa-grande e senzala: Formação da família brasileira sob o regime da economia patriarcal*. 20th ed. Rio de Janeiro: Livraria José Olympio Editora, [1933] 1980.

———. *The Masters and the Slaves: A Study in the Development of Brazilian Civilization*. Trans. Samuel Putnam. New York: Alfred A. Knopf, 1964.

———. "Negritude, mística sem lugar no Brasil." Interview with Gilberto Freyre in the *Estado de Sao Paulo. Boletim do Conselho Federal de Cultura* 1, no. 2 (Apr.–June 1971): 16–23; accessed at http://prossiga.bvgf.fgf.org.br/portugues/obra /artigos/cientificos/negritude_mistica.html.

———. *Order and Progress*. Ed. and trans. Rod W. Horton. Berkeley & Los Angeles: University of California Press, 1986.

———. "The Racial Factor in Contemporary Politics." Published for the Research Unit for the Multi-Racial Societies at the University of Sussex by Mac-Gibbon & Kee, 1966.

García Canclini, Néstor. *Hybrid Cultures: Strategies for Entering and Leaving Modernity*. Trans. Christopher L. Chiappari and Silvia L. López. Minneapolis: University of Minnesota Press, 1995.

García Icazbalceta, Joaquín. *Obras biográficas*. Mexico City: Antigua Librería Andrade y Morales, 1875.

García Jiménez, Francisco. *Así nacieron los tangos*. Buenos Aires: Editorial Losada, 1965.

García Saiz, María Concepción. *Las castas mexicanas: Un género pictórico americano = The Castes: A Genre of Mexican Painting*. [Italy]: Olivetti, 1989.

Garcilaso de la Vega, el Inca. *Comentarios reales*. 2nd ed. Mexico City: Editorial Porrúa, 1990.

Gilroy, Paul. *Against Race: Imagining Political Culture beyond the Color Line*. Cambridge, MA: Harvard University Press, 2000.

Gist, Noel P., and Anthony Gary Dworkin, eds. *The Blending of Races: Marginality and Identity in World Perspective*. New York: Wiley-Interscience, 1972.

Glantz, Margo, ed. *La Malinche, sus padres y sus hijos*. Mexico City: Facultad de Filosofía y Letras, Universidad Nacional Autónoma de México, 1994.

Glissant, Édouard. *Caribbean Discourse: Selected Essays*. Trans. J. M. Dash. Charlottesville: University Press of Virginia, [1981] 1989.

———. *Poetics of Relation.* Trans. Betsy Wing. Ann Arbor: University of Michigan Press, [1990] 1997.

Gobello, José. *Crónica general del tango.* Buenos Aires: Editorial Fraterna, 1980.

———. *Letras de tango: Selección (1897–1981).* Buenos Aires: Ediciones Nuevo Siglo, 1995.

———. "Lunfardo". In "El sur del sur." http://www.surdelsur.com/letras/lunfa /index.htm (accessed Jan. 27, 2004).

Gomes, Marco Aurélio Andrade de Filgueiras, org. *Pelo Pelô: História, cultura e cidade.* Salvador, Brazil: Editora da Universidade Federal da Bahia, 1995.

Gómez-Peña, Guillermo. *Dangerous Border Crossers.* New York: Routledge, 2000.

———. "The New World (B)order: A Work in Progress." *Third Text* 21 (Winter 1992–1993): 71–79.

———. *The New World Border.* San Francisco: City Lights, 1996.

———. *Warrior for Gringostroika: Essays, Performance Texts, and Poetry.* St. Paul, MN: Graywolf Press, 1993.

———, and Roberto Sifuentes. *Temple of Confessions: Mexican Beasts and Living Santos.* New York: powerHouse Books, 1996.

González, José Luis. "Literatura e identidad nacional en Puerto Rico." In *Puerto Rico: Identidad nacional y clases sociales: Coloquio de Princeton,* 45–79. Río Piedras, PR: Ediciones Huracán, 1979.

———. *El país de cuatro pisos y otros ensayos.* Río Piedras, PR: Huracán, 1980.

Graham, Richard, ed. *The Idea of Race in Latin America, 1870–1940.* Austin: University of Texas Press, [1990] 1999.

Grünewald, José Lino. *Carlos Gardel, lunfardo e tango.* Rio de Janeiro: Editora Nova Fronteira, 1994.

Gruzinski, Serge. *El pensamiento mestizo.* Trans. E. Folch González. Barcelona: Paidós, 2001.

Guayasamín, Oswaldo. *Algunas claves para Guayasamín.* Quito: Caspicara, 1972.

———. *Huacayñán: El camino del llanto = The Way of Tears.* Quito: Casa de la Cultura Ecuatoriana, 1953.

———. Interview, with María Gabriela Alemán, Dec. 10, 1996.

———. *Oswaldo Guayasamín.* Barcelona: Ediciones Nauta, 1992.

Gubar, Susan. *Racechanges: White Skin, Black Face in American Culture.* Oxford: Oxford University Press, 1997.

Guillén, Nicolás. *Cuba libre: Poems by Nicolás Guillén.* Trans. Langston Hughes and Ben Frederic Carruthers. Los Angeles: Ward Ritchie Press, 1948.

———. *Motivos de son.* Havana: Rambla, Bouza y Cía., 1930.

———. *El son entero.* In *Suma poética 1929–1946.* Buenos Aires: Editorial Pleamar, 1947.

———. *Sóngoro cosongo: Poemas mulatos.* Havana: Ucar, García y Cía., [1931] 1934.

———. *Summa poética.* Madrid: Cátedra, 1995.

Guzmán Ch., Jorge. *Contra el secreto profesional: Lectura mestiza de César Vallejo.* Santiago de Chile: Editorial Universitaria, 1991.

Handelsman, Michael. *Lo afro y la plurinacionalidad: El caso ecuatoriano visto desde su literatura.* University, MS: Romance Monographs, 1999.

Hernández, Luis Arturo. "Oswaldo Guayasamín: América, aparta de mí este cáliz." *Luke* (Sept. 2001) (http://www.espacioluke.com/Setiembre2001/Luis arturo-arte.html; accessed Dec. 23, 2003).

Hernández Franco, Tomás. *Apuntes sobre poesía popular y poesía negra en las Antillas.* San Salvador: Ateneo de El Salvador, 1942.

Herren, Ricardo. *Doña Marina, La Malinche.* Mexico City: Planeta, 1993.

Hoeg, Jerry. "Cultural Counterpoint: Antonio Benítez Rojo's Postmodern Transculturation." *Journal of Latin American Cultural Studies* 6, no. 1 (June 1997): 65–75.

Hughes, Langston. *The Collected Poems of Langston Hughes.* Ed. Arnold Rampersad. New York: Knopf, 1994.

———. *The Weary Blues.* New York: Knopf, 1926.

Hunsaker, Steven V. "Representing the Mulata: *El amor en los tiempos del cólera* and *Tenda dos milagres.*" *Hispania* 77 (May 1994): 225–234.

Icaza, Jorge. *El chulla Romero y Flores.* Ed. Manuel Corrales Pascual. Quito: Libresa, [1958] 1985.

———. *El chulla Romero y Flores.* Ed. Ricardo Descalzi, Renaud Richard. Nanterre, France: ALLCA XX, 1988.

———. *Huasipungo.* Bogotá: Editorial Oveja Negra, [1934] 1985.

Instituto Panamericano de Geografía e Historia. Comisión de Historia. *El mestizaje en la historia de Ibero-América.* Mexico City: Editorial Cultura, 1961.

Jaén, Dider T. "Introduction." *The Cosmic Race: A Bilingual Edition.* Baltimore: The Johns Hopkins University Press, [1979] 1997.

James, Conrad, and John Perivolaris, eds. *The Cultures of the Hispanic Caribbean.* Gainesville: University Press of Florida, 2000.

Jaramillo de Lubensky, María. *Diccionario de ecuatorianismos en la literatura.* Quito: Casa de la Cultura Ecuatoriana, 1992.

Joseph, May, and Jennifer Natalya Fink, eds. *Performing Hybridity.* Minneapolis: University of Minnesota Press, 1999.

Knight, Alan. *La revolución mexicana: Del porfiriato al nuevo régimen constitucional.* Mexico City: Grijalbo, [1986] 1996.

Knight, Franklin W. *Race, Ethnicity, and Class: Forging the Plural Society in Latin America and the Caribbean.* Waco, TX: Baylor University Press, Markham Press Fund, 1996.

Kusch, Rodolfo. *La seducción de la barbarie: Análisis herético de un continente mestizo.* Buenos Aires: Editorial Raigal, 1953.

Kutzinski, Vera M. *Against the American Grain: Myth and History in William Carlos Williams, Jay Wright, and Nicolás Guillén.* Baltimore: The Johns Hopkins University Press, 1987.

———. *Sugar's Secrets: Race and the Erotics of Cuban Nationalism.* Charlottesville: University Press of Virginia, 1993.

Lanuza, José Luis. *Morenada*. Buenos Aires: Emecé Editores, 1946.

Lara, Tomás de, and Inés Leonilda Roncetti de Panti. *El tema del tango en la literatura argentina*. Buenos Aires: Ediciones Culturales Argentinas, 1961.

Lara Martínez, Rafael. *Salarrué o el mito de la creación de la sociedad mestiza salvadoreña*. San Salvador: Dirección de Publicaciones e Impresos, 1991.

Larsen, Neil. *Reading North by South: On Latin American Literature, Culture, and Politics*. Minneapolis: University of Minnesota Press, 1995.

Lhamon, W. T. *Raising Cain: Blackface Performance from Jim Crow to Hip Hop*. Cambridge, MA: Harvard University Press, 1998.

Lienhard, Martin. "Of Mestizajes, Heterogeneities, Hybridisms and Other Chimeras: On the Macroprocesses of Cultural Interaction in Latin America." *Journal of Latin American Cultural Studies* 6, no. 2 (Nov. 1997): 183–200.

———. *La voz y su huella: Escritura y conflicto étnico-social en América Latina (1492–1988)*. Havana: Casa de las Américas, 1990.

Lionnet, Françoise. *Autobiographical Voices: Race, Gender, Self-Portraiture*. Ithaca, NY: Cornell University Press, 1989.

Lipschutz, Alejandro. *El problema racial en la conquista de América, y el mestizaje*. Santiago de Chile: Editorial Andrés Bello, 1967.

Lott, Eric. *Love and Theft: Blackface Minstrelsy and the American Working Class*. New York: Oxford University Press, 1993.

Lovell, Peggy A., and Charles H. Wood. "Skin Color, Racial Ideology, and Life Chances in Brazil." *Latin American Perspectives* 25, no. 3 (May 1998): 90–109.

Mabardi, Sabine. "Encounters of a Heterogeneous Kind: Hybridity in Cultural Theory." In Rita De Grandis and Zilà Bernd, eds., *Unforeseeable Americas: Questioning Cultural Hybridity in the Americas*, 1–20. Critical Studies 13. Amsterdam: Rodopi, 2000.

MacLachlan, Colin M., and Jaime E. Rodríguez O. *The Forging of the Cosmic Race: A Reinterpretation of Colonial Mexico*. Berkeley & Los Angeles: University of California Press, 1981.

Maingot, Anthony. "Race, Color and Class in the Caribbean." In Alfred Stepan, ed. *Americas: New Interpretive Essays*, 220–247. New York: Oxford University Press, 1992.

Mallon, Florencia E. "Constructing Mestizaje in Latin America: Authenticity, Marginality, and Gender in the Claiming of Ethnic Identities." *Journal of Latin American Anthropology* 2, no. 1 (Fall 1996): 170–181.

Manus, Carlos A. "El tango." *Gaceta Iberoamericana* (Jan.-Feb. 1999): 14–16.

Manzatto, Antonio. *Teologia e literatura: Reflexão teológica a partir da antropologia contida nos romances de Jorge Amado*. São Paulo: Edições Loyola, 1994.

Mariátegui, José Carlos. *Siete ensayos de interpretación de la realidad peruana*. Caracas: Biblioteca Ayacucho, 1979.

———. *Temas de nuestra América*. Lima: Editorial Amauta, 1960.

Marras, Sergio. *América Latina, marca registrada: (Conversaciones con Jorge Amado*

... *et al./sostenidas con Sergio Marras).* Chile: Editorial A. Bello; Buenos Aires: Ediciones B, Grupo Zeta; Mexico City: Universidad de Guadalajara, 1992.

Martí, José. *José Martí Reader: Writings on the Americas.* Ed. Deborah Shnookal and Mirta Muñiz. Melbourne: Ocean Press, 1999.

———. *Our America: Writings on Latin America and the Struggle for Cuban Independence.* Trans. Elinor Randall; additional trans. Juan de Onís and Roslyn Held Foner; ed., intro., notes Philip S. Foner. New York: Monthly Review Press, 1977.

Martínez-Echazábal, Lourdes. *Para una semiótica de la mulatez.* Madrid: Ediciones José Porrúa Turanzas, 1990.

Masiello, Francine. *The Art of Transition: Latin American Culture and Neoliberal Crisis.* Durham, NC: Duke University Press, 2001.

———. *Between Civilization & Barbarism: Women, Nation, and Literary Culture in Modern Argentina.* Lincoln: University of Nebraska Press, 1992.

Mattoso, Kátia M. de Queirós. *To Be a Slave in Brazil, 1550–1888.* Trans. Arthur Goldhammer. New Brunswick, NJ: Rutgers University Press, 1986.

McNeill, William H. *Keeping Together in Time: Dance and Drill in Human History.* Cambridge, MA: Harvard University Press, 1995.

Melhuus, Marit, and Kristi Anne Stølen, eds. *Machos, Mistresses, Madonnas: Contesting the Power of Latin American Gender Imagery.* London: Verso, 1996.

Mensing, Christian. Christian's bandoneon Web site. http://laue.ethz.ch/cm/band/node1.html (accessed Jan. 27, 2004).

Mignolo, Walter D. "Linguistic Maps, Literary Geographies, and Cultural Landscapes: Languages, Languaging, and (Trans)nationalism." *Modern Language Quarterly* 57 (June 1996): 181–196.

———. *Local Histories/Global Designs: Coloniality, Subaltern Knowledges, and Border Thinking.* Princeton, NJ: Princeton University Press, 2000.

Mikics, David. "Derek Walcott and Alejo Carpentier: Nature, History, and the Caribbean Writer." In Lois P. Zamora and Wendy B. Faris, eds., *Magical Realism: Theory, History, Community,* 371–404. Durham, NC: Duke University Press, 1995.

Miller, Marilyn. "(Gypsy) Rhythm and (Cuban) Blues: The Neo-American Dream in Guillén and Hughes." *Comparative Literature* 51 (1999): 324–342.

———. "Mixedblood Mediation and Territorial Re-Inscription in *Ceremony.*" *Meridians* 1 (2000): 157–178.

Montecino, Sonia. *Madres y huachos: Alegorías del mestizaje chileno.* Santiago: Editorial Cuarto Propio, 1991.

Morales, Jorge Luis. *Poesía afroantillana y negrista: Puerto Rico, República Dominicana, Cuba.* Río Piedras, PR: Editorial Universitaria, 1976.

Moraga, Cherríe, and Gloria Anzaldúa, eds. *This Bridge Called My Back: Writings by Radical Women of Color.* New York: Kitchen Table, Women of Color Press, 1983.

Morales Benítez, Otto. *Memorias del mestizaje.* Bogotá: Plaza y Janes, 1984.

Mörner, Magnus. "El mestizaje en la historia de Ibero-América: Informe preliminar." In Instituto Panamericano de Geografía e Historia, Comisión de Historia, *El mestizaje en la historia de Ibero-América*, 11–51. Mexico City: Editorial Cultura, 1961.

―――. *Race Mixture in the History of Latin America*. Boston: Little, Brown, 1967.

Morrison, Toni. *Playing in the Dark: Whiteness and the Literary Imagination*. Cambridge, MA: Harvard University Press, 1992.

Morson, Gary Saul, ed. *Bakhtin: Essays and Dialogues on His Work*. Chicago: University of Chicago Press, 1986.

Mumford, Kevin J. *Interzones: Black/White Sex Districts in Chicago and New York in the Early Twentieth Century*. New York: Columbia University Press, 1997.

Museo de Monterrey, San Antonio Museum of Art, and Museo Frantz Mayer. *La pintura de castas*. Mexico City: Artes de México, 1990.

Nano Lottero, Rómulo. *Palabras para América*. [Montevideo]: [Imprenta Nacional Colorada], 1931.

Nascimento, Abdias do. *Brazil, Mixture or Massacre?: Essays in the Genocide of a Black People*. Trans. Elisa Larkin Nascimento. Dover, MA: Majority Press, 1989.

Natale, Oscar. *Buenos Aires, negros y tangos*. Buenos Aires: Peña Lillo, 1984.

Nicotra Di Leopoldo, G. *Pensamientos inéditos de José Vasconcelos*. Mexico City: Ediciones Botas, 1970.

Nudler, Julio. "El tango. Cosa de negros. El último CD de Juan Carlos Cáceres. Un argentino en París." From *Tres Puntos* (May 1999) (http://www.todotango .com/spanish/biblioteca/cronicas/negros.html; accessed Jan. 27, 2004).

Ojeda, Enrique. *Cuatro obras de Jorge Icaza*. Quito: Casa de la Cultura Ecuatoriana, 1961.

Olinto, Antônio. " 'Tenda dos Milagres,' magia e revolução na literatura de língua portuguêsa." In *Jorge Amado, povo e terra*, 203–209. São Paulo: Livraria Martins, 1972.

Ordaz, Luis. *Inmigración, escena nacional y figuraciones de la tanguería*. Buenos Aires: Editores de América Latina, 1997.

Ortega, Julio. "Nacimiento del discurso crítico." *Cuadernos Americanos* 3, no. 18 (Nov.–Dec. 1989): 178–189.

Ortega y Medina, Juan A. *Reflexiones históricas*. Mexico City: Consejo Nacional para la Cultura y las Artes, 1993.

Ortiz, Fernando. *Contrapunteo cubano del tabaco y azúcar*. Havana: Editorial de Ciencias Sociales, [1940] 1983.

―――. *Cuban Counterpoint: Tobacco and Sugar*. Trans. Harriet de Onís. Durham, NC: Duke University Press, 1995.

―――. *Estudios etnosociológicos*. Comp. Isaac Barreal Fernández. Havana: Editorial de Ciencias Sociales, 1991.

―――. *Hampa afro-cubana: Los negros brujos*. Prol. C. Lombrosio. Madrid: Librería de F. Fe, 1906.

―――. "Martí y las razas." In *Vida y pensamiento de Martí: Homenaje de la ciudad de la Habana en el cincuentenario de la fundación del Partido Revolucionario Cubano*,

1892–1942, II: 335–367. Colección Histórica Cubana y Americana 4. Havana: Municipio de la Habana, 1942.

———. "Más acerca de la poesía mulata. Escorzos para su estudio." In Isaac Barreal Fernández, comp., *Estudios etnosociológicos*, 172–198. Havana: Editorial de Ciencias Sociales, 1991; reprinted from *Revista Cubana* 37, no. 2 (1936): 218–227.

———. *Los negros esclavos*. Havana: Editorial de Ciencias Sociales, [1916] 1975.

———. "La religión en la poesía mulata." In Isaac Barreal Fernández, comp., *Estudios etnosociológicos*, 141–175. Havana: Editorial de Ciencias Sociales, 1991.

———. "La transculturación blanca de los tambores de los negros." *Archivos Venezolanos de Folklore* 1, no. 2 (July–Dec. 1952): 235–265.

———. "Los últimos versos mulatos." In Oscar Fernández de la Vega and Alberto N. Pamiés, comps., *Iniciación a la poesía afro-americana*, 156–171. Miami: Ediciones Universal, 1973; reprinted from *Revista Bimestre Cubana* 35, no. 3 (1935): 321–336.

Ortiz, Renato. *Cultura brasileira e identidade nacional*. São Paulo: Editora Brasiliense, 1985.

Ortiz Nuevo, José Luis, and Faustino Núñez. *La rabia del placer: El origen cubano del tango y su desembarco en España, 1823–1923*. Seville: Diputación de Sevilla, 1999.

Pabón, Carlos. *Nación postmortem*. San Juan, PR: Ediciones Callejón, 2002.

Palés Matos, Luis. *La poesía de Luis Palés Matos*. Ed. Mercedes López-Baralt. San Juan, PR: Editorial de la Universidad de Puerto Rico, 1995.

———. *Selected Poems: Poesía selecta*. Trans., intro. Julio Marzán. Houston: Arte Público Press, 2000.

———. *Túntun de pasa y grifería*. San Juan: Biblioteca de Autores Puertorriqueños, 1950.

———. *Túntun de pasa y grifería*. Ed. Mercedes López-Baralt. San Juan: Editorial de la Universidad de Puerto Rico, 1993.

———. *Tuntún de pasa y grifería: Poemas afroantillanos*. San Juan: Biblioteca de Autores Puertorriqueños, 1937.

Paoletti, Mario. "Borges y Gardel." In Ramón Pelinski, comp., *El tango nómade: Ensayos sobre la diáspora del tango*, 445–455. Buenos Aires: Corregidor, 2000.

Papastergiadis, Nikos. "Tracing Hybridity in Theory." In Pnina Werbner and Tariq Modood, eds., *Debating Cultural Hybridity: Multi-Cultural Identities and the Politics of Anti-Racism*, 257–281. London: Zed Books, 1997.

Parker, Richard G. *Bodies, Pleasures, and Passions: Sexual Culture in Contemporary Brazil*. Boston: Beacon Press, 1991.

Parsons, James J. *La colonización antioqueña en el occcidente colombiano*. Bogotá: Banco de la República, 1961.

Paz, Octavio. *The Labyrinth of Solitude and Other Writings*. Trans. Lysander Kemp, Yara Milos, and Rachel Phillips Belash. New York: Grove, 1985.

Pedreira, Antonio S. *Insularismo: Ensayos de interpretación puertorriqueña*. Madrid: Tipografía Artística, 1934.

———. *Obras completas*. San Juan: Instituto de Cultura Puertorriqueña, 1970.

Pelinski, Ramón, comp. *El tango nómade: Ensayos sobre la diáspora del tango*. Buenos Aires: Corregidor, 2000.

Pérez de Barradas, José. *Los mestizos de América*. Madrid: Espasa-Calpe, 1976.

Perus, Françoise. "El dialogismo y la poética histórica Bajtinianos en la perspectiva de la heterogeneidad cultural y la transculturación narrativa en América Latina." *Revista de Crítica Literaria Latinoamericana* 23, no. 42 (Segundo semestre, 1995): 29–44.

Pierri, Ettore. *Chicanos: El poder mestizo*. Mexico City: Editores Mexicanos Unidos, 1979.

Poupeney-Hart, Catherine. "Mestizaje: 'I Understand the Reality, I Just Do Not Like the Word:' Perspectives on an Option." In Rita De Grandis and Zilà Bernd, eds., *Unforeseeable Americas: Questioning Cultural Hybridity in the Americas*, 34–55. Critical Studies 13. Amsterdam: Rodopi, 2000.

Pratt, Mary Louise. *Imperial Eyes: Travel Writing and Transculturation*. London: Routledge, 1992.

———. " 'Yo Soy la Malinche': Chicana Writers and the Poetics of Ethnonationalism." In Peter Verdonk, ed., *Twentieth-century Poetry: From Text to Context*, 171–187. London: Routledge, 1993.

Querino, Manuel. *The African Contribution to Brazilian Civilization*. Trans. and intro. E. Bradford Burns. Tempe: Arizona State University Center for Latin American Studies, 1978.

———. *O africano como colonisador*. Salvador, Brazil: Editora Progresso, 1954.

———. *A arte culinária na Bahia*. Salvador, Brazil: Editora Progresso, 1951.

———. *A raça africana e os seus costumes na Bahia*. Salvador, Brazil: Editora Progresso, [1916] 1955.

Raeders, George. *O conde Gobineau no Brasil*. 2nd ed. Rio de Janeiro: Paz e Terra, 1988.

Rama, Ángel. *Transculturación narrativa en América Latina*. Mexico City: Siglo Veintiuno, 1982.

Ramírez, Manuel. *Psychology of the Americas: Mestizo Perspectives on Personality and Mental Health*. New York: Pergamon Press, 1983.

Ramos, Julio. *Desencuentros de la modernidad en América Latina: Literatura y política en el siglo XIX*. Mexico City: Fondo de Cultura Económica, 1989.

———. *Divergent Modernities: Culture and Politics in Nineteenth-century Latin America*. Trans. John D. Blanco. Durham, NC: Duke University Press, 2001.

Ramos Mejía, José María. *Rosas y su tiempo*. Vol. 3. Buenos Aires: La Cultura Argentina, [1907] 1942.

Regan, Margaret. " 'Robert Colescott: Recent Paintings' Is a Sumptuous Display of Politically Charged Narrative." *Tucson Weekly* (Nov. 19, 1998). http://www.tucsonweekly.com/tw/11-19-98/review1.htm (accessed Dec. 23, 2003).

"Resources. Afro-Caribbean Rhythm Glossary." http://www.projectdrum.com (accessed Oct. 16, 2003); http://www.projectdrum.com/news/article_35.html (accessed Jan. 8, 2004).

Reuter, Edward Byron. *The Mulatto in the United States: Including a Study of the Role of Mixed-Blood Races throughout the World.* Boston: Badger Press, 1918.

Rice, John. "Fidel Wows Smokers at the Tropicana, Takes Pot Shots at Clinton" (Mar. 2, 1997). http://www.freep.com/news/nw/qcastro2.htm (accessed July 31, 1998; site discontinued).

Richard, Nelly. "The Latin American Problematic of Theoretical-Cultural Transference: Postmodern Appropriations and Counter-appropriations." *South Atlantic Quarterly* 92, no. 3 (1993): 453-459.

Ríos Ávila, Rubén. *La raza cómica: Del sujeto en Puerto Rico.* San Juan, PR: Ediciones Callejón, 2002.

———. "La raza cómica: Identidad y cuerpo en Pedreira y Palés." *La Torre* 7, nos. 27-28 (July-Dec. 1993): 559-576.

Rivas, Mercedes. *Literatura y esclavitud en la novela cubana del siglo XIX.* Seville: Escuela de Estudios Hispano-Americanos de Sevilla, 1990.

Roberts, Peter. "The (Re)construction of the Concept of 'Indio' in the National Identities of Cuba, the Dominican Republic and Puerto Rico." In Lowell Fiet and Janette Becerra, eds., *Caribe 2000: Definiciones, identidades y culturas regionales y/o nacionales,* 99-120. San Juan: Caribe 2000, Universidad de Puerto Rico, Facultad de Humanidades, 1997.

Robles, Humberto E. "Review of Jorge Icaza, *El Chulla Romero y Flores,* ed. crítica, 1988." In Samuel Gordon, ed., *La Colección Archivos: Hacia un nuevo canon: Reseñas aparecidas en la Revista Iberoamericana,* 70-75. Revista Iberoamericana, 1993.

Rodó, José Enrique. *Ariel.* Mexico City: Editorial Novaro-México, [1900] 1957.

Rodríguez, Ileana, ed. *The Latin American Subaltern Studies Reader.* Durham, NC: Duke University Press, 2001.

Roig, Arturo Andrés. *El pensamiento social de Juan Montalvo.* Quito: Universidad Andina Simón Bolívar, 1995.

Romano Magnavita, Pasqualino. "Quando a história vira espectáculo: Palco Móvel do Pelô." In Marco Aurélio Andrade de Filgueiras Gomes, *Pelo Pelô: História, cultura e cidade,* 121-131. Salvador, Brazil: Editora da Universidade Federal da Bahia, 1995.

Romero, Enrique. Liner notes, Celia Cruz, *Tributo a los orishas.* Música del Sol, MSCD 7050.

Rossi, Vicente. *Cosas de negros: Los oríjenes del tango y otros aportes al folklore rioplatense. Rectificaciones históricas.* Río de la Plata, Arg. 1926.

Sábato, Ernesto. *Tango: Discusión y clave.* Buenos Aires: Editorial Losada, 1997.

Sackett, Theodore Alan. *El arte en la novelística de Jorge Icaza.* Quito: Editorial Casa de la Cultura Ecuatoriana, 1974.

Sagás, Ernesto. *Race and Politics in the Dominican Republic.* Gainesville: University Press of Florida, 2000.

Salas, Horacio. *El tango.* Buenos Aires: Planeta, 1995.

———. *El tango: Una guía definitiva.* Buenos Aires: Aguilar, 1996.

Saldaña-Portillo, Josefina. "Who's the Indian in Aztlán? Re-Writing Mestizaje, Indianism, and Chicanismo from the Lacandón." In Ileana Rodríguez, ed., *The Latin American Subaltern Studies Reader*, 402-423. Durham, NC: Duke University Press, 2001.

Saldívar, José David. *The Dialectics of Our America: Genealogy, Cultural Critique, and Literary History*. Durham, NC: Duke University Press, 1991.

Salessi, Jorge. "Medics, Crooks, and Tango Queens: The National Appropriation of a Gay Tango." In Celeste Fraser Delgado and José Esteban Muñoz, eds., *Everynight Life: Culture and Dance in Latin/o America*, 141-174. Durham, NC: Duke University Press, 1997.

Sánchez, Luis Alberto. "El Vasconcelos que conozco." *Nueva Democracia* 40, no. 4 (Oct. 1960): 45-47.

Sánchez Macgrégor, Joaquín. "La estética de Vasconcelos como proyecto utópico." *Cuadernos Americanos* 31 (Jan.-Feb. 1992): 246-251.

Santos Rodrigues, João Jorge. "Carnaval." http://www2.uol.com.br/olodum /indexcarnaval.htm (accessed Jan. 8, 2004).

Sardinha, Carl Dennis. *The Poetry of Nicolás Guillén: An Introduction*. London: New Beacon Books, 1976.

Sarmiento, Domingo Faustino. *Facundo, or, Civilization and Barbarism*. Trans. Mary Mann; intro. Ilan Stavans. New York: Penguin Books, 1998.

Savigliano, Marta. *Tango and the Political Economy of Passion*. Boulder, CO: Westview Press, 1995.

Schultz, Alfred P. *Race or Mongrel*. New York: Arno Press, [1908] 1977.

Schwarcz, Lilia Moritz. *The Spectacle of the Races: Scientists, Institutions, and the Race Question in Brazil, 1870-1930*. Trans. Leland Guyer. New York: Hill and Wang, 1999.

Skidmore, Thomas E. *Black into White: Race and Nationality in Brazilian Thought*. New York: Oxford University Press, 1974.

———. *The Politics of Military Rule in Brazil, 1964-85*. New York: Oxford University Press, 1988.

Skirius, John. *José Vasconcelos y la cruzada de 1929*. Mexico City: Siglo XXI, 1978.

Smith, Carol A. "Myths, Intellectuals, and Race/Class/Gender Distinctions in the Formation of Latin American Nations." *Journal of Latin American Anthropology* 2 (1996): 148-169.

Sodré, Muniz. *Claros e escuros: Identidade, povo e mídia no Brasil*. Petrópolis, Brazil: Editora Vozes, 1999.

Solaún, Mauricio, and Sidney Kronus. *Discrimination without Violence: Miscegenation and Racial Conflict in Latin America*. New York: John Wiley & Sons, 1973.

Spitta, Silvia. *Between Two Waters: Narratives of Transculturation in Latin America*. Houston, TX: Rice University Press, 1995.

Spivak, Gayatri Chakravorty. "Can the Subaltern Speak?" In Patrick Williams and Laura Chrisman, eds., *Colonial Discourse and Post-Colonial Theory: A Reader*, 66-111. New York: Columbia University Press, 1994.

Stam, Robert. "Palimpsestic Aesthetics: A Meditation on Hybridity and Garbage." In May Joseph and Jennifer Natalya Fink, eds., *Performing Hybridity*, 59–78. Minneapolis: University of Minneapolis Press, 1999.

———. *Tropical Multiculturalism: A Comparative History of Race in Brazilian Culture and Cinema*. Durham, NC: Duke University Press, 1997.

Stastny, Francisco. "¿Un arte mestizo?" In Damián Bayón, ed., *América Latina en sus artes*, 154–170. Mexico City: Siglo XXI/UNESCO.

Tamayo Vargas, Augusto. "Interpretaciones de América Latina." In César Fernández Moreno, coord., *América Latina en su literatura*, 441–461. Mexico City: Siglo Veintiuno, 1978.

Tapscott, Stephen. *Twentieth-century Latin American Poetry: A Bilingual Anthology*. Austin: University of Texas Press, 1996.

Taracena, Alfonso. *José Vasconcelos*. Mexico City: Editorial Porrúa, 1982.

Todorov, Tzvetan. *The Conquest of America: The Question of the Other*. Trans. Richard Howard. New York: Harper Perennial, 1992.

Torres-Saillant, Silvio. "The Tribulations of Blackness: Stages in Dominican Racial Identity." *Latin American Perspectives* 100, 25, no. 3 (May 1988): 126–146.

Trigo, Abril. "Shifting Paradigms: From Transculturation to Hybridity: A Theoretical Critique." In Rita De Grandis and Zilà Bernd, *Unforeseeable Americas: Questioning Cultural Hybridity in the Americas*, 85–111. Critical Studies 13. Amsterdam: Rodopi, 2000.

Tur Donatti, Carlos M. "La utopía del regreso y la estética de la barbarie. (Vasconcelos, Riva Agüero y los nacionalistas argentinos)." *Cuadernos Americanos* 77 (1999): 167–176.

Valdés-Cruz, Rosa E. *La poesía negroide en América*. New York: Las Américas, 1970.

Vallejo, Fernando. *Our Lady of the Assassins*. Trans. Paul Hammond. London: Serpent's Tail, 2001.

Vasconcelos, José. *Bolivarismo y Monroísmo: Temas iberoamericanos*. Santiago de Chile: Ediciones Ercilla, 1937.

———. "El bronce del indio mexicano se apoya en el granito bruñido del Brasil." *El Maestro* III (May 1923): 255–258.

———. *The Cosmic Race: A Bilingual Edition*. Trans. and intro. Didier T. Jaén. Baltimore: The Johns Hopkins University Press, [1979] 1997.

———. *El desastre: Tercera parte de Ulises criollo*. Mexico City: Ediciones Botas, 1938.

———. *Discursos: 1920–1950*. Mexico City: Ediciones Botas, 1950.

———. *Estética*. Mexico City: Botas, 1936.

———. *Hernán Cortés: Creador de la nacionalidad*. Mexico City: Editorial Jus, 1985.

———. *Indología: Una interpretación de la cultura ibero-americana*. Paris: Agencia Mundial de Librería, 1926.

———. "The Latin-American Basis of Mexican Civilization." In José Vasconcelos and Manuel Gamio, *Aspects of Mexican Civilization*, 3–102. Chicago: University of Chicago Press, 1926.

———. *Obra selecta*. Caracas: Biblioteca Ayacucho, 1992.

———. *Prometeo vencedor: Tragedia moderna en un prólogo y tres actos*. Mexico City: Lectura Selecta, 1920.

———. *Qué es la revolución*. Mexico City: Ediciones Botas, 1937.

———. *La raza cósmica, misión de la raza iberoamericana*. Paris: Agencia Mundial de Librería, 1925.

———. *La raza cósmica: Misión de la raza iberoamericana, Argentina y Brasil*. Mexico City: Espasa-Calpe Mexicana, 1948.

———. *La raza cósmica: Misión de la raza iberoamericana, Argentina y Brasil*. 3rd ed. Mexico City: Espasa-Calpe Mexicana, 1966.

Vásquez Rubiños, Naghim, and Iván A. Soca Pascual. "80 años de vida." http://www.guegue.net/guayasamin/bloque.htm (accessed Jan. 27, 2004).

Vázquez Arce, Carmen. "*Tuntún de pasa y grifería*: A Cultural Project." In Conrad James and John Perivolaris, eds., *The Cultures of the Hispanic Caribbean*, 86–103. Gainesville: University Press of Florida, 2000.

Veloso, Caetano. *Tropicália 2*. Polygram/Warner, 1993.

Vento, Arnoldo Carlos. *Mestizo: The History, Culture, and Politics of the Mexican and the Chicano: The Emerging Mestizo-Americans*. Lanham, MD: University Press of America, 1998.

Verdonk, Peter, ed. *Twentieth-century Poetry: From Text to Context*. London: Routledge, 1993.

Vetrano, Anthony J. *La problemática psico-social y su correlación lingüística en las novelas de Jorge Icaza*. Miami: Ediciones Universal, 1974.

Vidarart, Daniel. *El tango y su mundo*. Montevideo: Ediciones Tauro, 1967.

Villaverde, Cirilo. *Cecilia Valdés*. Prol. and chron. Ivan A. Schulman. Caracas: Biblioteca Ayacucho, [1882] 1981.

Villegas, Benjamín, ed. *Mestizo America: The Country of the Future*. Bogotá: Villegas Editores, 2000.

Wade, Peter. *Blackness and Race Mixture: The Dynamics of Racial Identity in Colombia*. Baltimore: The Johns Hopkins University Press, 1993.

Wagley, Charles. "On the Concept of Social Race in the Americas." In Jorge I. Domínguez, ed., *Race and Ethnicity in Latin America*, 13–27. New York: Garland Publishing, 1994.

Warhol, Robyn R., and Diane Price Herndl, eds., *Feminisms: An Anthology of Literary Theory and Criticism*. New Brunswick, NJ: Rutgers University Press, 1997.

Werbner, Pnina, and Tariq Modood, eds. *Debating Cultural Hybridity: Multi-Cultural Identities and the Politics of Anti-Racism*. London: Zed Books, 1997.

Whitefield, Bernard. *Beginner's Book on the Tango, Conga, Rumba and Samba*. Boston, 1943.

"Who Invented the Tango?" Rediff on the net. http://www.rediff.com/news/1996/1812tang.htm (accessed Jan. 8, 2004).

Williams, Claudette. *Charcoal and Cinnamon: The Politics of Color in Spanish Caribbean Literature*. Gainesville: University Press of Florida, 2000.

Williams, Patrick, and Laura Chrisman, eds. *Colonial Discourse and Post-colonial Theory: A Reader.* New York: Columbia University Press, 1994.

Young, Robert J. C. *Colonial Desire: Hybridity in Theory, Culture, and Race.* London: Routledge, 1995.

———. *White Mythologies: Writing History and the West.* London: Routledge, 1990.

Zamora, Lois Parkinson, and Wendy B. Faris, eds. *Magical Realism: Theory, History, Community.* Durham, NC: Duke University Press, 1995.

Zapata Olivella, Manuel. *¡Levántate mulato!* Bogotá: REI, 1990.

———. *La rebelión de los genes: El mestizaje americano en la sociedad futura.* Bogotá: Altamir Ediciones, 1997.

Zavala, Iris. *Colonialism and Culture.* Bloomington: Indiana University Press, 1992.

Zea, Leopoldo. *Precursores del pensamiento Latinoamericano contemporáneo.* Mexico City: SEP Diana, 1979.

———. *Regreso de las carabelas.* Mexico City: Universidad Nacional Autónoma de México, 1993.

———. "Vasconcelos y la utopía de la raza cósmica." *Cuadernos Americanos* 37 (Jan.–Feb. 1993): 23–36.

Zotto, Miguel Ángel. "An Interview with Miguel Ángel Zotto by Fabiana Basso, Buenos Aires, December 1994." http://lancelot.bio.cornell.edu/matej/tango/zotto.html (accessed Feb. 17, 2000).

Zubillaga, Carlos. *Carlos Gardel.* Prol. Jorge Luis Borges. Madrid: Ediciones Júcar, 1976.

INDEX